Lecture Notes in Computer Science 15565

Founding Editors

Gerhard Goos
Juris Hartmanis

W0193275

The series Lecture Notes in Computer Science (LNCS), including its subseries Lecture Notes in Artificial Intelligence (LNAI) and Lecture Notes in Bioinformatics (LNBI), has established itself as a medium for the publication of new developments in computer science and information technology research, teaching, and education.

LNCS enjoys close cooperation with the computer science R & D community, the series counts many renowned academics among its volume editors and paper authors, and collaborates with prestigious societies. Its mission is to serve this international community by providing an invaluable service, mainly focused on the publication of conference and workshop proceedings and postproceedings. LNCS commenced publication in 1973.

Mousa Al-kfairy · Monther Aldwairi ·
Kim-Kwang Raymond Choo ·
Mohammad Tubishat · Saed Alrabaee ·
Omar Alfandi
Editors

Security and Privacy in Social Networks and Big Data

10th International Symposium, SocialSec 2024
Abu Dhabi, United Arab Emirates, November 20–22, 2024
Proceedings

 Springer

Editors
Mousa Al-kfairy 🆔
Zayed University
Abu Dhabi, United Arab Emirates

Monther Aldwairi 🆔
Zayed University
Abu Dhabi, United Arab Emirates

Kim-Kwang Raymond Choo 🆔
University of Texas at San Antonio
San Antonio, TX, USA

Mohammad Tubishat 🆔
Zayed University
Abu Dhabi, United Arab Emirates

Saed Alrabaee 🆔
United Arab Emirates University
Al Ain, United Arab Emirates

Omar Alfandi 🆔
Zayed University
Abu Dhabi, United Arab Emirates

ISSN 0302-9743   ISSN 1611-3349 (electronic)
Lecture Notes in Computer Science
ISBN 978-981-96-3773-7   ISBN 978-981-96-3774-4 (eBook)
https://doi.org/10.1007/978-981-96-3774-4

This Springer imprint is published by the registered company Springer Nature Singapore Pte Ltd.
The registered company address is: 152 Beach Road, #21-01/04 Gateway East, Singapore 189721, Singapore

If disposing of this product, please recycle the paper.

Preface

Social networks and big data have become integral to our daily lives. These platforms have evolved from simple communication and news-sharing tools into essential resources for professional networking, social recommendations, marketing, and online content distribution. As social networks combine with various activities, they generate big data that surpasses the capacity of conventional computer software and hardware to capture, manage, and process in a reasonable timeframe. It is widely acknowledged that security and privacy pose significant challenges for social networks and big data applications due to their scale, complexity, and diversity.

The 10th edition of the International Symposium on Security and Privacy in Social Networks and Big Data (SocialSec 2024) was held at Zayed University, Abu Dhabi, UAE, from November 20–22, 2024, co-located with the 18th International Conference on Network and System Security (NSS 2024). It followed the success of SocialSec 2015 in Hangzhou, China; SocialSec 2016 in Fiji; SocialSec 2017 in Melbourne, Australia; SocialSec 2018 in Santa Clara, CA, USA; SocialSec 2019 in Copenhagen, Denmark; SocialSec 2020 in Tianjin, China; SocialSec 2021 in Fuzhou, China, SocialSec 2022 in Xi'an, China, and SocialSec 2023 in Canterbury, UK. The SocialSec conference series aims to provide a leading-edge forum to foster interactions among researchers and developers within the security and privacy communities in social networks and big data.

The conference's technical program included 10 research papers (8 full papers and two short papers) selected by the Technical Program Committee (TPC) from 22 submissions received in response to the call for papers. The review process was organized and managed through EasyChair. All the papers were peer-reviewed by at least three reviewers by the TPC members. The submission process was anonymous, and author names were not visible to the reviewers. Received reviews were also anonymized to other TPC members, as well as to the paper's authors. The reviewers were asked to declare any conflicts of interest for all submissions at the beginning of the process, and the EasyChair system was configured to ensure TPC members (including TPC chairs) could see neither the reviewer assignments nor the reviews of the papers for which they had a conflict of interest. If one TPC Co-Chair had a conflict of interest, a discussion on each document was held, and the decision was made between the other two TPC Co-Chairs without a conflict of interest.

SocialSec 2024 and the co-located NSS 2024 shared three invited keynote talks for both conferences' participants, given by Mohamed Al Kuwaiti, Head, UAE Cyber Security Council, Lin Zhiqiang, Ohio State University, USA, and Nir Kshetri, University of North Carolina-Greensboro, USA.

The SocialSec 2024 TPC selected one paper for the Best Paper Award; the winner of the best paper award received a certificate and a gift kindly sponsored by Zayed University.

The SocialSec 2024 TPC was co-chaired by Kim-Kwang Raymond Choo, University of Texas at San Antonio, USA, Monther Aldwairi, Zayed University, UAE, and Mousa Al-kfairy, Zayed University, UAE; they selected the TPC members and led their efforts in choosing the papers that appear in this volume. The organization of SocialSec 2024 and the co-located NSS 2024 was led by Omar Alfandi, Zayed University, UAE, Saed Alrabaee, United Arab Emirates University, UAE, and Mousa Al-kfairy, Zayed University, UAE as both conferences' joint General Chair & Co-Chairs. The conferences were also made possible due to the professional work of Huwida Said, Zayed University, UAE, Samia Loucif, Zayed University, UAE, Abdallah Tubaishat, Zayed University, UAE, Feras Al-Obeidat, Zayed University, UAE, Dheya Mustafa, Hashemite University, Jordan, and Maurantonio Caprolu, King Abdullah University of Science & Technology, KSA as the Publicity Co-Chairs. Mohammad Tubishat, Zayed University, UAE and Thangavel Murugan, United Arab Emirates University, UAE were the Publication Chairs, and April Maramara, Zayed University, UAE was the Web Chair.

As the TPC Co-Chairs of SocialSec 2024 and the Publication Chair of both SocialSec 2024 and NSS 2024, we thank everyone who made this conference successful. We thank all the authors for submitting their manuscripts to the conference. We would also like to extend special thanks to members of the joint Organizing Committee for making SocialSec 2024 and NSS 2024 successful events. Last but not least, we also thank all participants of SocialSec 2024 and NSS 2024 for their active participation during the three days of the conferences.

November 2024

Mousa Al-kfairy
Monther Aldwairi
Kim-Kwang Raymond Choo
Mohammad Tubishat
Saed Alrabaee
Omar Alfandi

Organization

General Chair

Omar Alfandi   Zayed University, UAE

General Co-chairs

Saed Alrabaee   United Arab Emirates University, UAE
Mousa Al-kfairy   Zayed University, UAE

Program Committee Chairs

Kim-Kwang Raymond Choo   University of Texas at San Antonio, USA
Monther Aldwairi   Zayed University, UAE
Mousa Al-kfairy   Zayed University, UAE

SocialSec Steering Committee

Yang Xiang   Swinburne University of Technology, Australia
Jeremy Blackburn   Binghamton University, USA
Shujun Li   University of Kent, UK
Michael Sirivianos   Cyprus University of Technology, Cyprus
Anna Cinzia Squicciarini   Pennsylvania State University, USA
Tianqing Zhu   University of Technology Sydney, Australia

Publicity Co-chairs

Huwida Said   Zayed University, UAE
Samia Loucif   Zayed University, UAE
Abdallah Tubaishat   Zayed University, UAE
Feras Al-Obeidat   Zayed University, UAE

| Dheya Mustafa | Hashemite University, Jordan |
| Maurantonio Caprolu | King Abdullah University of Science & Technology, KSA |

Publication Chairs

| Mohammad Tubishat | Zayed University, UAE |
| Thangavel Murugan | United Arab Emirates University, UAE |

Web Chair

| April Maramara | Zayed University, UAE |

Local Organizing Committee

Rima Grati	Zayed University, UAE
Nadia Dahmani	Zayed University, UAE
Sarra Almessabi	Zayed University, UAE

Sponsorship Co-chairs

Fatma Taher	Zayed University, UAE
Mousa Al-kfairy	Zayed University, UAE
Yaser Khamayseh	Zayed University, UAE
Dina Tbaishat	Zayed University, UAE

Registration Chair

| Abeer Alhasan | Zayed University, UAE |

Technical Program Committee

Martin Andreoni	Technology Innovation Institute, UAE
Pietro Tedeschi	CY4GATE S.p.A., Italy
Sven Dietrich	City University of New York, USA

Yazan Alahmed   Al Ain University, UAE
Nisha Madathil   UAE University, UAE
Muhusina Ismail   UAE University, UAE
Omar Darwish   Eastern Michigan University, USA
Kyungbaek Kim   Chonnam National University, South Korea
Samer Khamaiseh   Miami University, USA
Claude Fachkha   Concordia University, Canada
Edwin Dauber   Widener University, USA
Christoforos Ntantogian Ionian University, Greece
Bo Luo   University of Kansas, USA
Paria Shirani   University of Ottawa, Canada
Wenjia Li   New York Institute of Technology, USA
Claudio Ardagna   Università degli Studi di Milano, Italy
Sergio Pastrana   Universidad Carlos III de Madrid, Spain
Khaled Shuaib   Al Ain University, UAE
Lianying Zhao   Carleton University, Canada
Christos Xenakis   University of Piraeus, Greece
Kuo-Hui Yeh   National Yang Ming Chiao Tung University,
                           Taiwan

Adel Abusitta   Polytechnique Montréal, Canada
Nora Cuppens-Boulahia   Polytechnique Montréal, Canada
Mahmoud Khasawneh   Al Ain University, UAE
Nikos Salamanos   Cyprus University of Technology, Cyprus
Kallol Krishna Karmakar University of Newcastle, Australia
Elias Bou-Harb   Louisiana State University, USA
Dima Alhadidi   University of Windsor, Canada
Irfan Ahmed   Virginia Commonwealth University, USA
Josep Domingo-Ferrer   Universitat Rovira i Virgili, Spain
Matthew Edwards   University of Bristol, UK
Helei Cui   Northwestern Polytechnical University, China
Dheya Mustafa   Hashemite University, Jordan
Chan Yeob Yeun   Khalifa University, UAE
Inah Omoronyia   University of Glasgow, UK
Azadeh Tabiban   Concordia University, Canada
Chiara Boldrini   Consiglio Nazionale delle Ricerche, Italy
Wenjuan Li   Education University of Hong Kong, China
Yunsheng Wang   California State Polytechnic University Pomona,
                           USA
Weizhi Meng   Technical University of Denmark, Denmark
Mengyuan Zhang   Vrije Universiteit Amsterdam, Netherlands
Xingliang Yuan   University of Melbourne, Australia
Changyu Dong   Newcastle University, UK

Stefano Cresci	Consiglio Nazionale delle Ricerche, Italy
Zhiqiang Lin	Ohio State University, USA
George Pallis	University of Cyprus, Cyprus
Luca Davoli	University of Parma, Italy
Thangavel Murugan	UAE University, UAE
Patrizio Dazzi	University of Pisa, Italy
Amr Youssef	Concordia University, Canada
Ximeng Liu	Singapore Management University, Singapore
Richard Chbeir	Université de Pau et des pays de l'Adour, France
Ersin Uzun	University of California, Irvine, USA

Contents

Analysis of Social Media Perspectives

Investigating Influential COVID-19 Perspectives: A Multifaceted Analysis of Twitter Discourse

Shadaab Kawnain Bashir[1](✉), Hossein Shirazi[2](✉), Noushin Salek Faramarzi[3],
Thomas Harris[1], Ashmita Shishodia[2], Hajar Homayouni[2],
and Indrakshi Ray[1](✉)

[1] Colorado State University, Fort Collins, CO, USA
{shadaab,indrakshi.ray}@colostate.edu
[2] San Diego State University, San Diego, CA, USA
{hshirazi,ashishodia2546,hhomayouni}@sdsu.edu
[3] Stony Brook University, Stony Brook, NY, USA
nsalekfarama@cs.stonybrook.edu

Abstract. Social media influencers, those with verified accounts or with more than 10,000 followers, played a crucial role in the propagation of narratives during the COVID-19 pandemic. We investigate their impact by characterizing and contrasting the differences in content patterns between influential individuals versus public organizations during the pandemic, analyzing emotions, sentiments, and scientific claims expressed in their Tweets. Advanced machine learning approaches, including customized transformer models, few-shot learning, and large language models such as GPT-3.5, were used. The findings reveal a stark contrast in sentiment usage across sub-domains like vaccines and lockdowns, with organizations predominantly employing neutral tones while individuals displaying a significant negative sentiment bias. Individuals often conveyed more negative emotions, whereas organizations exhibited greater optimism. However, many claims from both groups were not verified, highlighting the need to combat misinformation.

Keywords: COVID-19 · Emotion Detection · Sentiment Analysis · Scientific Claim Identification · User Profiling

1 Introduction

The emergence and pervasiveness of social media have transformed the way information is disseminated and consumed globally [18]. Particularly, in the context of the COVID-19 pandemic, social networks have played a vital role in informing public sentiment and influencing behaviors [8]. It has acted as an indispensable conduit for disseminating health advisories and updates on the virus's progress. Twitter[1] has become a hotbed for spreading rumors and false claims about the

---

[1] Now known as X, we collected and executed the experiments while it was known as Twitter.

M. Al-kfairy et al. (Eds.): SocialSec 2024, LNCS 15565, pp. 3–22, 2025.
https://doi.org/10.1007/978-981-96-3774-4_1

virus, exacerbating public confusion and anxiety. However, the rapid spread of information and the omnipresent nature of the platform has also fueled misinformation, creating a "digital infodemic" parallel to the pandemic [29] and making it difficult for the public to make informed decisions [14]. Influencers, defined by individuals or organizations with a substantial following base, can amplify messages, influence opinions, and mold social narratives [13]. The sharing of questionable information by influential figures on Twitter has played a substantial role in shaping misconceptions and distorting public understanding of the pandemic.

While the influence of social media is undeniable, there exists a nuanced divergence in the approach and impact of individual versus organizational influencers. Individual influencers, comprising celebrities, thought leaders, and other public figures, often present personal and subjective points of view. Their content tends to reflect personal opinions, experiences, or endorsements, which can vary widely in terms of accuracy and reliability [4]. On the other hand, organizational influencers, such as official accounts of entities like the World Health Organization (WHO), focus on disseminating verified information and official updates. Their content is typically more factual, objective, and aligned with public health guidelines [7]. This distinction is critical in understanding the landscape of social media discourse during the pandemic, as the type of influencer can significantly influence the nature and impact of the information being disseminated.

The current situation prompts a study of how individual and organizational influencers uniquely shape the social media landscape during the COVID-19 pandemic. There exists a notable research void in thoroughly examining and contrasting the content, sentiment, and impact of these distinct influencer categories. Understanding this discrepancy is essential to understanding the broader effects of social networks on public opinions and behaviors during health crises. Initial studies have delved into characteristics of COVID-19 Twitter data, tracking the emotional evolution expressed in Tweets during the pandemic by jointly analyzing both the types of emotion and the overall polarity of sentiment [20, 24, 33, 41, 43]. However, as far as our knowledge extends, existing studies have not undertaken a thorough analysis of the distinctions between organizational and individual influencers for COVID-19-related Tweets.

This research categorizes influencers into individual and organizational entities, examining content, sentiment, and emotional responses. It also evaluates the influence of these Tweets on public sentiment and trust in scientific information. This will help in understanding influencers' roles and communication strategies during the pandemic. In this study, we examine the following research questions.

- **RQ1:** *How do individual influencers and organizational influencers express their opinions and communicate their perspectives about the COVID-19 pandemic on Twitter and what are the differences?* This inquiry aims to investigate the differences between individuals and organizations in terms of the emotional appeals they use, the overall sentiment they portray, and the degree to which they rely on scientific evidence.

– **RQ2:** *To what extent deep learning algorithms can effectively profile individuals' and organizations' accounts on social media?* This question focuses on the identification and categorization of influencers in the dataset as either individuals or organizations, based on their characteristics and communication styles using deep learning algorithms.

To bridge the gap between these research questions and actionable analysis, four specific tasks were designed: *user profiling, emotion detection, sentiment analysis,* and *scientific content identification.* We need these tasks to understand the nuanced dynamics of Twitter discourse and also to leverage computational methods to systematically categorize and evaluate the content. User profiling is essential for distinguishing between individual users and organizations, facilitating an analysis that considers the source of each Tweet. This differentiation is crucial for RQ1, as it allows for an investigation into the unique communication styles and content preferences of these two groups. Emotion detection and sentiment analysis further enrich this understanding by quantifying the emotional and sentimental dispositions conveyed in Tweets, enabling a nuanced analysis of the emotional appeals and overall sentiment portrayed by different users. These tasks directly support the exploration of how opinions and perspectives are expressed, as outlined in RQ1. Finally, the scientific content identification task aligns closely with both RQ1 and RQ2 by evaluating the extent to which Tweets rely on scientific evidence, a factor that can significantly influence the credibility and reception of the information shared. Together, these tasks form a comprehensive framework for addressing the posed research questions, leveraging deep learning and computational linguistics to uncover insights into the digital discourse surrounding the COVID-19 pandemic on Twitter.

Due to the lack of a ground-truth labeled dataset, we developed a labeled dataset by collecting 1875 influential Twitter posts related to COVID-19 and annotating them using a multi-step pipeline. Each Tweet was manually labeled by human annotators for user profile (*individual* or *organization*), emotion (*joy, sadness, fear, surprise, anger*), sentiment (*positive, negative,* or *neutral*), and presence of scientific claims (*scientifically verifiable claims, scientific knowledge reference, general scientific research*) as illustrated in Fig. 1.

In our study, we used an automated approach to analyze the annotated dataset using NLP algorithms. The core of our methodology involved applying Bidirectional Transformer Encoder Representations (BERT) [9] for general text encoding, providing crucial foundational contextual embeddings for nuanced language interpretation. To address the specificity of scientific content, we integrated SciBERT, a BERT variant trained on scientific corpora, enhancing the accuracy of scientific claim detection. Furthermore, we used large language models like LLAMA2 and GPT-3.5 for their conversational understanding capabilities, helping to analyze emotions and sentiments. These models were instrumental in interpreting communicative intentions and subtleties within Tweets. This multifaceted NLP framework allowed for a comprehensive analysis of influencer categorization, sentiment, and scientific claim detection in the context of

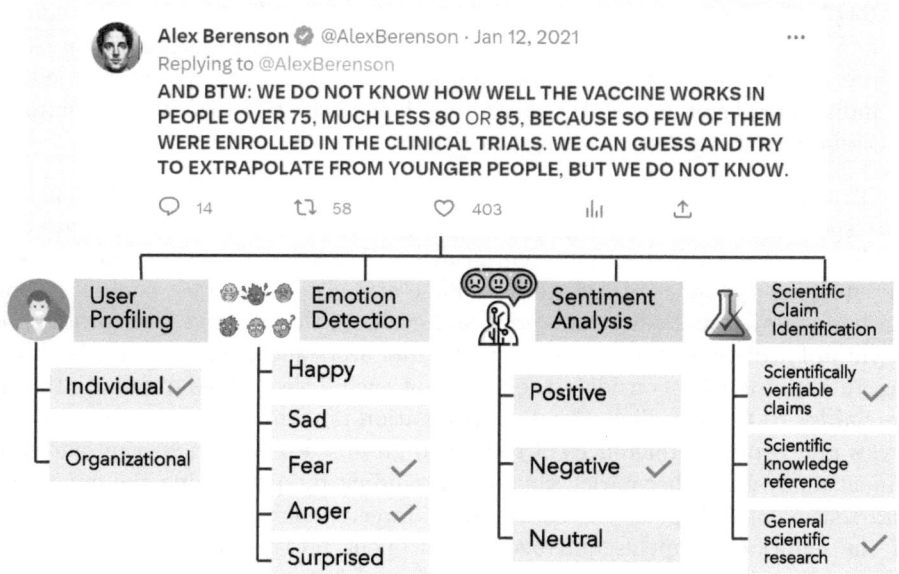

Fig. 1. Example Annotated Tweet From Our Annotated Dataset Demonstrating Multilayer Analysis Across Dimensions of User Profiling, Emotion Detection, Sentiment Analysis, and Scientific Claim Identification.

COVID-19, leveraging the strengths of each model to fulfill our specific research goals.

Our Contribution

– We created a unique dataset of manually annotated influential COVID-19 Tweets labeled for user profiles, emotions, sentiments, and scientific claims.
– We leveraged this new dataset in conjunction with advanced machine learning approaches including customized transformer models, few-shot learning, and Large Language Models. The GPT-3.5 model showcased impressive F1 scores, excelling with 0.91 for sadness, 0.89 for surprise, and SetFit performed best for fear with an F1 of 0.85, 0.91 for anger and 0.92 for joy. In sentiment analysis, RoBERTa$_{Twitter}$ emerged as a standout performer, achieving leading F1 scores of 0.72 for negative, 0.89 for neutral, and 0.78 for positive sentiment. Domain-specific language models like SciBERT demonstrated notable proficiency, with F1 scores of 0.87 for references, and 0.92 for general scientific claims and SetFit achieved an F1 score of 0.97 for verifiable claims.
– Key findings reveal individuals exhibit more subjective sentiment compared to organizations' impartiality; however, organizations disseminate higher overall volumes of pandemic-related content. Across both groups, many assertions lack rigorous verification, highlighting the imperative for validation to combat misinformation. Additionally, we observed a marked polarity in individual Tweets (positive or negative sentiments), in contrast to the more neutral

stance of organizations. The sheer volume of organizational Tweets, however, outweighs individual Tweets. By empowering nuanced investigation across these facets, this research significantly enhances the ability to decode complex perspectives and narratives that shape the discourse on social media crises.

– Our study advances beyond traditional sentiment analysis and topic modeling by integrating a multi-dimensional approach. This includes user profiling, emotion detection, sentiment analysis, and scientific claim identification, providing a holistic understanding of COVID-19-related discourse on social media.

The rest of this paper is structured as follows: Sect. 2 reviews relevant literature. Section 3 describes the data collection methodology and the annotation process. Sections 4, 5, 6, 7 present the experimental approach and results for each dimension of the analysis: user profiling, emotion detection, sentiment analysis, and identification of scientific claims respectively. Finally, Sect. 8 concludes the paper.

2 Related Work

Related work pertaining to user profiling, emotion detection, sentiment analysis, and scientific claim identification are described below.

2.1 User Profiling

User profiling involves creating detailed profiles of users based on their social media activity and behavior. Several related works have addressed various aspects of user profiling, including the identification of individuals and organizations and the clustering of Twitter users.

Kappus *et al.* [19] leveraged network analysis and hashtag clustering to group Twitter users based on their pandemic-related Tweets. Their study revealed highly insular communities on the platform. Furthermore, Egger and Yu [11] evaluated topic modeling approaches for COVID-19 Tweets related to cluster travel, demonstrating the effectiveness of BERTopic. However, in contrast to their approach of analyzing individual Tweets, our work aims to utilize user profile attributes rather than focusing solely on their Tweets. Our research extends existing methodologies by leveraging the power of transformer models, specifically BERT and BERTopic, to profile Twitter users. By examining their overall behavior and engagement patterns, we gain a deeper understanding of users' interests, preferences, and potential connections within the Twitter ecosystem.

One notable work is the development of the "demographer" Python package [39], which focuses on identifying gender and ethnicity, and distinguishes between accounts belonging to individuals or organizations. Another relevant study by Liang *et al.* [23] introduced DUWE, a dynamic user profiling model that tracks the interests of Twitter users over time using their Tweet history.

2.2 Emotion Detection and Sentiment Analysis

The COVID-19 pandemic has led to several studies on the emotional impact of the pandemic on individuals. Prior studies [1,26,30] have employed natural language processing techniques to analyze emotions and sentiments expressed in COVID-19-related Twitter data. While sentiment and emotion are commonly examined in tandem, it is noteworthy that there exist research endeavors dedicated to investigating these phenomena individually. For example, Nandal *et al.* [27] leveraged lexicon-based approaches to identify specific emotions like fear, sadness, and anger in Tweets. Similarly, Manguri *et al.* [25] used TextBlob for analysis and observed that over 50% of the Tweets showed neutral sentiment. Ainapure *et al.* [2] categorized Tweet sentiment as positive, negative, or neutral using VADER sentiment analysis. Yu *et al.* [42] found increased engagement with negative sentiment about COVID-19. Wrycza and Jacek [40] analyzed the topic of working from home which highlighted a predominantly positive response.

Several works have tracked emotional evolution over the timeline of the pandemic. Jalil *et al.* [17] revealed fluctuating positive and negative sentiments towards vaccines using supervised learning classifiers. Storey and O'Leary [33] demonstrated a shift from predominantly negative linguistic sentiments in early 2020 to more positive expressions by 2021 using the NRC Emotion Lexicon.

Previous research [6,10,36] focused on sentiment and emotion recognition utilizing lexicon-based Python tools. Our technique, on the other hand, employs transformers and LLMs to efficiently solve both sentiment and emotion detection tasks. Our study specifically aims to analyze the sentiment conveyed within Twitter, employing gold-standard data for this analysis.

2.3 Scientific Claim Identification

Recent works have sought to develop methods for the identification of scientific claims, with a particular focus on claims related to COVID-19. Saakyan *et al.* [32] presented COVID-Fact, a system designed specifically for verifying COVID-19 claims using the CORD-19 corpus. Wadden *et al.* [37], on the other hand, proposed a general framework for scientific claim identification using semantics to model claims and evidence. While promising, current scientific claim identification methods have limitations to address moving forward. Wadden *et al.* [38] improved claim identification in LONGCHECKER by considering full abstract context rather than isolated sentences. However, as noted by Landers *et al.* [22], existing frameworks still face challenges with scientific terminology and reasoning.

The SciTweets annotation framework by Hafid *et al.* [16] provides a valuable foundation for our scientific claim identification task. Their taxonomy categorizes Tweets as direct scientific claims, references to sources, or general terminology. We adopt this multi-label approach in our COVID-19 Twitter dataset, annotating for scientific claims, sources, and terms.

While previous works have predominantly concentrated on general Tweets across the platform, our research places emphasis on COVID-19 Tweets. In contrast to most prior studies [32,37,38] that rely on transformer based models such as BERT and its variations, our work encompasses a diverse set of models by leveraging LLMs in addition to transformers.

3 Data Collection and Annotation

The data collection from Twitter was tailored to capture a diverse array of discussions related to COVID-19 which was subsequently annotated.

3.1 Data Preparation

We used a dataset created by Zuo *et al.* [44] that contains more than 447 million Tweets collected from September 2020 to October 2021.

Influencers Accounts. We defined *influencers* as individuals and organizations that have verified accounts or those who have accounts with more than 10,000 followers.

Data Sampling. To create manageable samples for annotation and analysis, we employed iterative, targeted sampling strategies. After initial random sampling, we used keyword filtering to focus on Tweets about key topics like "face mask", "vaccine", and "quarantine", compiling corpus subsets specific to different analysis tasks. Using BERT and cosine similarity, we removed semantically similar Tweets to avoid annotation overlap. Through this multi-stage sampling approach, we arrived at final samples of 1875 Tweets only from influencers' accounts.

3.2 Manual Data Annotation

The study used a manual annotation process for Tweets, with three Computer Science undergraduate students proficient in English working together. For each task, annotators were given clear and step-by-step instructions. Each Tweet was randomly assigned to two, with a third adjudicated if needed. The consistency of annotations was evaluated using an inter-annotator agreement score.

User Profiling. To classify influencers into two distinct groups of *individuals* and *organizations*, we extracted user biographies and usernames associated with each Tweet. Subsequently, we tasked our annotators with determining the classification of each account into either group. Individual profiles are identified by personal narratives, experiences, milestones, and interests, while organizational accounts focus on professional accomplishments, formal tone, and references to collective entities or roles within organizations. The analysis yielded a Cohen's Kappa score of 0.96, indicating near-perfect agreement and reliability among annotators.

Emotion Detection. Emotion detection, aimed to identify the emotions expressed in Tweets. Emotion detection is split into two sub-tasks: whether a Tweet contains emotion or not, and if yes, what is the type of emotion? Ekman *et al.* [12] categorized human emotions into anger, surprise, disgust, enjoyment, fear, and sadness. We noticed many occurrences within these categories, except for disgust, where there were fewer samples available. As a result, we adjusted our framework to cover five primary emotional categories: *joy, sadness, surprise, fear,* and *anger* for investigating emotions expressed in Tweets. The consistency of the annotation task was assessed using a Jaccard Index score of 0.47 which represents moderate agreement among annotators for multi-categorical annotations. Also, to address the challenges of annotating emotions in a large dataset, we employed text augmentation techniques. We used back-translation, translating Tweets into foreign languages and back into English. This approach resulted in an augmented dataset with over 11,000 Tweets.

Sentiment Analysis. Our team of annotators analyzed each Tweet from the author's perspective to identify clear expressions of sentiment polarity. They classified Tweets into three categories: *positive* (hope, support, optimism), *negative* (fear, frustration, sadness), and *neutral* (no emotional expressions). We categorize Tweets based on the author's intended emotion rather than solely isolated linguistic components. For instance, we labeled the following Tweet as neutral in sentiment:

"We have jobs at serious risk NOW ! 67 of our industry cannot survive another lockdown! That is 32k high at salons amp; 251k jobs! amp; 21 billion lost to gdp So businesses are on their knees trading at 40! So please listen uk."

Despite negative phrasing like "at serious risk" and "cannot survive", our annotation process deemed the Tweeter's perspective as more objective than emotional. This exemplifies why we categorize based on holistic authorial intent rather than isolated linguistic components. By annotating based on intended emotion rather than isolated syntax, our methodology enables richer sentiment analysis. The Cohen's Kappa value of 0.46 indicates moderate alignment in sentiment annotation among our annotators. This level of agreement is considered reasonable, given that sentiment analysis involves a certain degree of subjectivity as a result of the inherent complexities of human emotions and language.

Scientific Claim Identification. To identify the type of scientific information present in Tweets, we adopted the annotation scheme established in prior work by Hafid *et al.* scheme [16] to identify and label Tweets for (i) Scientific claims or assertions of direct knowledge about COVID-19, (ii) References or citations to external scientific sources such as journals, reports, or news articles related to COVID-19, (iii) General scientific lexicon (e.g. "study", "data", "researchers") without specific factual claims. For each Tweet, our annotators assigned binary indicator values denoting the presence or absence of each scientific content type. We found that Tweets can display multiple categories simultaneously, and a score of 0.88 was obtained for Krippendorff's alpha, indicating strong agreement considering multi-categorical annotations.

Table 1 and Fig. 2 demonstrate the distribution of labels in different tasks in our dataset. While individual and organizational accounts are nearly equally represented, individuals exhibit higher rates of detected emotions and subjective positive/negative sentiment compared to organizations' prevailing neutral-

Table 1. An Overview of Annotations and Labels in the Dataset Across 4 Tasks, Including a Breakdown of [Ind]ividual and [Org]anizational Profiling.

Task	Label	Total (%)	Ind.(%)	Org.(%)
User	Individual	893 (48.0%)	–	–
Profiling	Organization	964 (52.0%)	–	–
	Emotion Existence	709 (38.2%)	28.1	10.1
	Joy	243 (13.1%)	8.7	4.4
Emotion	Sad	138 (7.4%)	5.6	1.8
Detection	Fear	143 (7.7%)	5.4	2.3
	Anger	278 (15.0%)	12.7	2.3
	Surprised	97 (5.2%)	3.9	1.3
Sentiment	Negative	364 (19.6%)	15.3	4.3
Detection	Neutral	1194 (64.3%)	23.1	41.2
	Positive	299 (16.1%)	9.6	6.5
	Claim Existence	922 (49.6%)	25.1	24.5
Scientific	Verifiable	729 (39.2%)	19.9	19.3
Claim	Reference	205 (11.0%)	5.3	5.7
	General	143 (7.7%)	4.4	3.3

ity. This evinces a contrast between the more emotional, subjective perspectives of individuals versus the objective stances organizations maintain.

Additionally, despite nearly half of Tweets containing declarative claims, most claims resist categorical verification, underscoring the need for rigorous validation to prevent misinformation, especially invoking scientific credibility. Further examination shows unreferenced claims are common among individual and organizational users. Individuals exhibit a higher percentage of general claims lacking citations. However, organizations have a slightly higher rate of referenced claims. This highlights the imperative of verifying unchecked assertions invoking scientific credibility across all user groups.

Our analysis reveals revealing contrasts in how individuals and organizations engage on Twitter. As seen in Table 1, individuals are more emotionally expressive overall, conveying greater anger while organizations project more joy. This pattern extends to sentiment as well, with organizations maintaining an impartial, neutral stance while individuals adopt more negative tones. The greater subjectivity of individuals is juxtaposed with the detached objectivity organizations pursue. Additionally, our claim analysis flags a concerning trend - a substantial number of assertions across both groups are categorized as verifiable, yet lack citations or factual references. Organizations hold a slight edge in propounding these unsubstantiated but potentially verifiable claims.

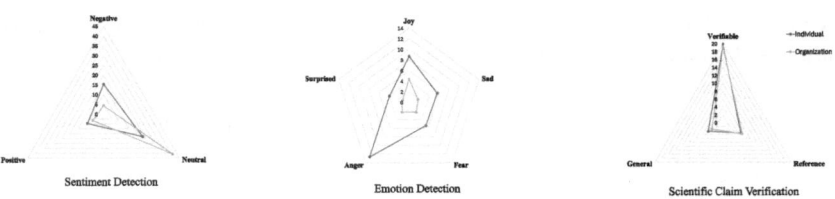

Fig. 2. Percentage Breakdown of Individual and Organizational Accounts in Sentiment Detection (Left), Emotion Detection (Middle), and Scientific Claim Identification (Right) Tasks.

4   Task 1: User Profiling

Identification of Twitter Account Ownership. Profiling the ownership of Twitter accounts allows us to distinguish between official accounts representing companies, institutions, or brands, and influencers with personal views and experiences.

To classify Twitter accounts into distinct categories of individuals and organizations, we leverage Tweet metadata. Our account identification process is based on three key features: *Twitter name*, *Twitter handle*, and *Twitter biography*. Although this approach has its limitations, such as not utilizing the actual Tweets posted by the account, it offers the benefit of requiring minimal information for the model to generate accurate predictions. Concatenating these features provides a condensed input for our BERT classifier to categorize accounts as either individual users or organizations. The data is divided into training and testing sets, with a split of 80% for training and 20% for testing. To convert the Tweet content into textual embeddings, a BERT layer is employed. Subsequently, these embeddings are fed into a single dense output layer to facilitate the classification process.

In addition to the BERT model, we also incorporated the Demographer [21] in our experiments. As an established approach for demographic inference, the Demographer extracts user metadata, linguistic cues, and network patterns to predict age, gender, and location. However, empirical results revealed BERT's overwhelming advantage. BERT outperformed Demographer in key metrics, achieving an F1 of 0.95 and an accuracy of 0.96, highlighting its proficiency in encoding semantic and contextual information from sparse text. Its self-attention mechanism can effectively model complex user attributes, despite lacking extensive feature engineering.

Topic of Occupation of the Users. User bios on Twitter offer a chance to understand the interests and occupations of the Twitter population. Occupation provides valuable insight into a user's knowledge base, credibility, authority, and sphere of influence, thereby contributing to a nuanced understanding of how Twitter influences vary across different professional segments. If an influencer's occupation is known, for instance, their Tweets might be given more weight if they are considered experts in their field, influencing not only individ-

Table 2. Top 5 Topics and Key Terms Identified Through Biography Clustering of Individual and Organization Accounts.

	Identified Topics	# Accounts	% Accounts
Individual	KAG, Trump, Trump2020	15048	4.5
	18, NSFW, Onlyfans	14730	4.2
	Periodista, Politica, Cuenta	10769	3.1
	Film, Actor, Director	8977	2.6
	Resist, BLM, Bidenharris2020	5015	1.4
Organization	Marketing, Business, Digital Tech.	7985	7.1
	Content, 18, Onlyfans Promo	6112	5.4
	Sports, Basketball, Athletics	4333	3.8
	Football, Club, League	4210	3.7
	Financial, Investment, Trading	4152	3.7

ual perspectives but also shaping collective societal discourse. Similarly, detecting occupation can also shed light on potential bias or vested interests, providing an additional layer of contextual information that is important in analyzing the authenticity and reliability of an influencer's content. From a socio-economic standpoint, knowing a user's occupation can help discern how information and influence diffusion patterns on Twitter correspond to various job sectors, thereby enhancing our understanding of societal impact. Moreover, this knowledge could be used to optimize targeted communication strategies, drive professional engagement, and develop policy-making processes that effectively address the real-time societal implications of Twitter-based influences.

By applying clustering techniques to textual descriptions in the user's biography, we can extract the most salient topics. Our approach leverages BERTopic [15] to cluster Twitter bios. First, we categorize accounts as individuals or organizations using BERT. This allows specialized clustering based on how each group crafts bios. For individuals, we extract professions, hobbies, and interests. For organizations, we identify their core purpose.

To address the issue of BERTopic producing an excessive number of outlier results, we used a technique that reduces outliers using probabilities obtained from the HBDSCAN [5]. Twitter biographies are classified into a certain topic cluster or an outlier group using the BERTopic algorithm, then the HBDSCAN model groups the data based on the most relevant subject and determines the likelihood that a Twitter bio belongs to any other cluster. Although these probabilities were not included in the initial topic clustering procedure, we reduced the number of outlier bios by choosing the topic with the highest likelihood and allocating the outlier to that category. To evaluate our optimized BERTopic approach, we compared the silhouette and coherence metrics [31] to a baseline. Silhouette quantifies cluster cohesion and separation. Our score of 0.52 confirms distinct, tightly clustered topics. Coherence measures topic interpretability. Our high score of 0.80 indicates coherent, semantically aligned topics.

Our topic clustering analysis revealed distinct trends in interests and occupations between individuals and organizations on Twitter. Table 2 displays the top 5 topics identified for each group along with selected representative words and the number of accounts per cluster. For individuals, politically-oriented topics like "KAG, Trump, Trump2020" and "Resist, BLM, Bidenharris2020" feature prominently, underscoring Twitter's role in civic discourse. Entertainment interests like "Film, Actor, Director" also rank highly. Organizations showcase more commercial themes, including "Marketing, Business, Digital Tech" and "Financial, Investment, Trading". Sports-related accounts also comprise a major cluster, consistent with the prevalence of teams and leagues on the platform.

The bifurcation between individuals and organizations is clearly evidenced in these topic profiles. By categorizing accounts before clustering bios, we can extract key themes unique to each group's priorities and intentions on Twitter. This table summarizes our core findings on the primary spheres of interest emerging from biography text analysis.

5   Task 2: Emotion Detection

For this task, we developed a pipeline system to categorize emotions in Tweets. First, a preliminary model filters Tweets to detect any emotions, while those with detectable emotions are passed to the next phase. In the second stage, five specialized classifiers evaluate each distinct emotion, identifying *joy*, *sadness*, *surprise*, *fear*, or *anger* specifically.

To train models for our pipeline architecture, we partitioned the Tweet dataset into three subsets - 70% for training, 20% for testing, and 10% for validation. With the goal of classifying individual emotions, we implemented six distinct binary classifiers. Five of these models focus on identifying the presence of one specific emotion: joy, sadness, surprise, fear or anger. The sixth classifier serves as a preliminary filter, detecting if a Tweet contains any emotion at all before passing it to the specific emotion classifiers.

In our quest to determine the best classifier, we employed a BERT model consisting of a BERT layer followed by a dense output layer. We evaluated the performance of this model using both augmented and non-augmented training sets. Moreover, to overcome the limitations posed by limited training data, we harnessed the power of SetFit [35] as a few-shot learning technique. Additionally, we have used LLMs like GPT-3.5 [28] and LLaMA-2-70B [34] and to probe these models we have used the following prompt:

"Classify the emotion of the Tweet. Does this Tweet contain any emotion? Yes or No. Does this Tweet contain Joy emotion? Yes or No. Does this Tweet contain Sad emotion? Yes or No. Does this Tweet contain Surprise emotion? Yes or No. Does this Tweet contain Anger emotion? Yes or No. Does this Tweet contain Fear emotion? Yes or No."

This comprehensive approach enabled us to thoroughly explore and compare various classifier configurations. Table 4 presents a comparative evaluation of emotion detection performance using BERT, SetFit, GPT-3.5, and LLaMA-2-70B models. Experiments were conducted using the both original dataset and an augmented version expanded via back-translation. The results demonstrate SetFit's effectiveness as a few-shot learning technique, achieving the top F1 scores for the existence of emotion. The model maintains consistent performance across all categories as it uses sentence transformers to generate semantically meaningful sentence embedding preserving the semantic integrity of entire sentences, unlike traditional models such as BERT which uses individual tokens. BERT, on the original dataset, exhibits high variance, for the F1 score. Its performance is lowest for sadness and surprise. Augmenting the training data substantially improves BERT's performance, reducing its gap with SetFit. The augmented BERT model attains a comparable F1 score to that of SetFit for emotion existence and for specific emotions. Furthermore, GPT-3.5 achieved the highest F1 score for detecting emotions like sadness and surprise.

Analysis indicates joy is detected most accurately by all models. This emotion likely has a more recognizable linguistic pattern. Intrinsically more complex emotions like sadness and surprise pose greater challenges for the BERT-based model but the chat-based models were able to make better inferences of these emotions as it is trained on a diverse range of text data. However, the chat-based models were not able to detect the emotions from Tweets efficiently, and hence by using better prompts the performance of these models can be improved. Overall, GPT-3.5 demonstrates proficiency in multi-label Tweet emotion detection and good choice for emotion-based tasks.

6 Task 3: Sentiment Analysis

Our main focus in the analysis was on assigning sentiment labels to the Tweets, classifying them into three categories: *positive*, *negative*, and *neutral*. We performed pre-processing steps to replace emojis and remove hashtags from Tweets. Additionally, we replace usernames with "USER_HANDLE", URLs with "URL_TOKEN", and substitute special characters with NULL characters. To ensure consistency, the entire text of the Tweets was converted to lowercase. These preprocessing steps aimed to clean the data and standardize the text for further analysis. We use BERT, RoBERTa$_{\text{Twitter}}$ [3], SetFit, GPT-3.5, and LLaMA-2-70B to conduct sentiment analysis on our dataset. RoBERTa$_{\text{Twitter}}$ is a RoBERTa-base model trained on 58 million Tweets and fine-tuned for sentiment analysis using the TweetEval benchmark. The BERT model was fine-tuned by adding a single dense layer with three outputs representing negative, neutral, and positive sentiments. Additionally, SetFit was employed, which is designed to train models with limited amounts of data. For the LLMs we have used the following prompt for sentiment detection:

Classify the sentiment of the author behind the Tweet as "Negative", "Neutral", or "Positive".

Table 4 shows that our task-specific model, RoBERTa$_{Twitter}$ achieved the highest F1 scores for identifying negative sentiment, and positive sentiment, and performed competitively on neutral sentiment compared to SetFit. In contrast, LLaMa-2-70B achieved the lowest F1 score in neutral sentiment. Conversely, GPT-3.5 achieved the lowest score in negative sentiment.

Our findings demonstrate the effectiveness of using a model fine-tuned on informal, social media text for accurate classification of sentiment polarity and intensity. The social media-optimized RoBERTa architecture was best able to capture the nuances and variances in how sentiment is expressed on such platforms. This highlights the importance of using task and domain-specific models for optimized performance on sentiment analysis versus general pre-trained models like BERT, SetFit, or LLMs alone.

Nevertheless, it is worth noting that our experimentation with TextBlob and VADER lexicon-based models had subpar results in Tweet sentiment analysis due to their limitations in contextual learning. These models were less suitable for sentiment analysis than contextual models like BERT and RoBERTa. The analysis also revealed that neutral Tweets were classified most accurately, while negative Tweets posed the greatest challenges.

Table 3. COVID-19 Keywords for 6 Topics that were used for Sentiment and Scientific Claim Analysis.

Topic	Keywords
Face Mask	mask, face, N95, KN95, covering, nose wire, adjustable strap, breathable fabric
Travel	travel, border, closures, hotel, passport
WFH	wfh, home, remote, hotel, telecommuting, virtual, video, zoom
Social Distancing	social, distancing, six feet, physical, close contact
Lockdown	lockdown, stay home, curfew, restricted movement, quarantine, isolation
Vaccine	vaccine, vaccination, vaccinated, pfizer, moderna, astraZeneca, johnson, sinopharm, sputnik

Topic-Targeted Sentiment Analysis. To analyze the polarity of the sentiments for specific discussion topics on Twitter, we filtered the full dataset to extract relevant subsets of Tweets. As shown in Table 3, we focused on six key topics and curated custom datasets for each one. For example, the "Lockdown" topic, we searched for Tweets containing related terms like "stay home", "curfew". This coarse-grained, keyword-based approach produced subsets containing only relevant Tweets for each discussion theme. The sentiment expressed in these subsets was classified using our top-performing model.

Figure 3 depicts the polarity of sentiments expressed by influencers over a 220-day period on six crucial themes. The graph reveals that influencers, including individuals and organizations, predominantly express neutral feelings for all key topics, indicating that influencers are primarily focused on distributing information to their followers during a crisis. Individuals tend to display more negative attitudes than organizations, as organizations represent a collective entity with goals, objectives, and brand images. They often maintain a professional demeanor to avoid negativity in discussions. On the other hand, individuals are more subjective towards their feelings. Furthermore, it can be noted that the topic of face masks is rated least positively by both individuals and organizations. There were instances of misinformation and conspiracy theories involving face masks throughout the pandemic and influencers may have been afraid to market face masks for fear of endorsing or spreading inaccurate information.

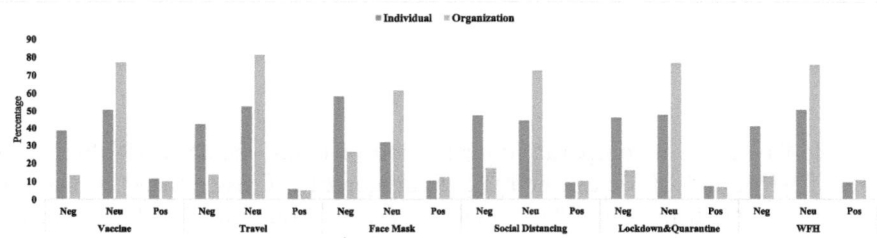

Fig. 3. Individual vs. Organization Sentiment Polarity on Significant Topics Related to COVID-19. Individuals are more subjective towards their opinions whereas organization tries to maintain a professional demeanor by posting neutral Tweets.

7   Task 4: Scientific Claim Identification

The task of identifying scientific content on Twitter involves categorizing them based on their scientific information. The annotation scheme labels Tweets for *scientifically verifiable claims*, *scientific knowledge references*, and *general scientific claim*. Each Tweet was assigned binary values representing the presence or absence of these scientific content types, and multiple categories could be present in a single Tweet.

In this work, we utilize a SciBERT-based [16] classifier for categorizing the diversity of scientific content on Twitter. We implemented a multi-label system to categorize scientific Tweet content. Tweets were assigned to one or more of the three categories (similar to our annotation). Similar to the prior tasks, we conducted experiments with both BERT, SetFit, and LLMs as well. Tweets received a 0/1 label for each category indicating exclusion/inclusion. In another branch of experiments, we evaluated the model on a binary scientific classification task. Rather than multi-label categorization, this setup predicted whether Tweets were related to science or not.

Table 4. Comparative Performance Analysis of BERT, SetFit, Task Specific, and LLMs in Emotion Detection, Sentiment Analysis, and Scientific Claim Identification. Task Specific Models, for Emotion Detection, we employed BERT with augmented data and for Sentiment Analysis, RoBERTa$_{Twitter}$ was utilized and SciBERT was employed for Scientific Claim Identification.

Task	Label	BERT				SetFit				Task Specific Model				GPT-3.5				LLaMA-2-70B			
		P	R	A	F1	P	R	A	F1	P	R	A	F1	P	R	A	F1	P	R	A	F1
Emotion Detection	Emotion Existence	0.85	0.77	0.77	0.81	0.83	0.82	0.83	0.83	0.85	0.79	0.84	0.83	0.75	0.70	0.70	0.70	0.76	0.59	0.59	0.56
	Joy	0.79	0.81	0.93	0.80	0.93	0.91	0.94	0.92	0.85	0.79	0.90	0.82	0.91	0.91	0.91	0.91	0.91	0.81	0.81	0.84
	Sadness	0.67	0.61	0.89	0.63	0.76	0.81	0.86	0.78	0.74	0.63	0.89	0.67	0.91	0.93	0.93	0.92	0.93	0.66	0.66	0.75
	Surprised	0.45	0.26	0.88	0.33	0.79	0.79	0.87	0.79	0.77	0.48	0.86	0.59	0.91	0.87	0.87	0.89	0.91	0.66	0.66	0.75
	Fear	0.64	0.46	0.88	0.53	0.87	0.83	0.89	0.85	0.80	0.64	0.87	0.71	0.88	0.80	0.80	0.83	0.90	0.56	0.56	0.64
	Anger	0.84	0.86	0.93	0.84	0.90	0.91	0.91	0.91	0.84	0.92	0.89	0.88	0.89	0.89	0.89	0.89	0.89	0.78	0.78	0.80
Sentiment Detection	Negative	0.68	0.53	0.53	0.60	0.64	0.66	0.66	0.65	0.77	0.68	0.67	0.72	0.47	0.73	0.73	0.57	0.35	0.69	0.46	0.69
	Neutral	0.80	0.93	0.93	0.86	0.86	0.86	0.87	0.86	0.86	0.91	0.91	0.89	0.88	0.54	0.54	0.67	0.75	0.39	0.52	0.39
	Positive	0.76	0.46	0.46	0.58	0.75	0.72	0.72	0.74	0.81	0.75	0.75	0.78	0.48	0.88	0.88	0.62	0.40	0.74	0.54	0.74
Scientific Claim	Claim Existence	0.85	0.69	0.77	0.76	0.88	0.80	0.85	0.84	0.85	0.76	0.81	0.80	0.60	1.00	0.60	0.67	0.68	0.88	0.67	0.67
	Verifiable	0.85	0.83	0.85	0.84	0.95	0.99	0.97	0.97	0.86	0.93	0.82	0.80	0.70	0.72	0.71	0.70	0.72	0.71	0.72	0.71
	Reference	0.77	0.51	0.87	0.49	0.64	0.78	0.89	0.70	0.88	0.84	0.88	0.87	0.67	0.71	0.72	0.67	0.77	0.74	0.71	0.73
	General	0.80	0.66	0.93	0.70	0.53	0.70	0.92	0.61	0.94	0.92	0.93	0.92	0.71	0.71	0.72	0.67	0.61	0.70	0.71	0.64

Table 4 presents a comparative evaluation of task-specific model SciBERT, BERT, SetFit, and LLMs on the task of categorizing Tweets based on the type of scientific content present. The models are assessed on multi-label classification for detecting Tweets scientific claims. containing: (1) verifiable scientific claims, (2) references to scientific sources, and (3) general scientific terminology. Our study indicates that SetFit excels in recognizing scientific claims, particularly in identifying those that are verifiable. Nonetheless, for categorizing reference and general claim types, the SciBERT model, tailored specifically for scientific text, demonstrates superior efficacy. Conversely, GPT-3.5 and LLaMA-2-70B exhibit limited capability in detecting scientific claims.

Topic-Targeted Scientific Claim Analysis. To investigate the dissemination of scientific information about COVID-19 issued by individuals and organizations based on Table 3 across six topics, we conducted an analysis and the results are provided in Table 5. Results showed that individuals and organizations had the lowest percentage of Tweets without factual assertions. On the other hand, organizations shared the most scientifically verifiable Tweets, complete with authentic references, outnumbering individual Tweets across these six topics except for Travel. As a result, it is evident that organizations propagated more credible claims than individuals since they have established reputations to sustain.

Table 5. Scientific Claims classified into [Ver]ifiable, [Ref]erences to Scientific sources, and [Gen]eral categories on Topics Related to COVID-19 for Individual vs. Organization.

Topic	Ver		Ref		Gen	
	Ind(%)	Org(%)	Ind(%)	Org(%)	Ind(%)	Org(%)
Vaccine	41.00	48.91	46.73	53.24	28.17	34.28
Travel	45.96	39.30	55.86	44.12	30.22	25.65
Face Mask	30.47	58.00	34.78	65.20	19.21	34.91
Social Distancing	37.24	44.81	41.99	47.99	25.03	29.71
Lockdown & Quarantine	39.90	47.97	47.01	52.97	26.76	32.32
Work From Home	42.75	47.75	48.54	51.44	28.88	33.52

8   Conclusion

Analysis of COVID-19 Twitter discourse in this paper offers valuable insights into how influential voices shape public narratives during global crises. By developing an integrated framework to characterize Tweets across multiple facets-including user profiles, emotions, sentiment, and scientific claims-this research enables a nuanced investigation of influencer's role amidst the pandemic. Using BERT embeddings, we improved account classification between individuals and organizations. Through biography clustering with BERTopic, we revealed influencer communities' Tweets about COVID-19, benefiting marketing research and dataset curation. Additionally, we pioneered an emotion detection model for Tweets, released on HuggingFace. We further constructed a tailored sentiment classifier to track attitude trajectories throughout the pandemic. Uniquely, our approach identifies author sentiment, while prior works relied solely on textual polarity. This nuanced technique provides richer insights into Twitter's emotional landscape. Scientific claim verification involved training a custom SciBERT-based classifier on domain-specific COVID-19 data. Key findings reveal notable differences between individuals and organizations in emotion expression, engagement patterns, and claim verification. The techniques developed in this work can inform communication strategies to promote healthy public discussions as online platforms grow increasingly influential.

Limitations include dataset constraints like language and scope. The dataset is restricted to English Tweets from influencers above 10,000 followers, limiting generalizability. Inherent subjectivity in annotating textual emotions also poses challenges. Additionally, the models rely solely on textual content without contextual cues. Nonetheless, the toolkit offers unprecedented capacity to investigate the complex, far-reaching impacts of COVID-19 across the digital landscape over time. Moving forward, we plan investigations into follower influence dynamics stemming from influencer content. We intend to develop a quantifiable metric assessing the degree of impact influencers have on followers. Formally evaluating the sway held by influencers via this proposed index would significantly advance comprehension of how impactful their messaging proves. Our forthcoming work seeks to unravel the mechanisms and effects at play following the publication of questionable influencer posts. Pinpointing the relationships between influencer content and audience groups represents an open research question warranting rigorous inspection using computational methods we aim to pioneer.

Acknowledgement. This work was partially supported by the U.S. National Science Foundation under Grant No. 1822118 and 2226232, Award Numbers DMS 2123761, the member partners of the NSF IUCRC Center for Cyber Security Analytics and Automation - AMI, NewPush, Cyber Risk Research, NIST and ARL, by NIST under Award No. 60NANB23D152, the State of Colorado (grant #SB 18-086) and the authors' institutions. Any opinions, findings, and conclusions or recommendations expressed in this material are those of the authors and do not necessarily reflect the views of the National Science Foundation, or other organizations and agencies.

References

1. Abd-Alrazaq, A., Alhuwail, D., Househ, M., Hamdi, M., Shah, Z.: Top concerns of tweeters during the COVID-19 pandemic: infoveillance study. J. Med. Internet Res. **22**(4), e19016 (2020)
2. Ainapure, B.S., et al.: Sentiment analysis of COVID-19 tweets using deep learning and lexicon-based approaches. Sustainability **15**(3), 2573 (2023)
3. Barbieri, F., Camacho-Collados, J., Anke, L.E., Neves, L.: TweetEval: unified benchmark and comparative evaluation for tweet classification. In: Findings of the Association for Computational Linguistics: EMNLP 2020, pp. 1644–1650 (2020)
4. Bruns, A., Harrington, S., Hurcombe, E.: 'Corona? 5G? or Both?': the dynamics of COVID-19/5G conspiracy theories on Facebook. Media Int. Aust. **177**(1), 12–29 (2020)
5. Campello, R.J.G.B., Moulavi, D., Sander, J.: Density-based clustering based on hierarchical density estimates. In: Advances in Knowledge Discovery and Data Mining, PAKDD 2013, pp. 160–172 (2013)
6. Chakraborty, K., Bhatia, S., Bhattacharyya, S., Platos, J., Bag, R., Hassanien, A.E.: Sentiment analysis of COVID-19 tweets by deep learning classifiers-a study to show how popularity is affecting accuracy in social media. Appl. Soft Comput. **97**, 106754 (2020)
7. Chau, M., Xu, J.: Business intelligence in blogs: understanding consumer interactions and communities. MIS Q. **36**(4), 1189–1216 (2012)
8. Cinelli, M., et al.: The COVID-19 social media infodemic. Sci. Rep. **10**(1), 1–10 (2020)
9. Devlin, J., Chang, M., Lee, K., Toutanova, K.: BERT: pre-training of deep bidirectional transformers for language understanding. CoRR abs/1810.04805 (2018)
10. Dubey, A.D.: Twitter sentiment analysis during COVID-19 outbreak. Available at SSRN 3572023 (2020)
11. Egger, R., Yu, J.: A topic modeling comparison between LDA, NMF, Top2Vec, and BERTopic to demystify twitter posts. Front. Sociol. **7**, 886498 (2022)
12. Ekman, P., et al.: Basic emotions. Handb. Cogn. Emot. **98**(45–60), 16 (1999)

13. Freberg, K., Graham, K., McGaughey, K., Freberg, L.A.: Who are the social media influencers? A study of public perceptions of personality. Public Relat. Rev. **37**(1), 90–92 (2011)
14. Ghebreyesus, T.A.: Munich security conference. World Health Organ. **15** (2020)
15. Grootendorst, M.: BERTopic: neural topic modeling with a class-based TF-IDF procedure. arXiv preprint arXiv:2203.05794 (2022)
16. Hafid, S., Schellhammer, S., Bringay, S., Todorov, K., Dietze, S.: Scitweets - a dataset and annotation framework for detecting scientific online discourse. In: Proceedings of the 31st ACM International Conference on Information & Knowledge Managemen, pp. 3988–3992 (2022)
17. Jalil, Z., et al.: COVID-19 related sentiment analysis using state-of-the-art machine learning and deep learning techniques. Front. Public Health **9**, 2276 (2022)
18. Kaplan, A.M., Haenlein, M.: Users of the world, unite! The challenges and opportunities of social media. Bus. Horiz. **53**(1), 59–68 (2010)
19. Kappus, P., Groß, P.: Finding clusters of similar-minded people on twitter regarding the Covid-19 pandemic. arXiv preprint arXiv:2203.04764 (2021)
20. Kaur, H., Ahsaan, S.U., Alankar, B., Chang, V.: A proposed sentiment analysis deep learning algorithm for analyzing COVID-19 tweets. Inf. Syst. Front. 1–13 (2021)
21. Knowles, R., Carroll, J., Dredze, M.: Demographer: extremely simple name demographics. In: Proceedings of the First Workshop on NLP and Computational Social Science, pp. 108–113 (2016)
22. Landers, E., et al.: An assessment of scientific claim verification frameworks: final presentation. Comput. Inf. Sci.: Res. Exp. Undergr. Disinf. Detect. Anal. **8** (2022)
23. Liang, S., Zhang, X., Ren, Z., Kanoulas, E.: Dynamic embeddings for user profiling in twitter. In: Proceedings of the 24th ACM SIGKDD International Conference on Knowledge Discovery & Data Mining, pp. 1764–1773 (2018)
24. Lopez, C.E., Vasu, M., Gallemore, C.: Understanding the perception of COVID-19 policies by mining a multilanguage twitter dataset. CoRR abs/2003.10359 (2020)
25. Manguri, K.H., Ramadhan, R.N., Amin, P.R.M.: Twitter sentiment analysis on worldwide COVID-19 outbreaks. Kurd. J. Appl. Res. 54–65 (2020)
26. Mansoor, M., Gurumurthy, K., U, A.R., Prasad, V.R.B.: Global sentiment analysis of COVID-19 tweets over time. CoRR abs/2010.14234 (2020)
27. Nandal, N., Tanwar, R., Pathan, A.S.K.: Sentiment analysis based emotion extraction for COVID-19 using crawled tweets and global statistics for mental health. Procedia Comput. Sci. **218**, 949–958 (2023)
28. OpenAI: Models (2023). https://platform.openai.com/docs/models/gpt-3-5. Accessed 18 Nov 2023
29. Pennycook, G., McPhetres, J., Zhang, Y., Lu, J.G., Rand, D.G.: Fighting COVID-19 misinformation on social media: experimental evidence for a scalable accuracy-nudge intervention. Psychol. Sci. **31**(7), 770–780 (2020)
30. Rajput, N.K., Grover, B.A., Rathi, V.K.: Word frequency and sentiment analysis of twitter messages during Coronavirus pandemic. CoRR abs/2004.03925 (2020)
31. Rousseeuw, P.J.: Silhouettes: a graphical aid to the interpretation and validation of cluster analysis. J. Comput. Appl. Math. **20**, 53–65 (1987)
32. Saakyan, A., Chakrabarty, T., Muresan, S.: COVID-fact: fact extraction and verification of real-world claims on COVID-19 pandemic. In: Proceedings of the 59th Annual Meeting of the Association for Computational Linguistics and the 11th International Joint Conference on Natural Language Processing (Volume 1: Long Papers), pp. 2116–2129 (2021)

33. Storey, V.C., O'Leary, D.E.: Text analysis of evolving emotions and sentiments in COVID-19 twitter communication. Cogn. Comput. **16**(4), 1834–1857 (2024)
34. Touvron, H., et al.: LLaMA 2: open foundation and fine-tuned chat models. arXiv preprint arXiv:2307.09288 (2023)
35. Tunstall, L., et al.: Efficient few-shot learning without prompts. arXiv preprint arXiv:2209.11055 (2022)
36. Vijay, T., Chawla, A., Dhanka, B., Karmakar, P.: Sentiment analysis on COVID-19 twitter data. In: 2020 5th IEEE International Conference on Recent Advances and Innovations in Engineering (ICRAIE), pp. 1–7 (2020)
37. Wadden, D., et al.: Fact or fiction: verifying scientific claims. In: Proceedings of the 2020 Conference on Empirical Methods in Natural Language Processing (EMNLP), pp. 7534–7550. Association for Computational Linguistics (2020)
38. Wadden, D., Lo, K., Wang, L.L., Cohan, A., Beltagy, I., Hajishirzi, H.: Longchecker: improving scientific claim verification by modeling full-abstract context. arXiv preprint arXiv:2112.01640 (2021)
39. Wood-Doughty, Z., Mahajan, P., Dredze, M.: Johns Hopkins or Johnny-Hopkins: classifying individuals versus organizations on twitter. In: Proceedings of the Second Workshop on Computational Modeling of People's Opinions, Personality, and Emotions in Social Media, pp. 56–61. Association for Computational Linguistics (2018)
40. Wrycza, S., Maślankowski, J.: Social media users' opinions on remote work during the COVID-19 pandemic. Thematic and sentiment analysis. Inf. Syst. Manage. **37**(4), 288–297 (2020)
41. Xavier, T., Lambert, J.: Sentiment and emotion trends in nurses' tweets about the COVID-19 pandemic. J. Nurs. Scholarsh. **54**(5), 613–622 (2022)
42. Yu, H., Yang, C.C., Yu, P., Liu, K.: Emotion diffusion effect: negative sentiment COVID-19 tweets of public organizations attract more responses from followers. PLoS ONE **17**(3), e0264794 (2022)
43. Zhou, J., Yang, S., Xiao, C., Chen, F.: Examination of community sentiment dynamics due to COVID-19 pandemic: a case study from a state in Australia. SN Comput. Sci. **2**, 1–11 (2021)
44. Zuo, C., Banerjee, R., Chaleshtori, F.H., Shirazi, H., Ray, I.: Seeing Should Probably Not be believing: the role of deceptive support in COVID-19 misinformation on twitter. ACM J. Data Inf. Qual. **15**(1), 1–26 (2022)

Influence Detection in Agetech on Social Platforms Using Machine Learning and Classifier Calibration

Noel Khaemba[1]([✉]) [iD], Issa Traoré[1] [iD], and Mohammad Mamun[2] [iD]

[1] Department of Electrical and Computer Engineering, University of Victoria,
Victoria, BC V8P 5C2, Canada
noelk@uvic.ca
[2] National Research Council of Canada, Government of Canada, Ottawa,
ON K1A 0R6, Canada

Abstract. As seniors continue to age and look to age in place by utilizing smart devices with sensors, online platforms are a major resource for them and their care givers to socialize and search or look for information on agetech. This comes with a risk as they can be unfairly targeted or influenced in a certain way. Influence refers to information or action that can cause a change in direction, thought or action either positively or negatively, some sort of coordinated manipulation either positively or negatively. There are many influence campaigns propagated through social media and our focus is on information that targets the elderly particularly on the topic of agetech. This paper presents a review of existing work around influence campaigns in general, the methods used in influence detection and the obtained results. To our knowledge none of the existing work has addressed influence campaigns from agetech perspective. With that in mind, we developed a new approach for detecting influence campaigns aimed at agetech using machine learning and classifier calibration. We used machine learning to highlight influence campaign and misinformation in agetech. To develop and evaluate our approach, we collected an agetech dataset consisting of a set of tweets that contain the hashtag agetech. The evaluation yielded encouraging results.

Keywords: Agetech · Influence campaign · Aging in place · Fake news · Machine learning · Misinformation

1 Introduction

The number of seniors using the Internet and especially social media platforms is expected to grow over the years. One major area of interest to seniors using social platforms is agetech as they come across and consume information about Internet of Things (IoT) devices for aging in place. In as much as this information could be useful to them, there is also a risk of susceptibility to getting influenced either negatively or positively. Positive influence can, for instance,

M. Al-kfairy et al. (Eds.): SocialSec 2024, LNCS 15565, pp. 23–37, 2025.
https://doi.org/10.1007/978-981-96-3774-4_2

make them get to know about a certain product or a meeting through which they can gain beneficial information about agetech while negative influence could be a case where they become victims of misinformation or disinformation and get scammed. With the evolving tactics of malicious actors tools like ChatGPT and Gemini which process textual input and generate human-like text can be used in influence campaigns. Influence campaigns can be propagated on social media platforms using for instance URLs, text and images.

An influence campaign occurs when a set of users' posts have a common objective and talking points, for instance, to promote a product, meeting, conference or to criticize a person, product or to promote disinformation in a given online discussion. This implies that the text in the posts is the same or similar. Coordinated campaigns are non-organic and mainly consist of spam and promotional messages that are driven by few accounts flooding messages to the platform.

1.1   Our Contributions

In this paper, we present an approach to detect influence campaigns targeted at senior citizens. The goal being to protect them from online social media manipulation by providing a filtering system that detects influence campaigns, for instance, in marketing or forums where seniors are targeted in an unfair way. Our approach consists of determining the factors and characteristics underlying influence campaign susceptibility which can be used to assess the impact of the influencer and the impact on the influenced elderly person. This entails understanding what kind of content do the elderly engage with and the patterns that make them susceptible to manipulations stemming from influence campaigns. It involves analyzing the susceptibility of an individual to influence campaigns based on their personal account profile, viewed content, interactions or engagement history, social connections so as to provide risk alerts and assessments that are personalized.

To develop and evaluate the proposed model, we harvested a dataset consisting of 6825 tweets that contain #agetech. The dataset was manually labelled by assigning an influence campaign label in the range 0 to 1. We trained machine learning (ML) models on this labelled dataset to automatically detect agetech influence campaign.

The core contributions of our work are summarized as follows:

- We present a labelled tweets dataset for agetech influence campaign which is unique to our case because there are no existing resources with this kind of data.
- We use classifier calibration to demonstrate automatic influence campaign detection achieving great performance that outperforms the standard machine learning methods.

The remaining sections are structured as follows. Section 2 discusses related work in the area of influence campaign. Section 3 presents our dataset, outlines data labeling process, and preliminary analysis. Section 4 presents our approach and model for influence detection using machine learning models. Section 5 outlines the experimental evaluation. Sect. 6 presents the concluding remarks and areas for future study that we intend to further explore.

2   Related Work

2.1   On Detecting Coordinated Campaigns

Cao et al. [3] emphasized in their work the fact that URLs can be used to share both beneficial and malicious artifacts or detrimental knowledge. URL sharing can be organic but sometimes it could be strategically organized with the intention, for example, to promote a certain product or person. Cao et al. [3] conducted a study that explored URL sharing by investigating user behaviour among individuals and groups. The authors proposed a method to model, identify, characterize, and classify organic and organized groups that are involved in URL sharing. The proposed approach is guided by the premise that the patterns of individual-based behavioral signals observed in their URL posting activities can be used to reveal groups of accounts that participate in similar activities.

Mesnards et al. [13] developed an approach to detect coordinated influence campaigns performed by bots on twitter. The authors observed that bots interact with people more than with each other. Considering such observation, they developed a probability model based on the Ising model from statistical physics to represent the network structure and bot labels. The aim is to simultaneously detect multiple bots engaged in coordinated influence campaigns, which distinguishes their approach from methods that identify bots individually. The proposed algorithm utilizes the Ising model to find the maximum likelihood assignment of bot labels through solving a minimum cut problem. By validating the approach against human-labeled ground truth, the authors claimed it can accurately detect bots compared to existing methods. Their study also revealed that the content posted by the identified bots, suggested a coordinated agenda related to geopolitical issues [12,13].

Mesnards et al. [13] proposed a bot detection algorithm considered to be language-agnostic which means that it is applicable to various social networks across different countries without requiring prior knowledge of language, specific individuals or culture. The authors compared their approach with previous bot detection algorithms, emphasizing its efficiency in handling large networks. The proposed algorithm was evaluated on different Twitter datasets related to various events, such as elections and conspiracy theories. The results showed that the proposed algorithm performed better than an existing bot detection algorithm called BotOrNot, in terms of the area under the ROC curve (AUC) while achieving competitive run time in the cases tested [13].

Lee et al. [9] focused on detecting coordinated free text campaigns in social media, particularly campaigns including spamming, advertising, and political astroturfing. They extracted campaigns from large-scale social media based on a content-driven framework that links free text posts with common "talking points". The key steps of the proposed framework include isolating coherent campaigns using graph mining techniques, then identifying correlation in text, based on the message and user and eventually analyzing temporal behaviors of various campaign types [9]. By studying twitter messages, the authors identified five campaign types which are Promotion, Spam, Celebrity, News and Template. They then demonstrated how these campaigns can be extracted with high recall and precision. The posts consist of duplicate messages with different accounts tagged and trending keywords, and may also contain a link to a malicious site [9].

Assenmacher et al. [2] used unsupervised stream clustering to detect coordinated campaigns which are engineered by malicious manipulation versus normal trend evolution. They were able to distinguish whether a campaign is organic/automatic or orchestrated/human-driven. They emphasized that it is important to also establish the origin and motive of a campaign, observed topic, and who are the participants and means used in placing a topic.

Weber et al. [17] presented an approach for detecting campaigns such as organized trolling and astroturfing by evaluating account meta data and interactions. This involved determining how campaign actors coordinate their activities and establishing that there are anomalous levels of coincidental behaviour.

Social media influence is dependent on information dissemination and engagement. The proposed approach involves analyzing the activities between accounts to construct latent connection networks (LCNs) and using these to detect highly coordinating communities (HCCs). The highest coordinating communities are identified using a community detection algorithm called FSA_V which is a variation of focal structures analysis (FSA) because of its ability to reveal influential sets of users instead of individuals. LCNs are constructed based on links between accounts like co-retweets where the same tweet is retweeted, co-URL where the same URL is used in different tweets, co-hash tag or co-conv where a set of accounts join the same conversation.

Besides FSA_V, the authors used two other campaign detection methods based, respectively, on k-nearest neighbors (KNN) algorithm and a simple threshold which maximizes the mean edge weight (MEW) to HCC size ratio. There were large discrepancies in the HCCs extracted by the three methods, therefore tuning and significant pre-processing is recommended in order to obtain interpretable results.

Hui et al. [6] developed a tool called BotSlayer that can detect coordinated campaigns in real time on twitter. They underscored the fact that social media platforms can be manipulated in different ways including trolling, astroturfing and misinformation. This is achieved through bots or accounts that are not authentic and might be controlled by software deployed to push certain narrative such as influencing an election. The BotSlayer tool uses an anomaly detection model that flags specific entities like trending accounts, phrases, media, links or hashtags that are propagated in a coordinated manner. Using its dashboard one can submit some query terms to collect data on tweets that meet the query criteria. It then outputs the most suspicious entities which can be sorted based on mean bot score, and number of accounts or tweets containing the entity.

Chen et al. [4] noted that in the past few years there has been a significant increase in bots or automated accounts and hijacked accounts on Twitter which have clickbait posts or send spam to influence public opinion on certain topics, spread malware through links or generate traffic to specific sites in promotional campaigns. It is estimated that about 9% to 17% of accounts on Twitter are bots sending out more than 15% of the tweets [4]. They also noted that bots send out tweets which contain URLs three times more than human accounts implying that bots mostly send out tweets that consist of URLs. The authors developed an unsupervised method for detecting spam campaigns in real time, which relies on identifying bots using shortened URLs and having duplicate tweets over a given time. Using the approach, they built a blacklist of URLs, Twitter accounts and email addresses with the goal of sharing the threat findings in real time.

2.2   On Detecting Influence Campaigns

In an effort to address the challenges posed by social media influence campaigns to public discourse and democracy, Luceri et al. [11] proposed a novel influence campaign detection method that utilizes Large Language Models (LLMs) The authors analyzed influence campaigns from four countries by utilizing open-source LLMs to detect drivers of these operations. The study benchmarked the proposed method against existing techniques and highlighted the effectiveness of LLM-based approaches in identifying influence campaigns. The study acknowledged current state-of-the-art methods and emphasized their diminishing performance when applied to new influence campaigns, highlighting the need for dynamic detection methods. The proposed methodology addresses this challenge by incorporating content, network structures, and user metadata, which are transformed into a textual format compatible with LLMs. The results demonstrated the model's success in identifying influence campaigns while adapting to the multilingual and diverse nature of social media, thus providing a robust detection mechanism [11].

Mostafa et al. [14] presented an approach for detecting spam campaigns based on tweet text using deep learning methods. They first represent each of the tweets as a sentence embedding (Sen2Vec), check for text similarity and as a result build a graph with content that has similar intention or purpose. Thereafter they perform cohesive campaign extraction. The data is then classified using text clustering and Siamese Recurrent Network. They were able to achieve high precision and recall using these techniques in classifying the samples as spam or non-spam. According to the authors, the proposed method improves the accuracy and speed of spam detection compared to existing techniques. They suggested that for future work, it would be interesting to add the tweet timestamp so as to obtain similar content with a consideration of the time, also there is a need to enhance similarity extraction so as to tell text similarity even when strange words are used in tweets. They also recommended using more diverse datasets with less bias and using ensemble learning as a way to fix the spam drift problem considering that the characteristics of spam keep changing over time [14].

Varol et al. [16] focused on developing a method for early detection of information campaigns using trending memes particularly for advertisement. They mentioned that the three main challenging questions around information campaigns are what information can be trusted as verified facts versus fake news or rumours, how is the campaign propagated in terms of tools or strategies used like trolls, social bots and manipulated accounts, and lastly who are the concealed entities behind the campaigns. They also stated that there are challenges in discriminating influence campaigns from grassroot conversations, and even defining when a campaign occurs is difficult because there are various factors to be considered like user engagement dynamics, the nature of the content and the intended purpose of the source.

Tussyadiah et al. [15] established that there is a relationship between the engagement of consumers in social media platforms and their susceptibility to global consumption influence. They investigated how the level of connectedness and social influence between consumers and their peers can cause higher susceptibility to global consumption influence particularly in the area of restaurant consumption. According to the authors, influence susceptibility is heightened through factors like social prestige, conformity to trend, and quality perception.

Alizadeh et al. [1] focused on extracting coordinated influence operations from organic social media activity using content based features. They used a Reddit dataset about Russian influence and a publicly available twitter dataset on Venezuelan, Chinese and Russian trolls targeting the United States. They trained and tested their models over monthly time windows for the different campaigns to assess its effectiveness in differentiating influence efforts from political or general users.

For feature engineering they expanded the shortened URLs and applied some preprocessing on the text. For each post and its URL, they compute five features that can be easily interpreted by humans. The first feature is content which consists of number of words in the URL and post, sentiment, topic of the post and Linguistic Inquiry and Word Count (LIWC) scores. The second feature is meta-content which refers to the proportion of top 25 words or bigrams commonly used in trolls per post. The third feature is URL domain where they specify the type of domain, for example political, news, sport website or commercial. The fourth feature is meta URL domain whereby they check if the URL domain is among the top 25 domains that trolls shared. The fifth feature is Timing which refers to hour, day and week on which the post was made. They also emphasize on the fact that besides account age-related features, they do not use user-level features like followers and posts count. This is so that the approach can be robust enough to be used for data from other social media platforms like Facebook. They used the random forest model without doing hyperparameter tuning like grid search because their intention was to mainly evaluate if a simple out-of-the-box classifier can identify the content of coordinated influence campaigns on social media [1].

Zhang et al. [19] observed that with the growth in the use of social media platforms, there is also an increase in the spread of fake news. They conducted a survey on fake news and noticed that most of the detection methods focus on identifying features of the content, users, and context that indicate misinformation. They also noted that one of the major challenges to fake news detection is that there is limited access to good quality labelled datasets. They proposed to detect fake news using unsupervised methods including unsupervised news embedding, cluster analysis, and semantic similarity analysis.

Dinh et al. [5] developed a software framework for spam detection in real time that can extract important security insights and can be used for cyber criminal investigations. They also introduced some spam campaign labeling techniques which involves creating a spam campaign labeling server that listens to particular network ports using Wikipedia Miner toolkit libraries. The approach involves extracting frequent words from the spam emails in a campaign and feeding them to the spam campaign labeling server. The response, which consists of a list of topics relevant to the specific spam campaign, is saved back into the central database. Their method for spam detection is based on the frequent-pattern tree (FP-Tree) technique with the premise that the more frequent an attribute is shared, the higher the likelihood that it is shared in spam emails. The less frequent attributes are considered to be obfuscated by spammers and can be unearthed within the FP-Tree thus exposing the strategies used by spammers [5].

2.3   Summary

As per the related work, there are various studies on influence campaign and coordinated campaigns, and different shallow and deep machine learning methods were used to automatically detect influence.

The existing studies focus on detecting influence with regards to politics, bots, messaging spams, trolls or marketing. In contrast, our work focuses on detecting influence campaign in the area of agetech on content that targets the elderly. Also besides just using standard machine learning methods, we also apply classifier calibration to attain improved performance in influence detection in agetech.

3   Dataset

In this study we collected an agetech tweets dataset however we believe these methods can be applied to datasets from other platforms. It would entail extracting indicators or attributes of influence campaign in agetech from social media platforms. These patterns can be observed through the relationship between different elements in the posts like text, timing, topic or URL. For example, the hashtag used, content of the post, time at which it was sent out and quantity of traffic in terms of number of posts containing similar information that are sent around the same time. Influence campaign in agetech could therefore be analysed using other data resources besides tweets data. However the agetech tweets dataset came in handy for our study considering the scarcity of data in agetech [7,8].

3.1   Data Collection and Labeling

The data was collected from Twitter, by harvesting 6825 tweets that contain #agetech. The dataset captured all the tweets that contain #agetech because agetech is our area of focus. Using the dataset we performed URL classification by expanding tiny URLs and did domain check to determine if the URL is malicious or not. The expanded URLs were either not malicious or unknown meaning the domain no longer exists or is inaccessible.

Some of the tweets were in other languages so we translated all of them to English before doing further analysis. We also performed emotion analysis using TextBlob to determine the emotion portrayed in each tweet. The emotion analysis breakdown for the collected tweets are shown in Table 1. Most of the tweets were associated with the emotion of joy, followed by a good amount having the emotion of sadness. This implies that the tweets are likely to have extremes of either emotions of joy or sadness which is our focus in influence campaign because where there is influence, it is likely to be something very positive or negative.

Table 1. Emotion analysis breakdown for the collected dataset

Emotion	No. of tweets
joy	2995
sadness	1443
surprise	865
neutral	689
fear	526
anger	299
disgust	8

We applied topic modelling on the collected data using Latent Dirichlet Allocation (LDA) model to determine the objective in the tweet text. Figure 1 shows the main objectives or topics in the tweets where the tweets mostly talk about aging, care and ai. This is concurrent with the fact that the focus of the study is on agetech.

Additionally, we performed an analysis on the words used in the agetech tweets to understand what the most commonly used words are. We created a list of all the words in the agetech tweets excluding the stop words to identify the popular words. Figure 2 shows a plot of the word frequencies of the agetech

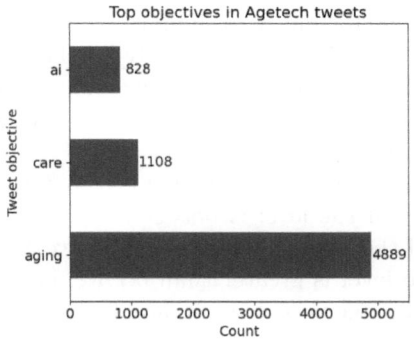

Fig. 1. Tweets objective analysis

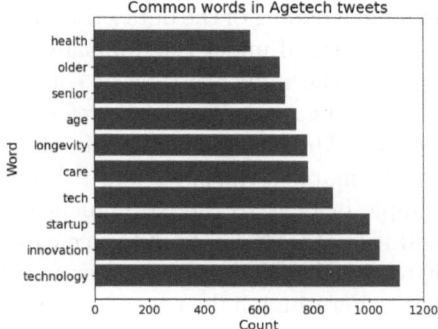

Fig. 2. Tweets text word frequencies

Table 2. Data labelling categories

Influence	Explanation	Influence score
Duplicate	Similarity in text or same URL - Exact same text or similar text with a few differences (same phrases). Also same URL linked in tweet - a way to try and have many people see the same post and click on the same link [19].	1
Exaggeration	Extremely captivating or catchy text. It might be very negative or positive.	0.2
Misinformation	Suspicious URL, incorrect figures, incorrect text or description - did not find any	1
Same_tagging	Same tagged account in different tweet text; the account, product or hashtag is mentioned many times especially of specific people or companies or product.	1
Meeting	Meeting, conference, event, workshop, roundtable, clubhouse meetup, podcast, collaboration or interview	0.6
Captivating	Nice catchy text or title. Interesting info that an elderly person or their caregiver may be persuaded to try and check. Post that is likely to cause engagement around agetech	0.2
No influence	No influence established	0

tweets without the stop words. It can be observed that the top three words used in most agetech tweets is technology, innovation and startup.

We also checked for text similarity, URL similarity and cosine similarity as a way of determining coordinated campaigns. Furthermore we opted to do manual labelling of the dataset, therefore the campaigns with similar text or URL were captured under the duplicate category. The data was manually labelled to indicate the influence type or source and the level of influence was assigned a score in the range 0 to 1. We refer to this labelled dataset as the agetech tweets dataset. The data labelling is further explained in Table 2.

We mapped the label values to four classes whereby if the label is 0 then the sample belongs to the No_influence category, if the level is between 0.1–0.5 we add it to the Moderate influence category, if the level is between 0.5–0.7 we add it to the High influence category, and if the level is greater than 0.7 we add it to the Very_high influence class. The labelled influence categories and breakdown are as shown in the Table 3

Table 3. Influence labels and breakdown

Labels and breakdown	No. of records
No_influence	5206
Very_high	1172
High	352
Moderate	95

The majority of the records fall under the No_influence class, about 76.28% while 17.17% are under Very_high influence, 5.16% are under High influence, and 1.39% are under Moderate influence. This is important to note as we can use it to track any class biases in our analysis and deploy some ways to offset the bias as we train the model.

4   Influence Campaign Detection Approach

In order to automatically predict influence in agetech, we applied different machine learning models to our dataset. We studied the following classifiers: XGB, Random Forest, Decision tree, CatBoost and LightGBM. We also applied different deep learning methods, however, the above shallow machine learning models outperformed the deep learning models. Therefore, the results presented in this paper are restricted to the above shallow ML models.

To further boost the performance of the models we performed classifier calibration on the classifiers. Classifier calibration involves using a calibrator which is a function that helps map the score from a classifier onto a probability estimate within the range [0,1] which is a posterior probability that an observation belongs to a specific class [18]. It helps refine the predictions of the classification model so that they can better align with the true underlying probabilities. So when fitting the model, the calibration compares the predicted probabilities with the actual outcomes and adjusts the probabilities to better align with the actual outcomes.

The calibration standardizes scores across different classifiers so that they are on the same scale for better comparison and interpretation. Probability estimates by many classifiers are not always well-calibrated so calibration helps enhance them [10,18]. We used the isotonic method when applying classifier calibration as it is good for an unbalanced dataset [10].

5   Experimental Evaluation

5.1   Performance Metrics

Our measures of performance are accuracy, F1 score, precision and recall. Accuracy is a great measure for the performance of the classifier, however, for an imbalanced dataset it is likely to give an inflated accuracy value for the dominant class. Therefore, we also use F1 score to evaluate the model performance which is more sensitive to the minority classes. F1 score also combines both precision and recall thus providing a more balanced measure that can help achieve high precision and recall without neglecting either of them.

5.2   Using Uncalibrated Classifiers

We applied 5 different ML classifiers on the dataset to assess their ability for influence detection. The tweet text was CountVectorizerized, which is an effective text data pre-processing technique for influence detection as it helps in determining frequency of certain words which can be indicative of the sentiment, class or nature of the text.

The data was split into 70% train dataset and 30% test dataset which was used to validate the influence detection performance of the different models. Table 4 shows the performance measures obtained in detecting influence campaign in agetech using the selected classifiers.

Table 4. Performance results for the classifiers without calibration

Model without calibration	Accuracy	F1 Score	Precision	Recall
Random Forest	0.8916	0.8653	0.8888	0.8916
XGBoost	0.8887	0.8671	0.8831	0.8887
CatBoost	0.8848	0.8611	0.8819	0.8848
LightGBM	0.8843	0.8634	0.8698	0.8843
Decision Tree	0.8804	0.8716	0.8645	0.8804

From Table 4, it can be observed that all models have an accuracy score way above the average, which means most of the records were correctly classified. Random Forest has the highest accuracy, precision and recall while Decision Tree classifier achieved the highest F1 score in detecting influence campaign.

Fig. 3 shows the confusion matrix of Random Forest with classifier calibration. The model achieves great performance especially in classifying records that belong to the "No influence" class while the rest of the classes have more misclassified samples most likely because they have fewer samples.

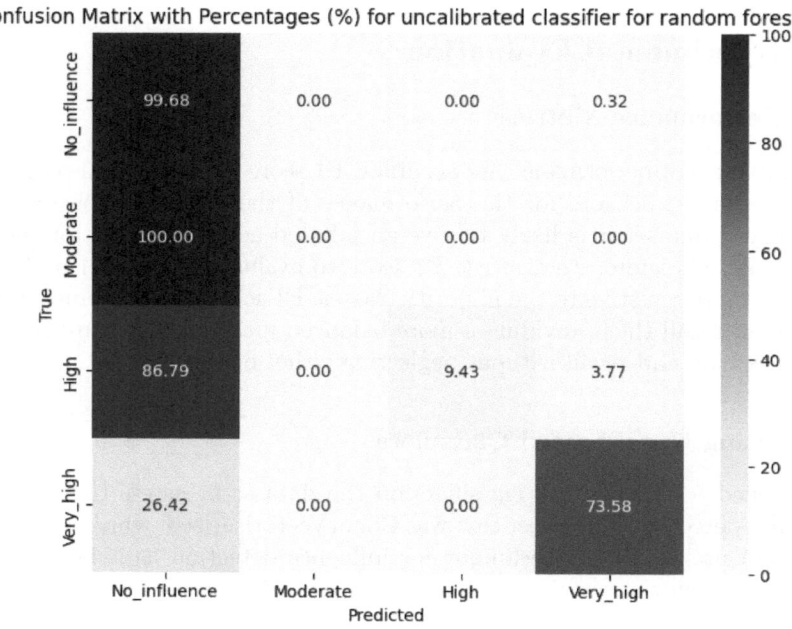

Fig. 3. Confusion matrix of Random Forest without classifier calibration

5.3   Using Classifier Calibration

Table 5 shows the performance measures obtained in detecting influence campaign in agetech using classifier calibration. There is improvement in model performance when classifier calibration is applied on the machine learning methods. The Random Forest classifier performs the best by achieving the highest accuracy, F1 score, precision, and recall.

We also explored classification using deep learning models like BERT, SimpleRNN and LSTM. Their performance is fairly good but lower than the shallow machine learning models. Considering the computational resources and processing power needed for deep learning models, we considered that shallow machine learning models are ideal and more effective.

Figure 4 shows the confusion matrix of Random Forest with classifier calibration.

The classifier performs very well in correctly classifying records that belong to the "No influence" class which had the highest number of samples. For the

Table 5. Performance results when using classifier calibration

Model with calibration	Accuracy	F1 Score	Precision	Recall
Random Forest	0.9033	0.8854	0.8900	0.9033
Decision Tree	0.8999	0.8820	0.8837	0.8999
CatBoost	0.8989	0.8803	0.8864	0.8989
XGBoost	0.8930	0.8713	0.8843	0.8931

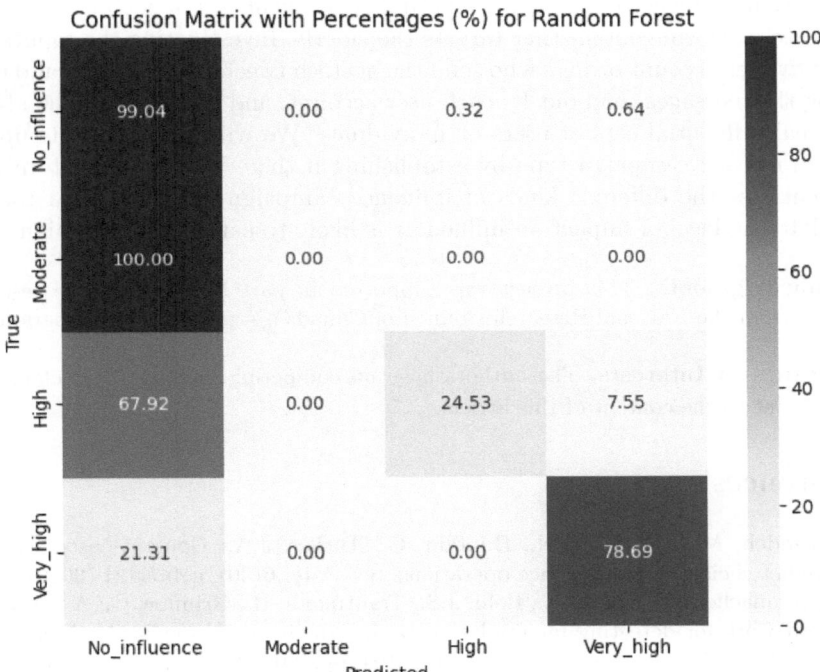

Fig. 4. Confusion matrix of Random Forest with classifier calibration

"Moderate influence" and "High influence" classes they have fewer samples and they are mostly misclassified to be of no influence. For the "Very high influence" class majority of the samples are correctly predicted, about 80%. Also it can be observed that with classifier calibration there are more samples correctly classified than without classifier calibration

6   Conclusion

Safeguarding seniors from direct or indirect social media manipulation about agetech is important because influence campaigns can be detrimental to them. The study investigated the problem of campaign detection in agetech on social media platforms, focusing on Twitter data. We performed preliminary analysis on the agetech tweets data to understand the emotion behind the tweets, identify the tweets objectives and top keywords used across the tweets. The study also achieved high accuracy in detecting influence campaign using machine learning methods whereby the Random Forest model with classifier calibration performed best.

Some areas we intend to further explore include making use of Large Language Models (LLMs) in automatic or semi-automatic labelling of our dataset, as an alternative to the manual labelling we performed. Computing the security risk score of influence campaign susceptibility or likelihood of getting influenced by online platform content that targets the elderly. Investigating the reputation of the twitter account owners who send the agetech tweets, aggregating and evaluating the messages send out by each user account, and checking for the ability to reveal influential sets of users or individuals. We will explore the temporal pattern of each campaign type by establishing if there is a trend/pattern that differentiates the different kinds of influence campaign and develop a tool to calculate the level of impact an influencer is likely to cause in a campaign.

Acknowledgments. This project was supported in part by collaborative research funding from the National Research Council of Canada's Aging in Place Program.

Disclosure of Interests. The authors have no competing interests to declare that are relevant to the content of this article.

References

1. Alizadeh, M., Shapiro, J.N., Buntain, C., Tucker, J.A.: Content-based features predict social media influence operations. Sci. Adv. **6**(30), eabb5824 (2020)
2. Assenmacher, D., Clever, L., Pohl, J.S., Trautmann, H., Grimme, C.: A two-phase framework for detecting manipulation campaigns in social media. In: Meiselwitz, G. (ed.) HCII 2020, Part I. LNCS, vol. 12194, pp. 201–214. Springer, Cham (2020). https://doi.org/10.1007/978-3-030-49570-1_14
3. Cao, C., Caverlee, J., Lee, K., Ge, H., Chung, J.: Organic or organized? Exploring URL sharing behavior. In: Proceedings of the 24th ACM International on Conference on Information and Knowledge Management, pp. 513–522 (2015)
4. Chen, Z.: An unsupervised approach to detect spam campaigns that use botnets on twitter. Ph.D. thesis, Rice University (2018)
5. Dinh, S., Azeb, T., Fortin, F., Mouheb, D., Debbabi, M.: Spam campaign detection, analysis, and investigation. Digit. Investig. **12**, S12–S21 (2015)
6. Hui, P.M., Yang, K.C., Torres-Lugo, C., Menczer, F.: BotSlayer: DIY real-time influence campaign detection. In: Proceedings of the International AAAI Conference on Web and Social Media, vol. 14, pp. 980–982 (2020)
7. Khaemba, N., Traoré, I., Mamun, M.: Security and privacy of IoT devices for aging in place. In: Traore, I., Woungang, I., Saad, S. (eds.) Artificial Intelligence for Cyber-Physical Systems Hardening. Engineering Cyber-Physical Systems and Critical Infrastructures, vol. 2, pp. 181–201. Springer, Cham (2022). https://doi.org/10.1007/978-3-031-16237-4_8
8. Khaemba, N., Traore, I., Mamun, M.: A framework for synthetic agetech attack data generation. J. Cybersecur. Priv. **3**(4), 744–757 (2023)

9. Lee, K., Caverlee, J., Cheng, Z., Sui, D.Z.: Campaign extraction from social media. ACM Trans. Intell. Syst. Technol. (TIST) **5**(1), 1–28 (2014)
10. Lemaître, G., et al.: Calibration - scikit-learn (2024). https://scikit-learn.org/stable/modules/calibration.html. Accessed 22 July 2024
11. Luceri, L., Boniardi, E., Ferrara, E.: Leveraging large language models to detect influence campaigns in social media. arXiv preprint arXiv:2311.07816 (2023)
12. des Mesnards, N.G., Hunter, D.S., el Hjouji, Z., Zaman, T.: Detecting bots and assessing their impact in social networks. Oper. Res. **70**(1), 1–22 (2022)
13. Mesnards, N.G.d., Zaman, T.: Detecting influence campaigns in social networks using the ising model. arXiv preprint arXiv:1805.10244 (2018)
14. Mostafa, M., Abdelwahab, A., Sayed, H.: Detecting spam campaign in twitter with semantic similarity. J. Phys: Conf. Ser. **1447**, 012044 (2020)
15. Tussyadiah, S.P., Kausar, D.R., Soesilo, P.K.: The effect of engagement in online social network on susceptibility to influence. J. Hosp. Tour. Res. **42**(2), 201–223 (2018)
16. Varol, O., Ferrara, E., Menczer, F., Flammini, A.: Early detection of promoted campaigns on social media. EPJ Data Sci. **6**, 1–19 (2017)
17. Weber, D., Neumann, F.: Who's in the gang? Revealing coordinating communities in social media. In: 2020 IEEE/ACM International Conference on Advances in Social Networks Analysis and Mining (ASONAM), pp. 89–93. IEEE (2020)
18. Yousef, W.A., Traoré, I., Briguglio, W.: Classifier calibration: with application to threat scores in cybersecurity. IEEE Trans. Dependable Secure Comput. **20**(3), 1994–2010 (2022)
19. Zhang, X., Ghorbani, A.A.: An overview of online fake news: characterization, detection, and discussion. Inf. Process. Manage. **57**(2), 102025 (2020)

Privacy and Security Issues

ChatGPT Through the Users' Eyes: Sentiment Analysis of Privacy and Security Issues

Mousa Al-kfairy[1]([envelope])[iD], Ahmed Al-Adaileh[2][iD], and Obsa Sendaba[1]

[1] College of Technological Innovation, Zayed University, Abu Dhabi,
United Arab Emirates
Mousa.al-kfairy@zu.ac.ae
[2] School of Computing, Skyline University College, Sharjah, United Arab Emirates

Abstract. This research investigates user perceptions of security and privacy in the context of AI technologies, focusing specifically on Chat-GPT. We conducted a sentiment analysis of approximately 11,000 tweets collected from X Platform (formerly Twitter) between November 2022 and January 2024. Advanced natural language processing techniques were employed to preprocess the tweets, eliminating irrelevant data and refining the text for analysis. Sentiment analysis tools were then used to categorize user sentiments as positive, negative, or neutral. The results reveal a complex duality in user attitudes towards ChatGPT. While users generally appreciate the functional benefits and innovative capabilities of ChatGPT, there is substantial concern regarding data privacy and the potential misuse of AI technologies. Positive sentiments often highlighted the efficiency and utility of ChatGPT in various applications, whereas negative sentiments were predominantly focused on privacy risks and ethical considerations. These findings underscore the need for developers to prioritize transparent data handling practices and incorporate robust security features to address user concerns. Additionally, the study highlights the importance of updated regulations that protect user data while fostering innovation. Policymakers are urged to develop comprehensive policies that balance the need for security with the benefits of technological advancement. This study contributes to a deeper understanding of user perceptions of AI technologies, emphasizing the importance of a balanced approach that considers both benefits and risks. The insights gained provide a foundation for future research and inform strategies to enhance user trust and acceptance of AI technologies like ChatGPT.

Keywords: User Perceptions · ChatGPT Security and Privacy · Data Privacy · User Sentiment · Privacy Risks

1 Introduction

ChatGPT has been used for multiple applications, including chatbots, language translation, and content creation which demonstrate its versatility and potential

M. Al-kfairy et al. (Eds.): SocialSec 2024, LNCS 15565, pp. 41–67, 2025.
https://doi.org/10.1007/978-981-96-3774-4_3

for innovation in natural language processing. ChatGPT's revolutionary shifts in accessing information could advantage sectors holding stakes, such as education, research, journalism, mass media, Information Technology (IT), and retail, among others [1]. However, its enhanced abilities introduce new risks, particularly the potential misuse of persuasive fake text in disinformation campaigns, deep fakes, and other malicious activities [2]. Despite ChatGPT's ability to reject inappropriate queries, hackers can manipulate it to produce malware or exploit vulnerabilities. Users are also uneasy about how OpenAI handles personal data, which includes an automatic collection of log data, usage data, device information, cookies, and analytics [3]. The privacy policy indicates that such information might be shared with third-party entities like cloud vendors, web analytics service providers, government authorities, and industry peers [3]. This data collection could lead to profiling individuals based on their interactions with ChatGPT which could raise privacy concerns, especially when the model learns from databases that might contain personal or inaccurate information. Furthermore, malicious users could exploit ChatGPT for social engineering attacks or harmful content creation.

Thus, this study aims to understand the user perspective on privacy and security issues surrounding ChatGPT, given its widespread adoption and potential for misuse. By conducting sentiment analysis on discussions from the X platform, this study aims to highlight users' key concerns, which can inform better practices and policies for developers and stakeholders in the AI community. Understanding user sentiments is crucial for enhancing trust and ensuring the responsible deployment of AI technologies.

Therefore, we seek to answer the following questions:

- What are the primary privacy and security concerns expressed by users of ChatGPT on the X platform?
- How do these concerns vary across different user demographics and contexts?
- What are the most common sentiments associated with privacy and security issues in user discussions about ChatGPT?

The remainder of this paper is structured as follows: In Sect. 2, we review the relevant literature on privacy and security concerns related to ChatGPT. Section 3 describes the methodology used to conduct the sentiment analysis on discussions from the X platform. Section 4 presents the sentiment analysis results, highlighting key privacy and security concerns users express. In Sect. 5, we discuss the implications of our findings for developers, stakeholders, and policymakers in the AI community. Finally, Sect. 6 concludes the paper with a summary of the main points and suggestions for future research.

2   Literature Review

The field of AI, particularly with models like GPT, is evolving at an unprecedented rate. This swift progression means new versions and capabilities are frequently introduced, leaving little time for comprehensive security and privacy studies to catch up. This rapid development cycle creates a significant gap in the literature as the necessary in-depth analyses and peer-reviewed studies take time to conduct and publish. GPT models are inherently complex, and the "black box" nature means that even experts may not entirely understand how inputs are transformed into outputs, creating a barrier to developing a robust body of literature. Furthermore, a significant portion of the state-of-the-art work on GPT models is conducted by private companies like OpenAI, Google, and Microsoft. These companies often do not fully disclose their methodologies, training data, or security measures, limiting the amount of information available for public scrutiny and academic research. Consequently, the literature on the privacy and security of GPT models is less comprehensive than it could be if more data were available. An effective strategy for addressing the disparity involves examining users' perceptions of security and privacy associated with the technology.

Employing ML algorithms within ChatGPT leads to extensive data handling, thus exposing sensitive information to potential theft or misuse, which poses notable privacy and security risks [4]. Wu et al. [3] suggests users might continue to experience unease regarding the potential threats linked with OpenAI's storage and management of their data. The authors highlight that there is a chance that personal data might be stored in insecure data centers or shared with industry partners whose reliability is uncertain. The opacity of OpenAI's operations to users exacerbates the problem, as it hinders the ability to audit or confirm the handling of personal data. Due to concerns about consent and personal data privacy, Italy banned ChatGPT on March 31, 2023, cutting off server access to all IP addresses in Italy. After almost a month of dialogue and enhancements, Italian regulators permitted the service reinstated on April 28, 2023 [5]. Following this, OpenAI introduced modifications to address the privacy concerns, however, the swift reauthorization led to doubts about the thorough scrutiny of essential GDPR issues, which triggered a new investigation by other countries such as Canada, Germany, Sweden, and France [4].

Many studies have examined the broad societal impacts and specific domain applications of ChatGPT [4]. Dis et al. [6] discuss concerns with using large language models (LLMs) such as ChatGPT, including errors, biases, and potential plagiarism, as well as their tendency to amplify human cognitive biases. The authors found that ChatGPT often produces false and misleading information due to gaps in its training data and its inability to distinguish between credible and non-credible sources. Dwivedi et al. [4] indicate that the implementation of ChatGPT raises significant concerns regarding the gathering, retaining, and applying learner data, alongside worries over potential data breaches and unauthorized access to personally identifiable information. Huang et al. [7] shows that training data poisoning attacks pose a significant risk to AI models by corrupting data they are trained on, leading to inaccurate outputs and compromised decision-making. This manipulation creates opportunities for malicious insiders to introduce vulnerabilities and compromise the security and integrity of the LLM. Heiding et al. [8] found that both AI-generated and manually crafted personalized phishing emails, compared to generic ones, had higher click-through rates. Wu et al.[3] highlights through harnessing ChatGPT's code generation features, hackers can disseminate harmful software packages via forged code repositories. Once the malicious code is generated, hackers can distribute it through fabricated code libraries or repositories, disguising it as harmless or useful code for developers to use in their projects. Unsuspecting developers who incorporate this code into their projects may inadvertently introduce security vulnerabilities or install malware onto their systems when they run the code.

Since its launch, several studies have analyzed users' sentiments towards ChatGPT. One way to obtain insights into user feedback, perception, and public opinion is through sentiment analysis. Researchers have increasingly emphasized the analysis of emotions and opinions conveyed in tweets, comments, and various forms of textual content. According to Bian et al., [9], the analysis of sentiments on Twitter, which involves categorizing opinions as positive, negative, or neutral, has proven to be highly valuable for gauging the public or user perception toward a product, service, or technology. Korkmaz et al. [10] conducted a study that utilized tweets as the primary data source, focusing on two months following the launch of ChatGPT. The researchers employed AFINN, Bing, and NRC dictionaries to analyze the content of the tweets. Most ChatGPT users expressed satisfaction with their experience of using the technology, considering it successful. The study found that only a small portion of users reported encountering erroneous or false results from ChatGPT, leading to dissatisfaction with the situation. Likewise, according to Ul Haque et al. [11], most individuals who embraced the technology early exhibited highly positive attitudes regarding various subjects, including disruptions to software development, entertainment, and exercising creativity.

The adoption of ChatGPT in the business context was predominantly discussed positively, with 75% of views being positive, 5% negative, and 20% neutral, suggesting a sense of optimism for future possibilities [11]. In contrast to topics like software development, where the acceptance of ChatGPT is largely positive, the utilization of ChatGPT for educational purposes evoked a mixture of positive and negative perceptions among users [11]. The analysis revealed that regarding the use of ChatGPT in educational settings, 52% of views were positive, 32% were negative, and 16% were neutral. Mhlanga [12] suggests that before integrating ChatGPT into the educational setting, it is important for educators to communicate with students regarding the collection, utilization, and storage of their data and obtain their consent. Safeguarding users' personal information is a crucial consideration when employing ChatGPT in education [12].

This study distinguishes itself from previous research by focusing specifically on users' perceptions of security and privacy while using ChatGPT. Unlike earlier studies that may have broadly examined the functionality or utility of ChatGPT, our research focuses on the critical issue of how secure and private users feel their interactions are when engaging with ChatGPT. To achieve a comprehensive understanding, we gathered data from X (previously known as Twitter), a platform renowned for its diverse user base and rich discourse. By employing sophisticated sentiment analysis techniques, we assessed and categorized user sentiments. This allowed us to identify general perceptions and specific concerns and apprehensions users have regarding their privacy and security while interacting with ChatGPT. Our approach provides important views of users' sentiments and offers valuable insights into the areas where improvements are needed to enhance trust and confidence in ChatGPT.

3 Methodology

In this section, we present the methodology employed in our study. It starts by outlining the research design and then explains how the dataset is streamed, collected, examined, and improved. Subsequently, we delve into the pre-processing and cleaning techniques applied to the tweets, ensuring effective and efficient processing. Lastly, we discuss the technologies and methods utilized for sentiment analysis and topic modeling. These steps are illustrated in Fig. 1.

3.1 Research Design

As depicted in Fig. 2, this study collected approximately 11K tweets addressing ChatGPT privacy and security from the X platform. The data acquisition was conducted using Python scripts with the Basic Package of X API. It is noteworthy that the Twitter Downloader Tool, officially available, was unusable due to the revocation of our previously acquired academic license by the X platform administration. Consequently, the limitations imposed by the Basic Package, allowing retrieval of a maximum of 10K tweets per month, significantly hindered the data collection process. It is important to mention that alternative methods, such as utilizing scrapers or crawlers, are strictly prohibited without prior written consent according to X's Terms of Service [13]. Additionally, due to financial constraints, subscribing to other offered packages, such as the Pro Package, was not feasible. To enhance the quality of results and streamline the analysis process, the tweets underwent pre-processing to eliminate extraneous information.

A study was undertaken to gauge user sentiment and polarization concerning ChatGPT security and privacy. This was achieved by analyzing their tweets through Natural Language Processing (NLP) techniques to discern polarity (positive, negative, and neutral) [14]. As highlighted by Lin Yue et al. [15], sentiment analysis proves effective in uncovering patterns that elucidate users' emotions and perspectives on analyzed topics. In this research, we employed Stanford CoreNLP and the Vader tool for sentiment analysis [16], utilizing a lexicon-based approach that assigns sentiment scores to words for text evaluation. An advantage of this method is its efficiency and cost-effectiveness in handling relatively large datasets, such as tweets.

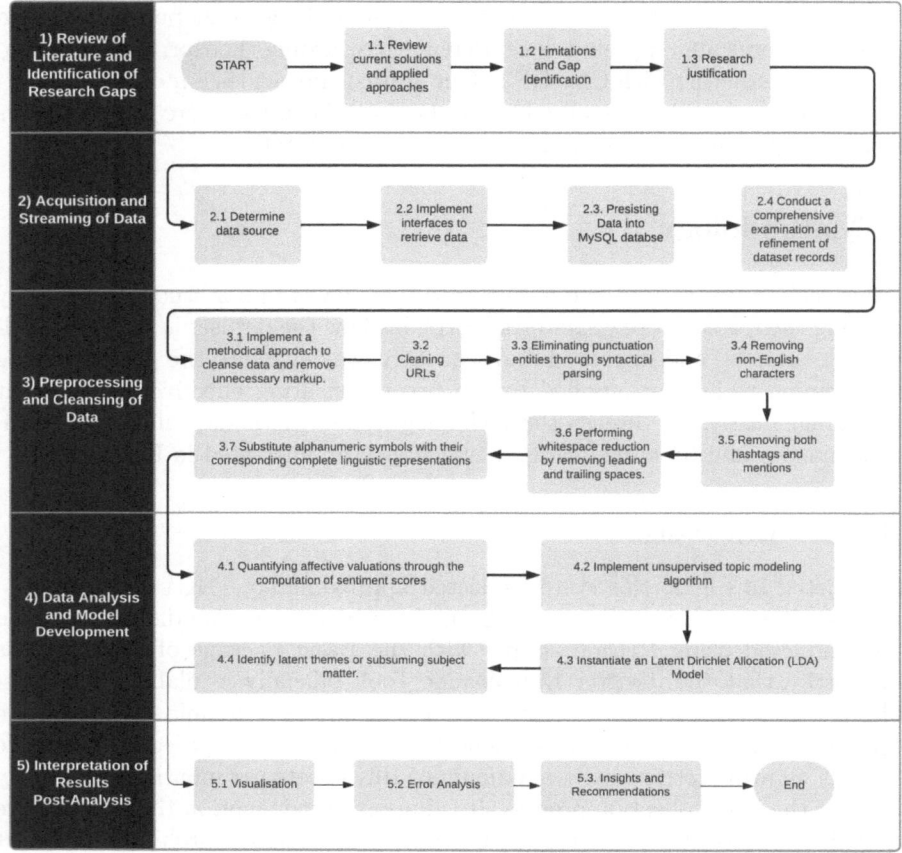

Fig. 1. Methodology Summary: A review of current solutions, identification of deficiencies and performing gap analysis, and the systematic streaming, purification, manipulation, and analysis of tweet data. Subsequently, the findings are subjected to further examination and explanation of their relevance.

3.2   Dataset Streaming and Construction

Due to restrictions from the X platform administration on searching and retrieving tweets via their official API, which included revoking the previously obtained Academic Research License and shutting down the Tweets Downloader API Tool, we had to develop our routines using Python to search and retrieve tweets using the basic version of the X API v2. We searched the X Platform for keywords such as "chatgpt" with "privacy," "security," "data protection," "ethics," "data security," "encryption," "data confidentiality," "misinformation," "user trust," "regulation compliance," "ethical use," "transparency," "cybersecurity," "trustworthiness," and "reliability" in English. We obtained 11K relevant tweets from November 2022 to January 2024 [13].

A dataset of 11K tweets, though not as large as some datasets, provides substantial data for sentiment analysis and topic modeling. It offers a diverse range of language patterns, sentiments, and topics, representing a broad Twitter user base. This diversity ensures the sentiment analysis and topic modeling capture a wide range of opinions and themes. The dataset size allows for robust statistical analysis, drawing meaningful insights from the data while balancing comprehensiveness and computational efficiency. Annotated with sentiment labels or topic categories, the quality of these annotations is crucial, with a higher likelihood of obtaining well-labeled data using automated techniques with selective human verification. The original dataset included fields like "author id," "created at," "geo," "id," "lang," "like count," "quote count," "reply count," and "retweet count." We tailored the dataset by removing irrelevant fields like "geo," "lang," "reply count," "retweet count," and "quote count," focusing on "like count" to indicate user agreement and support. Manual intervention was needed to address plural forms of words, such as "regulations" and "regulation."

The tweets were analyzed to assess the sentiment expressed by X platform users, offering insights into their attitudes towards topics related to ChatGPT security and privacy. Using machine learning methodologies like Latent Dirichlet Allocation (LDA), we scanned, aggregated, and categorized observations (e.g., words) into documents, classifying them into distinct topics, known as topic discovery or modeling [17,18]. The dataset was obtained in JavaScript Object Notation (JSON) format to avoid line-break issues in tweets. The process began with converting downloaded tweets from JSON to processable cells and saving them in a relational MariaDB database for further analysis.

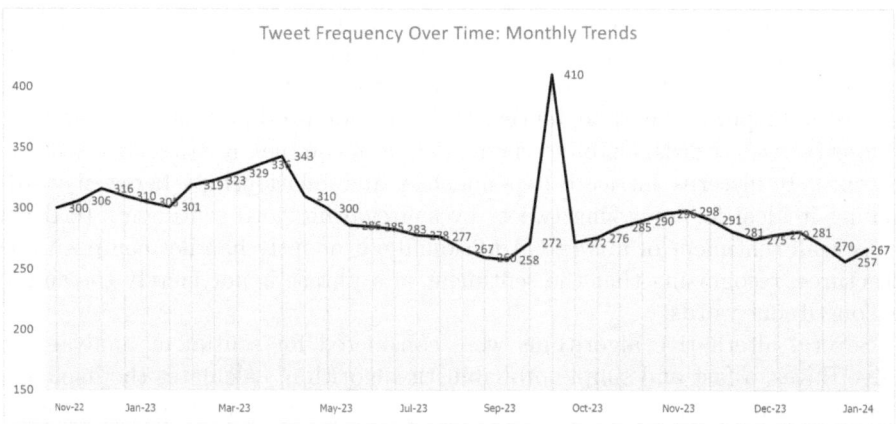

Fig. 2. The number of tweets related to the keyword "ChatGPT Privacy and Security" between November 2022 and January 2024.

3.3   Refining, Pre-processing, and Cleansing Tweet Data

Data preparation is crucial for ensuring accurate and dependable results while also streamlining computation and processing efforts by excluding irrelevant data in advance. The data preparation process involved several steps. Firstly, eliminating irrelevant phrases and codes, such as HTML and XML tags, and subsequently converting letters to lowercase. Secondly, conducting spelling checks. Thirdly, given the prevalence of abbreviations and symbols across various industries, these elements were systematically searched and replaced within tweets to enhance message comprehension. This step was iteratively refined throughout the analysis to optimize the abbreviation list. Fourthly, tweets underwent parsing, with documents (words) being split and extracted, a critical step considering most traditional text analytics techniques operate at the word level. The resulting documents underwent cleaning to remove "Stop Words," which contribute noise to the data without adding substantive value. Although an attempt was made to normalize documents by lemmatizing words and reducing them to their roots, this approach yielded unreliable results, resulting in the loss of over 80% of the original documents due to repeated root words. Consequently, normalization was omitted from the preparation steps. Finally, part-of-speech tagging, noun phrase extraction, named entity recognition, and basic dependencies analysis were conducted, enabling the identification of grammatical structures and focusing primarily on verbs and nouns [19].

3.4   Modelling and Data Analysis Approach

Recursive Neural Tensor Network (RNTN) is a key algorithm utilized in this study, specifically designed for parsing and sentiment analysis tasks. The RNTN excels in understanding nuanced sentiment within sentences. It considers the sentiments of individual words and recursively combines them to derive the sentiment of phrases and sentences. Using tensor products, it captures interactions between words, enabling the modeling of complex relationships within a sentence. It discerns intricate dependencies and relationships between words, making it ideal for analyzing tweets by aggregating word sentiments to derive the overall sentiment of a tweet. Additionally, it adeptly handles compositional structures, recognizing that the sentiment of a phrase is not merely the sum of its constituent words.

Several alternative algorithms were considered for sentiment analysis: (1) Naive Bayes, a fast and simple probabilistic algorithm, calculates the likelihood of a document belonging to a particular sentiment class based on word occurrences and frequencies. However, it fails to capture complex word relationships, making it unsuitable for analyzing tweets. (2) Support Vector Machines (SVM) classify documents into sentiment classes by finding a hyperplane that separates them in a high-dimensional space. Although it handles non-linear relationships, SVM requires extensive parameter tuning, making it impractical for this research. (3) Long Short-Term Memory (LSTM), a type of Recurrent Neural Network (RNN), captures long-term dependencies and addresses the vanishing gradient problem. However, its computational complexity and the brevity of tweets limit its effectiveness in capturing nuanced sentiments. (4) Bidirectional Encoder Representations from Transformers (BERT) offers bidirectional context understanding and excels at grasping tweet context. Despite its state-of-the-art performance, BERT's computational intensity and resource demands are prohibitive for this research. Additionally, tweets' informal language, slang, and abbreviations challenge BERT's ability to handle non-standard grammatical structures without specialized fine-tuning or model architectures. Furthermore, understanding sarcasm and irony often requires domain-specific knowledge that BERT may not inherently capture without additional adjustments.

Unveiling Tweets Sentiment. The sentiment analysis process involved transforming tweets into numerical vectors using the Bag-of-Words (BoW) approach, enabling the construction of sentiment classification models. This method entails creating a vocabulary of unique words extracted from the corpus and representing each document as a vector denoting the frequencies of words within the vocabulary. This research utilized the Stanford CoreNLP library for sentiment analysis on tweets, known for its robustness across diverse application domains [20]. Employing a recursive neural network, the sentiment analysis component captures the hierarchical structure of sentences, considering the sentiments of individual words and their combinations within phrases and sentences. Sentiment evaluation assigns labels such as 'Very Negative,' 'Negative,' 'Neutral,' 'Positive,' and 'Very Positive,' represented by a score ranging from 0 to 4. Throughout the analysis, the toolkit determines the polarity of sentences using a supervised learning-based technique, establishing connections between nouns and predictors. To enrich the dataset for further analysis, two new columns, 'score' and 'sentiment,' were appended to each tweet entry.

The sentiment analysis model is trained on labeled datasets containing examples of sentences paired with corresponding sentiment labels, leveraging its dependency parsing capabilities to grasp the grammatical structure of sentences. Additionally, part-of-speech tagging aids in identifying the role of each word in a sentence. While transformer-based models like BERT and GPT have achieved remarkable success in various natural language processing tasks, including sentiment analysis, they have potential challenges and drawbacks. Training and fine-tuning transformer models require substantial computational resources, such as high-performance GPUs or TPUs, which may not be available for this research. Moreover, transformer models are large and resource-intensive for training and deployment. Effective fine-tuning on specific tasks typically requires task-specific labeled datasets that may not be present in the examined dataset. Lastly, transformer models are complex and lack interpretability, posing challenges in understanding how the model arrives at a particular decision, especially in distinguishing ads from real tweets.

Analysis of Phrases and Applying Topic Modeling Techniques. The analysis involves clustering or summarizing tweets to identify the topics within the dataset. Initially, this task includes identifying phrases within the tweets and visualizing them using a word cloud, revealing the frequency or significance of words within the text corpus [21]. Two critical decisions must be made: determining the degree of phrases, often n-grams, where "N" denotes the number of successive words to consider (e.g., single, double, triple), and discerning the number of topics present within the tweets. N-grams phrase analysis delves deeper into the tweets to encapsulate underlying topics. The n-gram selection depends on the dataset size, topic complexity, and language usage. Higher n-gram values (e.g., 3-gram or above) capture intricate word relationships but increase computational complexity, while lower n-gram values (e.g., 1-gram or 2-gram) yield broader topic assignments with less strain, suitable for smaller datasets.

Experimenting with different n-gram values helps determine the optimal balance between topic quality and computational efficiency. According to Abrigo et al. [22], the degree of N-grams depends on domain-specific knowledge and language characteristics. In our research, single, double, and triple N-grams were most effective in representing phrases within tweets. The number of topics can be identified based on domain expertise or feedback from subject matter experts. Alternatively, perplexity scores from training a topic model using techniques like Latent Dirichlet Allocation (LDA) assist in determining the optimal number of topics. LDA, chosen over Non-negative Matrix Factorization (NMF) for this research, is suitable for capturing diverse themes in tweets due to its generative probabilistic model, representing documents as mixtures of topics. Despite its reliance on a bag-of-words representation and sensitivity to hyperparameters, LDA's flexibility in modeling multiple subjects within tweets made it the preferred choice.

4 Results

After implementing the specified pre-processing steps, we identified a total of 17998 unique words and their frequencies within the analyzed dataset. Examination of these unique words, reveals that certain words occupy positions within the top 25 despite not providing significant meaningful information. For instance, words that are not nouns or verbs such as "like", "s", and "just" were removed because they don't have an added value in both sentimental analysis and topic modeling, moreover words like "chatgpt", "privacy" and "security" were initially included in the search query to construct the original tweets dataset. These words have been subsequently eliminated, and a set of various cleaning procedures applied. Moreover, since this research is focused on examining ChatGPT based on both categories "Security" and "Privacy", and as a preparation step for the upcoming sentimental analysis, we manually categorized the first most-repeated 25 keywords into these categories. We considered the following rules while attempting to target an appropriate categorization: firstly, all keywords related to user concerns, protection, confidentiality, trust, and ethical considerations generally align more closely with privacy, secondly: Keywords related to encryption, tech, and risks align more closely with security measures and threat mitigation, finally: many keywords like data, technology, tools, and artificial intelligence have significant overlaps between privacy and security, indicating their importance in both domains. The outcomes are presented in Table 1, which showcases the top keywords alongside their occurrences. The numerical representation of these keywords is also depicted in Fig. 3(a) and Fig. 3(b).

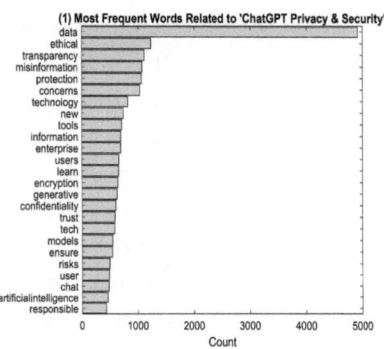

(a) Word Cloud of Top 25 bag-of-words.   (b) Histogram of the most frequent 25 Words.

Fig. 3. Various plotting of the top 25 repeated words related to 'Metaverse Marketplace'

Table 1. The top 25 words and their repetency within inspected tweets after applying various cleaning procedures, including the outcome of the manual categorization of keywords into "Privacy", "Security" or "Both"

No.	Word	Count	Category
1	data	3714	Privacy
2	ethical	1097	Both
3	misinformation	949	Both
4	transparency	907	Both
5	protection	889	Security
6	concerns	841	Privacy
7	technology	817	Security
8	new	738	Both
9	tools	708	Security
10	information	693	Privacy

continued

Table 1. continued

No.	Word	Count	Category
11	enterprise	688	Security
12	users	656	Privacy
13	learn	651	Both
14	encryption	642	Security
15	generative	625	Both
16	confidentiality	605	Privacy
17	trust	589	Security
18	tech	587	Security
19	models	550	Privacy
20	ensure	545	Both
21	risks	496	Security
22	artificial-intelligence	460	Both
23	responsible	437	Both
24	web	416	Both
25	latest	416	Both

4.1   Sentimental Analysis

After performing sentiment analysis on the collected and cleaned tweets using the Stanford CoreNLP toolbox, each tweet was classified as "negative," "neutral," or "positive." The sentiment results at the tweet level were then mapped to the keywords and categories levels, based on the established relationships between tweets and their corresponding keywords and categories. Table 2 provides examples of the sentiment analysis at the tweet level, while Fig. 4, Fig. 5 and Fig. 6 illustrate the sentiment analysis and their scores at the keywords and categories levels, respectively.

Figure 4 illustrates the sentiment analysis of the ten most frequently mentioned keywords in the inspected tweets. Sentiments were calculated for the tweets containing these keywords.

According to the graph, the keyword "data" was mentioned in 2011 positively, 619 negatively, and 1020 neutrally ranked tweets, which indicates that almost 3% of Twitter's users' perceptions are negative, 5.6% are neutral, and the majority about 11% are positive about aspects related to the 'data' which is strictly coupled with privacy aspects. Applying the same approach to other keywords such as "misinformation", and "transparency" reveals nearly similar results. However, this trend differs for some other keywords such as "ethical", and "tools" where the overall users' perceptions are more positive than neutral with about 92% and 69% for both keywords respectively, approximately less than 1% neutral for "ethical", and 15% for "tools", and 6% and 15% as negative perception.

Figure 6 illustrates the sentimental analysis of the examined categories and shows that the highest number of tweets in this category are positive (2453), suggesting that most discussions around privacy are perceived positively. Moreover, a notable amount of negative sentiment (814) indicates concerns or criticisms about privacy-related topics. However, many tweets (1277) are neutral, which could mean that many discussions are factual or non-opinionated. Examining the figures related to "Security" reveals that positive sentiments are prevalent but lower than privacy. This suggests that security topics are viewed positively, but not as strongly as privacy. Moreover, fewer tweets express negative sentiments (219) than privacy, indicating less criticism or fewer issues discussed. Finally, relatively few neutral tweets (310) show that discussions about security are less neutral and more opinionated. The figures shown, which are related to both categories, reveal a high frequency of positive sentiment (2307), indicating a generally favorable view when privacy and security are discussed together. With 453 negative tweets, the negative sentiment is lower than the positive, suggesting fewer criticisms or negative perceptions. A moderate number of neutral tweets (658) indicate some factual or balanced discussions.

Table 3 shows the related figures. The list of the discussed topics will be revealed and discussed in the next sections: topic modeling, and discussion.

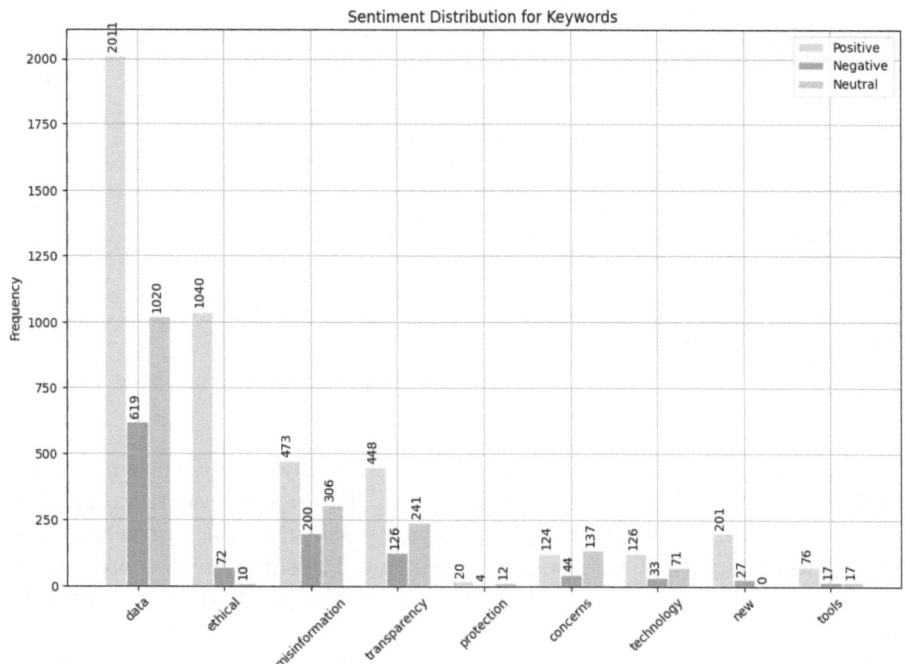

Fig. 4. Top 10 keywords and their sentiment calculated based on the sentiment of tweets where they found in the examined tweets.

Table 2. Example tweet data with cleaned text and corresponding attributes including their cleaned state,

Tweet (original)	Tweet (cleaned)	Category	Sentiment Score	Sentiment
ChatGPT is designed with security at its core! Whether you're exploring AI for business or personal use, you can trust its commitment to privacy and safe content generation. Discover how AI can enhance your workflows without compromising security. https://vist.ly/wgpp #AI #ChatGPT #Security	ChatGPT is designed with security at its core! Whether you're exploring AI for business or personal use, you can trust its commitment to privacy and safe content generation. Discover how AI can enhance your workflows without compromising security. https vist.ly wgpp AI ChatGPT Security	security	0.9921	Positive
The university said on Thursday it will get access to ChatGPT Enterprise, a version of the viral chatbot that offers more security, privacy and higher-speed access to OpenAI's technology (2/2)#ArizonaStateUniversity #ASU	The university said on Thursday it will get access to ChatGPT Enterprise, a version of the viral chatbot that offers more security, privacy and higher-speed access to OpenAI's technology (2/2)ArizonaStateUniversity ASU	privacy	0.9817	Pos.
#AI Puts 81.6% of Content Writers' Jobs at Risk, Say Digital Marketers #AIart #digitalart #TrendingNow #UnitedStates #attack #cyber #GPT4 #cloud #CyberAttack #coding #digital #Bitcoin #ElonMusk #Hacked #OpenAI #ChatGPT #Trending #networking #CyberSecurity #darkweb #web3 #Infosys https://t.co/VsbXdzHxbI	AI Puts 81.6% of Content Writers' Jobs at Risk, Say Digital Marketers AIart digitalart TrendingNow UnitedStates attack cyber GPT4 cloud CyberAttack coding digital Bitcoin ElonMusk Hacked OpenAI ChatGPT Trending networking CyberSecurity darkweb web3 Infosys https t.co VsbXdzHxbI"	security	−0.9783	Neg.

In sentiment analysis, both "polarity" and "subjectivity" provide crucial insights into the nature of the examined text. The polarity score ranges from −1.0 to 1.0, with −1.0 indicating very negative sentiment, 0 representing neutrality, and 1.0 signifying very positive sentiment. The subjectivity score, ranging from 0.0 to 1.0, measures how subjective or objective the text is. A score of 0.0 denotes highly objective, fact-based content, while a score of 1.0 indicates highly subjective, opinion-based content. As Fig. 7 and Fig. 8 illustrate, an analysis of the polarity and subjectivity of tweets reveals that most tweets exhibit a neutral to positive sentiment. Furthermore, the subjectivity scores lean towards the opinion-based end of the spectrum, with many approaching the maximum score

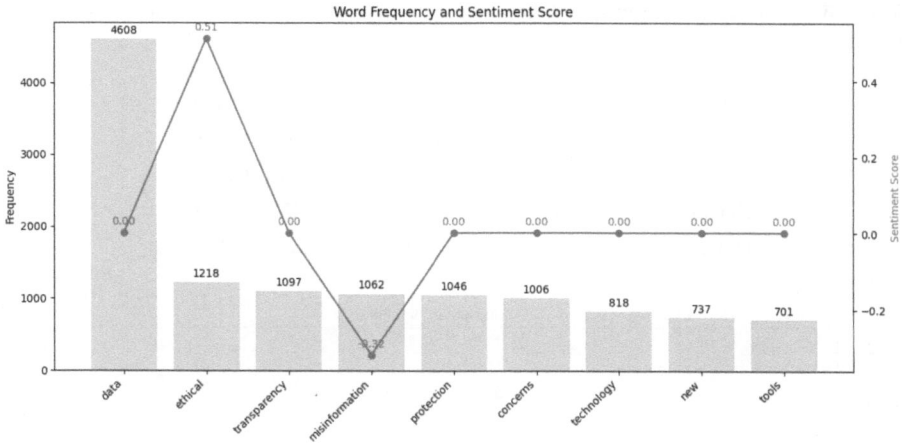

Fig. 5. Top 10 keywords. The total of tweets where they appear, and the calculated sentiment score is shown as the red line.

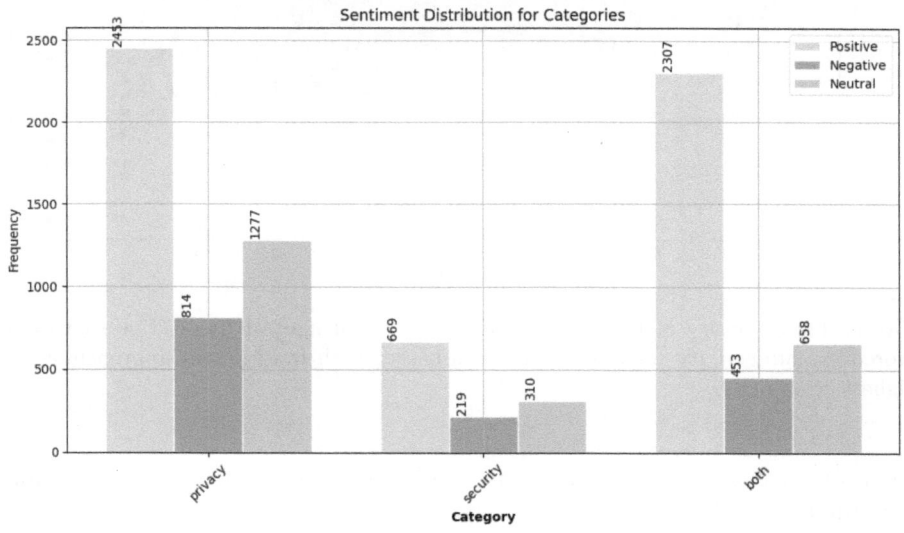

Fig. 6. The sentiment analysis based on the examined categories

of 1.0. This suggests that positive or neutral tweets typically do not contain negative opinions and are less likely to describe issues or problems.

4.2   Underlying Topic Modelling and Analysis

In this research, we generated a total of 90 word cloud graphs to explore underlying topics. These graphs were created for three inspected categories: security, privacy, and both categories combined. Each group consisted of 30 graphs (with

Table 3. List of the examined Categories showing the figures of their sentimental analysis

Category	Negative tweets (percentage)	Neutral tweets (percentage)	Positive tweets (percentage)
Security	219 (18%)	310 (26%)	669 (56%)
Privacy	814 (18%)	1277 (28%)	2453 (54%)
Both	453 (13%)	658 (19%)	2307 (67%)

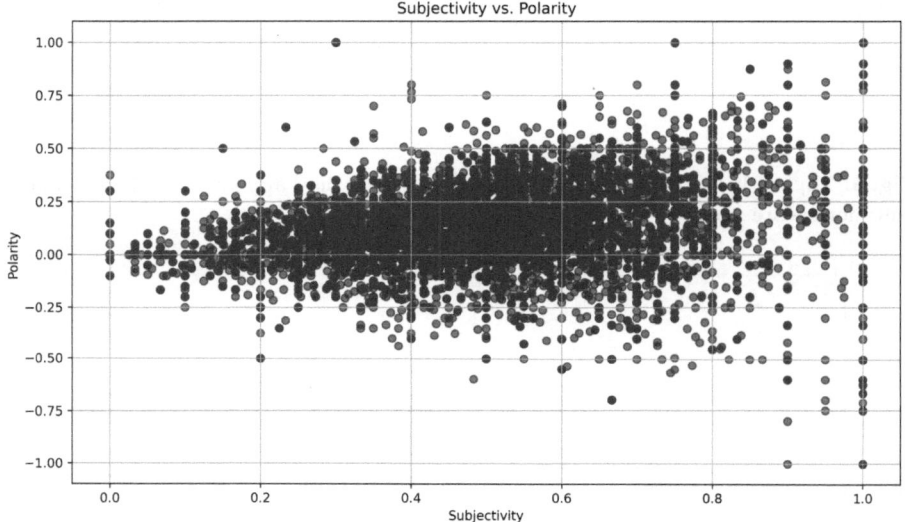

Fig. 7. The majority of tweets' polarities are overall neutral to positive sentiment. Moreover, subjectivity tends to be opinion-based, with most scores approaching the highest score of 1.0.

10 graphs per sentiment group: positive, negative, and neutral). The 10 graphs were further divided into "2-gram" and "3-gram" graphs, with 5 graphs for each type. Specifically, a 1-gram word cloud represents single words, a 2-gram combines two words, and a 3-gram combines three words. This division allowed us to analyze text data at both the phrase and sentence levels, capturing different levels of detail in the topics being explored. Notably, common words used for searching tweets, such as "chatgpt" and "security" and "privacy", ...etc., were intentionally retained, as they may contribute to revealing nuanced meanings. Example word cloud graphs can be seen in Fig. 9(a), Fig. 9(b), and Fig. 9(c).

The three-gram figures provide valuable insights at varying levels of detail. While a single-gram Fig. 9(a) displays keywords like 'data,' 'ethical,' 'transparency,' 'misinformation,' and 'protection,' the 2-gram word clouds Fig. 9(b) offer more specific information. For instance, they reveal phrases such as 'data protection,' 'generative ai,' 'ethical ai,' and 'ai governance.' Going further, the

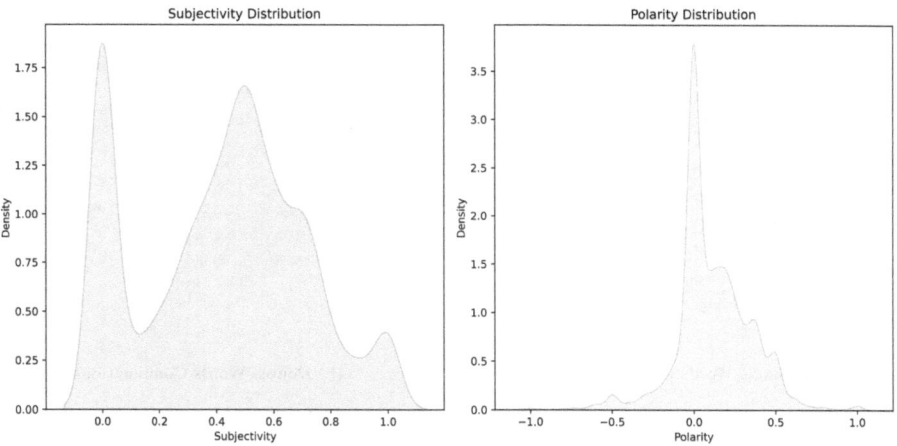

Fig. 8. Subjectivity & Polarity Plot (Diagram)

3-gram word clouds 9(c) delve into in-depth explanations of 2-gram phrases, providing even more specific details. For instance, consider learning about the latest developments in the field by exploring 'learn the latest development.' Additionally, responsible ethics play a crucial role, as indicated by the 3-gram phrase 'ensure responsible ethical.' Furthermore, understanding the current status of governance development, specifically 'development ai governance' and 'governance effective policies,' is essential. Our research highlights that both 2-gram and 3-gram analyses effectively uncover the underlying topics discussed in the examined tweets.

The process of underlying topics has been applied to all examined categories based on the previously explained sentimental analysis pictured in Fig. 6. In the following subsections, the results will be presented.

Security. Within the scope of the theme of security, as indicated in Table 3, 18% of the tweets related to security were negative. These are mostly associated with several topics, such as firstly: Cybersecurity threats, data breaches, and vulnerabilities in enterprise environments. Secondly: evolving on the potential misuse and security risks of AI technologies like ChatGPT. This topic was guessed based on the words such as "chatgpt", "llm (Large Language Models)", "chatbot", "Microsoft", "genre", "tool", "hacker", "exploit", "content", "code", "write", "intellig" (Artificial Intelligence)" which indicates the "AI technology and misuse". Moreover, phrases such as "hacker", "exploit", "lack", "critic", "warn", "problem", "remove", "arrest", "bad" point to negative connotations and security concerns. Here are some examples from observed related tweets:

– *"With the rising use of #AI-driven tools like #ChatGPT the number of #cyberattacks has doubled in the last year and became more sophisticated.*

(a) Single Words Combination.   (b) Double Words Combinations.

(c) Triple Words Combinations.

Fig. 9. Example Word-Cloud of Top 25 Presented using 1-, 2- and 3-gram Words Combinations representing the examined categories.

> *#Cybersecurity experts say AI-powered #ITsecurity tools could help protect your #privacy but are not a silver bull* https://bit.ly/4570Otf"
> – *"#CyberTuesdayNIST Warns of Security and Privacy Risks from Rapid AI System Deployment*
> *- At some point, ChatGPT was breached.*
> *The question is where does your breached data go?*
> *It goes to the dark web where it is sold?*
> *Always change your passwords."*

Moreover, several positively discussed topics were identified in the dataset, comprising the majority of tweets at 56%. These topics revolved around various themes such as firstly, "Proactive and Innovative Cybersecurity Practices" including "Ethical and Responsible Cybersecurity Practices", "Innovations in Cybersecurity Technologies", "Proactive Measures and Threat Prevention", "Integration of AI and Blockchain for Enhanced Security", "Continuous Learning and Staying Updated with Trends", "Development and Deployment of Secure Applications", "Advancements in Cybersecurity Policies and Governance". Secondly, "Supportive and Secure Digital Environment" which is the main title for subtitles such as "Support and Solutions for a Secure Digital Environment", "Promoting Safe Usage and Awareness", and "Fostering a Secure Workplace and Industry Environment".

Additionally, the positively oriented security topics in the dataset revolve around enhancing transparency and regulation, leveraging technological advancements, fostering collaboration and community engagement, securely managing digital assets, and combating misinformation to build trust. As an example, we can consider the following tweet which encapsulates positive security-related topics, emphasizing advancements, regulatory compliance, community engagement, digital asset management, and combating misinformation:

- *"Excited about @OpenAI's latest transparency report! Clear guidelines and regulatory compliance are essential for building trust.* ◉ 🔒 *Check it out here:* https://openai.com/transparency *#AI #Security #Transparency"*
- *"What's the best system for managing and monitoring #data? Comment if you think you know. For insight, watch this video showing @Microsoft #Azure tools and processes I that tackle malicious #security threats in real-time."*
- *"Have you heard about AI trends impacting the AEC industry but aren't sure how to embrace them at your firm? Register now for our AI Summit, focused on AI for AEC firms!* https://t.co/wZrrac22Hg
  #AISummit #BSTGlobal #AEC #AI #BigData #ChatGPT #LLM #ESG #Cybersecurity https://t.co/F7eY9PP1Pg"*
- *"Misinformation is a big threat, but @OpenAI's latest efforts to improve content authenticity are promising. Let's build a safer web together! Find out more: OpenAI Efforts #AI #Security #Trust"*

A closer look at tweets concerning perceived benefits shows that nearly 26% of them are neutral, without any clear polarization. Topics such as "Enterprise Security Solutions", "Encryption and Data Protection", "Ransomware and Cybercrime", "Training and Awareness", and "Technological Advancements in Security". This context can be seen in the following example tweets:

- *TODAY OpenAI Debuted ChatGPT Enterprise*

  OpenAI
  claims that its new solution gives enterprise-grade security for business use and unlimited access to a high-speed version of ChatGPT's underlying large language model #GPT4.
  The company mentioned it's the most powerful version of #ChatGPT yet. It also includes the ability to process longer inputs, advanced data analysis capabilities, and per-organization customization options.
  Future enhancements of #ChatGPTEnterprise include:
  ◆ *Custom connections to other enterprise applications*
  ◆ *ChatGPT #Business for smaller organizations*
  ◆ *Improved Advanced Data Analysis and browsing*
  ◆

Tools made specifically for data analysts, marketers, customer support and other roles.
#ai #ArtificialIntelligence #ChatGPT #chatbots #TechNews https://bit.ly/3x32WFE

- *Fmr. FTC Commissioner Noah Joshua Phillips on the FTC's investigation of OpenAI's ChatGPT:*
"They're interested in how the company is using its models, how its training those models, how its assessing risks, ... and they're also looking at privacy and data security."
https://bit.ly/3Vstt8B
- *"Cybersecurity 101: Encryption #education #archerawareness #ChatGPT*
https://bit.ly/4e2vrUN"
- *"The encryption malware code I wrote was done with ChatGPT's help after some coercion.*
This highlights the pointy end of the stick getting pointier when it comes to the sophistication of ransomware moving forward due to tech advancements such as ChatGPT and other LLMs"
https://bit.ly/4c5U4hr

Privacy. Analyzing users' views on privacy concerns showed that 18% of the tweets examined were negative and critical, 28% remained neutral without evident bias, and the majority, constituting 54%, expressed positivity. Investigating the specific topics that evoked negative, positive, or neutral responses among users provided insights into their sentiments and perspectives. These topics were identified as follows:

Topics related to users' positive perceptions, which compose almost more than half of tweets (54%), were retrieved from the observed 3-gram phrases such as "data privacy secure", "policy ensures response", "govern affect policy", "develop govern effect", "learn latest develop", "enhance secure privacy", "secure privacy unlimited", "release chatgpt enterprise", "user privacy secure", "privacy amp secure". The main topic is describing the exciting advancements in data privacy that are shaping the future of digital safety, with organizations adopting stronger protocols and policies to ensure robust protection of personal information. Government and corporate initiatives are paving the way for effective privacy policies, while the latest technological developments continue to enhance user privacy. Moreover, innovative privacy-focused software releases and enterprise solutions, like ChatGPT Enterprise, are setting new standards for secure communication and data protection. Together, these efforts underscore the commitment to safeguarding our digital world, providing users with the confidence that their information is well-protected. This can be seen in the following example tweets:

- *"8/ As we continue to witness advancements in AI, it's crucial to explore the ethical and responsible use of technologies like ChatGPT. Privacy, bias mitigation, and user consent should always be at the forefront of AI development and deployment.* 🔒🔐 "

- *"Learn about the latest developments in AI governance and having effective policies to ensure the responsible and ethical use of AI technology. #AIgovernance #AIethics #ChatGPT #AI #ML https://t.co/Rk5n6p61yN"*
- *"Brave Software, Inc., the company behind the privacy-focused browser, launched its own AI chatbot named "Leo." It works similar to ChatGPT, Bing, Bard and Claude but highlights its focus on prioritizing user privacy."*
- *"@OpenAI is partnering with Arizona State University to bring ChatGPT Enterprise tech to education. This enhances security, privacy and provides faster access to AI technology for academia ● ■ #OpenAI #AIinEducation ● ● https://t.co/SreAZtSupa"*

Since the total percentage of the tweets related to the negative users' perception regarding privacy issues consists of a very small portion, about 18% of the total dataset, discussed topics revolve around concerns and criticisms related to privacy, data protection, and ethical issues associated with the use of AI language models, specifically ChatGPT. Here are the inferred topics: firstly, concerns about the potential for AI, like ChatGPT, to dehumanize content, leading to ethical issues in communication and representation. Secondly, issues regarding the privacy and security of data when using AI services, particularly within enterprises using ChatGPT. Thirdly, specific focus on how AI services like Azure OpenAI comply with Italian data protection regulations and the role of Italian data protection authorities. Fourthly, criticism of the data analysis capabilities of AI models like ChatGPT, with concerns about potential violations of user privacy. Finally, risks associated with AI models having longer context windows, which may lead to greater exposure of sensitive information. The following example tweets illustrate some of these topics.

- *" ■ The UK Competition and Markets Authority is investigating whether AI development is in consumers' best interests, with a focus on chatbot software like ChatGPT. With concerns over job losses, privacy, and false information."*
- *"Italy Rules ChatGPT Violated European Privacy Laws*
  The country's data protection authority, known as Garante, said that it notified OpenAI of breaches of EU rules, known as General Data Protection Regulation."
- *"Pseudolangs might be more useful than DSLs for building apps on top of LLMs.*
  Since new model features (longer context windows, multimodality, code interpretation, web browsing) roll out in end-user facing GUIs like ChatGPT, http://Claude.ai, Bard *before* dev-facing APIs."

Finally, examining the neutral sentimental tweets, which compose one-third of tweets (approx. 28%) reveals that a good portion of discussed topics related to neutral users' perceptions, where users did not express polarized opinions rather they just mention them, seem to be associated with data privacy policies, government regulations, advancements in privacy technology, and the release of ChatGPT Enterprise with a focus on privacy features. Moreover, there were several advertising tweets promoting various technologies and platforms. Following are a couple of related examples of tweets:

- " 🌐 *Dive into the 2024 digital policy developments with #DWShorts episode 20:* https://youtu.be/5lqYy8aY2Bw!

  🚀 *Explore this year's digital landscape - from historic elections to global data privacy makeovers, AI's impact on the digital economy, and the latest in cybersecurity.* 🤖🔒 *Stay informed, stay ahead!"*
- *"By 2026, Gartner predicts 50% of governments worldwide will enforce use of responsible AI through regulations, policies and the need for data privacy." Learn in this Q&A about AI Regulations to Drive Responsible AI Initiatives:"*

5 Discussion

5.1 Theoretical Implications

This research makes significant contributions to the theoretical understanding of user perceptions of privacy and security in AI technologies, specifically in the context of ChatGPT. Several key theoretical implications emerge from this study.

First, this research extends Privacy Calculus Theory, which posits that individuals perform a cost-benefit analysis when deciding whether to adopt technology, weighing the perceived benefits against potential privacy risks. The study's findings align with this theory, revealing that users appreciate the innovative and functional benefits of ChatGPT while harboring significant concerns about privacy risks and data misuse. The duality in user sentiments-where positive perceptions of ChatGPT's utility coexist with apprehensions about privacy-underscores the relevance of privacy calculus in shaping user decisions regarding the adoption of AI technologies. This highlights the need for future theoretical models on AI adoption to place a stronger emphasis on the trade-offs between benefits and privacy risks in user decision-making.

Second, this study builds on the Diffusion of Innovations (DoI) Theory, which explains how a population adopts new ideas and technologies over time. According to DoI theory, privacy and security concerns can be significant barriers to adopting new technologies. Our findings indicate that, despite the rapid spread of ChatGPT, users' concerns about data security and privacy serve as obstacles to broader acceptance. In this context, DoI theory can be enriched by recognizing the role of privacy anxieties as a "rate-limiting" factor in the diffusion process. This implies that innovations in AI, like ChatGPT, might face slower adoption unless privacy and security concerns are addressed proactively. The research provides theoretical insights into how reducing privacy risks can accelerate the adoption of ChatGPT.

Additionally, this study touches on the concept of Trust in the technology, an emerging framework for understanding user interaction with AI systems. Trust is a critical component in technology acceptance, and this research shows that trust in the data-handling practices of AI developers, such as OpenAI, is a decisive factor in whether users feel comfortable engaging with AI technologies. The findings suggest that trust-building strategies, such as transparent communication about data security and the ethical use of AI, should be integrated into theoretical models of AI adoption. The role of trust, privacy concerns, and perceived benefits must be analyzed jointly in future studies to provide a more comprehensive framework for AI adoption and acceptance.

Lastly, this research highlights the importance of Sentiment Analysis as a Tool for Theoretical Exploration. Sentiment analysis allows researchers to understand user perceptions on a large scale and in real time, offering an empirical approach to understanding how users react to new technologies. The study demonstrates that sentiment analysis can complement traditional survey-based methodologies, offering a robust tool for measuring public opinion and theorizing about technology adoption patterns in dynamic environments like social media. However, as the study highlights the limitations of sentiment analysis, especially in misinterpreting sarcasm or informal language, future theoretical work should consider integrating more nuanced sentiment analysis techniques to handle these challenges better.

5.2   Practical Implications

This study's practical implications are particularly relevant for developers, policymakers, and organizations that are integrating or deploying AI technologies like ChatGPT. Several important areas for practical applications emerge from the findings.

First, AI Developers should prioritize transparency in data handling and privacy policies. The study shows that users are increasingly concerned about how AI systems collect, store, and use their data. Developers can build trust and mitigate privacy concerns by offering clear and easily accessible explanations of their data practices. For example, providing users with privacy management dashboards where they can control the data collected about them would not only empower users but also foster trust. Companies like OpenAI can improve user confidence by conducting regular transparency reports outlining their data protection measures and compliance with global privacy regulations, such as GDPR.

Second, Organizations using AI technologies, particularly in sectors like education, healthcare, and business, should be mindful of the privacy and security concerns identified in this study. These organizations must ensure that they use AI tools in ways that comply with data protection regulations and are transparent about how user data is handled. For instance, educational institutions using ChatGPT for academic purposes must communicate how student data is stored, processed, and protected and obtain explicit consent for any data collection. By addressing these concerns proactively, organizations can avoid legal and ethical issues while enhancing their reputation as responsible users of AI technology.

The study also emphasizes the importance of Robust Security Features in AI technologies. Developers should incorporate advanced encryption techniques, data anonymization, and other security protocols to minimize the risks of data breaches and unauthorized access. Continuous improvements in AI systems to safeguard data security will protect users and reduce their apprehension toward the technology. Focusing on developing privacy-enhancing technologies (PETs), such as differential privacy or federated learning, could make AI systems more acceptable to privacy-conscious users. Furthermore, developers should ensure that AI models like ChatGPT are regularly audited for vulnerabilities and equipped to handle emerging cybersecurity threats.

For Policymakers, this study provides clear evidence of the need for updated and comprehensive regulations governing AI technologies. As AI continues to evolve and integrate into more aspects of society, regulations must keep pace to protect user privacy while fostering innovation. Regulatory bodies should focus on creating flexible and adaptive frameworks that allow AI technology to thrive while ensuring user data is handled ethically and securely. This might include setting clearer standards for AI data usage, requiring AI companies to undergo regular privacy audits, and creating guidelines for transparency reporting. By creating strong, enforceable data privacy laws, policymakers can alleviate public concerns and encourage the broader adoption of AI tools.

Lastly, the study's insights can inform User-Centered Design approaches in AI development. Developers should consider involving users in the design of intuitive and user-friendly privacy features and interfaces. Engaging users through feedback loops can help refine privacy settings and features, ensuring that they meet the expectations and needs of different user groups. For example, developers could introduce customizable privacy settings that allow users to control what data is shared with AI systems, thereby enhancing the user's sense of control over their personal information.

In conclusion, the findings of this research provide a roadmap for developers, organizations, and policymakers to enhance the user experience and trust in AI technologies. By addressing privacy and security concerns head-on, the adoption of ChatGPT and similar technologies can be accelerated, benefiting both users and society at large.

6   Conclusion, Future Research and Research Limitations

In conclusion, this research significantly enhances the theoretical understanding of user perceptions regarding security and privacy in AI technologies, focusing specifically on ChatGPT. By employing sentiment analysis from social media platforms, we have identified how users balance the perceived benefits and risks of these advanced tools. The study offers valuable insights into technology acceptance and innovation diffusion, highlighting that while users acknowledge the transformative potential of AI, concerns about data privacy and misuse remain significant. These findings underscore the necessity for a balanced approach that promotes both innovation and robust privacy measures, setting a foundation for future research and theoretical development.

Future research should consider conducting longitudinal studies to track changes in user perceptions over time, providing insights into the evolving landscape of privacy and security concerns in AI technologies. Comparative studies across different AI platforms could reveal whether the identified concerns are specific to ChatGPT or reflect broader trends. Additionally, exploring how user perceptions vary across demographics, such as age and education, can help tailor more inclusive AI technologies.

Examining the impact of regulatory changes on user trust and the adoption of AI tools would provide valuable feedback on the effectiveness of data protection policies. Research should also focus on developing and testing new privacy-enhancing technologies to address user concerns proactively. Investigating the ethical implications of AI usage, including potential biases and societal impacts, would further deepen our understanding and help establish guidelines for responsible AI deployment.

While this study provides valuable insights into user perceptions of Chat-GPT's privacy and security issues through sentiment analysis, several limitations should be acknowledged.

First, the reliance on data from X (formerly Twitter) may not fully capture the diversity of ChatGPT users, limiting the generalizability of the findings. X users may not represent the broader population, and the discussions analyzed might be skewed toward more vocal or technologically literate individuals, potentially overlooking the sentiments of less active or non-users of social media platforms.

Second, while sentiment analysis provides a useful method for gauging public opinion, it is important to note that it can sometimes misinterpret the context or tone of social media posts. Social media language is often informal, ambiguous, and sometimes ironic, making it challenging for sentiment analysis tools to capture the true sentiment behind a post accurately. This potential for misinterpretation can lead to inaccuracies in the findings.

Third, although the sentiment analysis results are presented in aggregate terms, further granularity could have been explored. Specifically, the study did not differentiate between the types of users originating the posts-such as private citizens, media sources, or organizations. Such an analysis could have provided more nuanced insights into how different user groups perceive privacy and security issues related to ChatGPT. Future research could address this gap by categorizing the originators of posts and analyzing sentiment variations across different user groups.

Despite these limitations, this research provides a crucial foundation for understanding user perceptions of AI technologies, emphasizing the need for a balanced approach that addresses both benefits and risks. Future studies should build on these insights, exploring broader contexts and more detailed data to advance our knowledge and improve AI technology deployment in alignment with user expectations and ethical standards.

Acknowledgement. This research was supported by the Zayed University RIF grant activity code R22085.

The authors have no competing interests to declare relevant to this article's content.

References

1. Haleem, A., Javaid, M., Singh, R.P.: An era of ChatGPT as a significant futuristic support tool: a study on features, abilities, and challenges. BenchCouncil Trans. Benchmarks Stand. Eval. **2**(4), 100089 (2022)
2. Choudhury, A., Shamszare, H.: Investigating the impact of user trust on the adoption and use of ChatGPT: survey analysis. J. Med. Internet Res. **25**, e47184 (2023)
3. Xiandong, W., Duan, R., Jianbing, N.: Unveiling security, privacy, and ethical concerns of ChatGPT. arXiv (2023)
4. Dwivedi, Y.K., et al.: "so what if ChatGPT wrote it?" Multidisciplinary perspectives on opportunities, challenges and implications of generative conversational AI for research, practice and policy. Int. J. Inf. Manag. **71**, 102642 (2023)
5. Bertomeu, J., Lin, Y., Liu, Y., Ni, Z.: Capital market consequences of generative AI: early evidence from the ban of ChatGPT in Italy. Available at SSRN 4452670 (2023)
6. Van Dis, E.A.M., Bollen, J., Zuidema, W., Van Rooij, R., Bockting, C.L.: ChatGPT: five priorities for research. Nature **614**(7947), 224–226 (2023)
7. Huang, W.R., Geiping, J., Fowl, L., Taylor, G., Goldstein, T.: Metapoison: practical general-purpose clean-label data poisoning. In: Advances in Neural Information Processing Systems, vol. 33, pp. 12080–12091 (2020)
8. Heiding, F., Schneier, B., Vishwanath, A., Bernstein, J.: Devising and detecting phishing: large language models vs. smaller human models. arXiv preprint arXiv:2308.12287 (2023)
9. Bian, J., et al.: Mining Twitter to assess the public perception of the "internet of things". PLoS ONE **11**(7), e0158450 (2016)
10. Korkmaz, A., Aktürk, C., Talan, T.: Analyzing the user's sentiments of ChatGPT using Twitter data. Iraqi J. Comput. Sci. Math. **4**(2), 202–214 (2023)
11. Ul Haque, M., Dharmadasa, I., Sworna, Z.T., Rajapakse, R.N., Ahmad, H.: "i think this is the most disruptive technology": Exploring sentiments of ChatGPT early adopters using Twitter data (2022)
12. Mhlanga, D.: Open AI in education, the responsible and ethical use of ChatGPT towards lifelong learning. In: FinTech and Artificial Intelligence for Sustainable Development: The Role of Smart Technologies in Achieving Development Goals, pp. 387–409. Springer, Cham (2023)
13. Twitter: Twitter terms of service, Accessed 2024
14. Jurado, F., Cobos, R., Blázquez-Herranz, A.: A content analysis system that supports sentiment analysis for subjectivity and polarity detection in online courses. IEEE Revista Iberoamericana de Tecnologias del Aprendizaje **14**(4), 177–187 (2019)
15. Yue, L., Chen, W., Li, X., Zuo, W., Yin, M.: A survey of sentiment analysis in social media. Knowl. Inf. Syst. **60**, 617–663 (2019)
16. Elbagir, S., Yang, J.: Twitter sentiment analysis using natural language toolkit and Vader sentiment. In: In Proceedings of the International Multiconference of Engineers and Computer Scientists, Hong Kong. IMECS 2019 (2019)
17. Cambridge University Press: Cambridge dictionary. https://dictionary.cambridge.org/dictionary/english/tweeter?q=tweeters. Accessed 19 Feb 2024
18. Onah, D.F., Pang, E.L., El-Haj, M.: A data-driven latent semantic analysis for automatic text summarization using LDA topic modelling. arXiv (2022)
19. Kumar, T., Mahrishi, M., Nawaz, S.: A review of speech sentiment analysis using machine learning. In: Proceedings of Trends in Electronics and Health Informatics: TEHI 2021. TEHI (2022)

20. Manning, C., Surdeanu, M., Bauer, J., Finkel, J., Bethard, S., McClosky, D.: The Stanford core NLP natural language processing toolkit. In: Bontcheva, K., Zhu, J. (eds.) Proceedings of 52nd Annual Meeting of the Association for Computational Linguistics: System Demonstrations, pp. 55–60, Baltimore, Maryland. Association for Computational Linguistics (2014)

21. Turki Turki and Sanjiban Sekhar Roy: Novel hate speech detection using word cloud visualization and ensemble learning coupled with count vectorizer. Appl. Sci. **12**(13), 6611 (2022)

22. Abrigo, A.B.C., Estuar, M.R.J.E.: A comparative analysis of n-gram deep neural network approach to classifying human perception on dengvaxia. In: 2019 IEEE 2nd International Conference on Information and Computer Technologies (ICICT), pp. 46–51. IEEE (2019)

Extended Abstract: Evaluating Cross-Chain Platforms for EV Charging Payment Systems

L. K. Bang[1], P. H. T. Trung[1], N. B. Nam[1], H. G. Khiem[1], Bao Q. Tran[1], Hieu M. Doan[1], Duy D. X. Pham[1], and Ngan T. K. Nguyen[2(✉)]

[1] FPT University, Hanoi, Vietnam
banglkce160155@fpt.edu.vn
[2] FPT Polytechnic, Ho Chi Minh City, Vietnam
nganntkpc06789@fpt.edu.vn

Abstract. This paper examines the application of blockchain technology in electric vehicle (EV) charging payment systems, focusing on a comparative analysis of four EVM-supported platforms: Binance Smart Chain, Polygon, Fantom, and Celo. As the EV market expands, traditional payment methods struggle to meet the unique requirements of charging infrastructure, such as real-time pricing and seamless user experiences across networks. We analyze these platforms' performance in three key operations: transaction creation, NFT minting, and NFT transfer, considering factors like transaction fees, gas limits, gas usage, and gas prices. The study aims to provide insights into the suitability of each platform for real-world EV charging applications, addressing the challenges of implementing blockchain-based payment in this domain.

Keywords: Blockchain · Electric Vehicles · NFT · Payment Systems · Smart Contracts

1 Introduction

The rapid growth of electric vehicles (EVs) has led to an increased demand for efficient and reliable charging infrastructure. As the EV market expands, the need for robust payment systems to handle charging transactions has become increasingly apparent. Traditional payment methods often struggle to meet the unique requirements of EV charging, such as real-time pricing, dynamic load balancing, and seamless user experiences across different charging networks.

Blockchain technology has emerged as a potential solution to address these challenges in EV charging payment systems. The decentralized nature of blockchain offers improved transparency, security, and efficiency in managing transactions [10,11]. By leveraging smart contracts and distributed ledgers, blockchain-based systems can automate payments [15], ensure fair pricing [8], and provide a tamper-resistant record of all charging sessions [5]. Recent

M. Al-kfairy et al. (Eds.): SocialSec 2024, LNCS 15565, pp. 68–78, 2025.
https://doi.org/10.1007/978-981-96-3774-4_4

research has explored various aspects of blockchain integration in EV charging ecosystems. For instance, V2GNet incorporates blockchain to optimize energy distribution while safeguarding against potential attacks in Vehicle-to-Grid (V2G) networks [12]. Other studies have focused on developing auction mechanisms that utilize blockchain to facilitate efficient and transparent energy trading between EVs and the grid [13]. These advancements demonstrate the potential of blockchain to enhance the overall efficiency and reliability of EV charging payment systems.

The integration of blockchain with EV charging infrastructure also opens up new possibilities for peer-to-peer energy trading. This approach allows EV owners to participate in energy markets, potentially reducing the impact of charging on power systems while offering economic benefits to participants [4]. Furthermore, blockchain-based systems can enable more sophisticated pricing models that account for factors such as renewable energy availability, grid congestion, and time-of-use rates [7]. However, the implementation of blockchain-based payment systems for EV charging is not without challenges. One of the primary considerations is the choice of blockchain platform, as different networks offer varying levels of performance, cost-effectiveness, and features. To address this, our study focuses on evaluating four prominent EVM-supported platforms: Binance Smart Chain (BNB Smart Chain), Polygon, Fantom, and Celo. Each of these platforms presents unique characteristics that can significantly impact the efficiency and cost-effectiveness of EV charging payment processes.

Our analysis centers on three key operations crucial to EV charging payment systems: transaction creation, NFT minting, and NFT transfer. By examining these operations across the selected platforms, we aim to provide insights into their suitability for real-world EV charging applications. We consider various factors including transaction fees, gas limits, gas usage, and gas prices to offer a comprehensive comparison of the platforms' performance in the context of EV charging payments. The results of this evaluation will help stakeholders make informed decisions when selecting a blockchain platform for implementing EV charging payment systems. By understanding the trade-offs between transaction costs, processing speed, and overall efficiency, developers and network operators can choose the most appropriate platform for their specific use cases. This knowledge is crucial for the development of cost-effective and efficient blockchain-based solutions that can meet the growing demands of the EV charging market.

2 Related Work

2.1 Evolution of Energy Trading Systems for Electric Vehicles

The landscape of energy trading management systems for EVs has seen considerable development in recent years. Blockchain technology has emerged as a key component in enhancing the security and reliability of transactions within V2G networks. For instance, V2GNet incorporates an energy trading algorithm designed to optimize energy distribution while safeguarding against potential

attacks [12]. Efforts to protect user privacy have also been made, with the introduction of schemes that ensure transaction anonymity [5]. Auction mechanisms
leveraging blockchain have been proposed to facilitate energy trading between
EVs and the grid, aiming to improve efficiency and transparency [13]. Peer-to-
peer models have shown potential in mitigating the impact of EV charging on
power systems while offering economic advantages to participants [4].

The integration of smart grids with energy trading systems has demonstrated
promise in managing fluctuating EV demands. Cloud-based energy management services incorporating fair demand response models have been developed
to optimize electricity usage and trading [7]. Coordinated management strategies
involving V2G services and renewable energy sources have been explored to mitigate risks in day-ahead electricity markets [2]. Research has also focused on
optimizing peer-to-peer energy trading systems that incorporate vehicle-to-
home (V2H) modes, aiming to reduce community energy costs and enhance
energy independence [3]. Secure electricity trading models based on blockchain
have been proposed to improve the reliability of EV energy transactions [6].
Additionally, energy trading frameworks for smart campus parking lots have
been developed to enable efficient energy exchange among EVs [1].

2.2   Blockchain Applications in EV Energy Trading

The application of blockchain technology in the Internet of Electric Vehicles
(IoEV) has been explored as a potential solution to challenges in energy and data
trading. The decentralized nature of blockchain offers improved transparency and
trust in managing real-time vehicle data and facilitating secure energy trading.
Consortium blockchain models using smart contracts and advanced digital signatures have been proposed to enhance the security and efficiency of data and
energy transactions in the IoEV [14]. Vehicle-to-vehicle energy trading frameworks leveraging novel consensus mechanisms have been developed to improve
transaction throughput and security among EVs [16]. Researchers have also
designed secure and decentralized energy trading models using smart contracts
in V2G networks, aiming to address risks associated with centralized trading
systems [9]. Incentive contract models based on energy blockchain have been
explored, focusing on securing electricity trading among EVs and encouraging
participation through game theory-based rewards [6].

3   Approach

3.1   Traditional Approach for Electric Vehicle Charging
Infrastructure

Figure 1 illustrates a comprehensive EV charging infrastructure network, depicting the flow of energy from producers to end consumers. This system encompasses multiple components, including energy sources, various types of charging stations, and electric vehicles, all interconnected in a coherent ecosystem

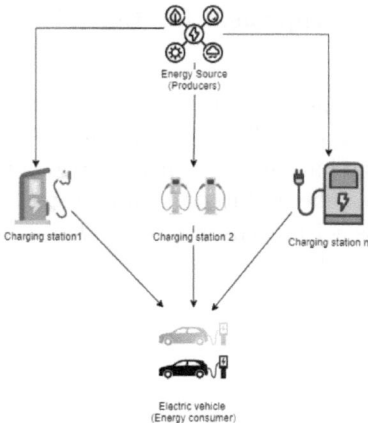

Fig. 1. Electric Vehicle Charging Infrastructure Network

designed to support the growing adoption of electric transportation. At the core of this infrastructure is the energy source, represented as "Energy Source (Producers)." This component serves as the foundation of the entire system, providing the necessary power to all downstream charging stations. The inclusion of renewable energy symbols suggests a focus on clean, sustainable energy production for powering the EV charging network. This approach aligns with the broader goals of reducing carbon emissions and promoting environmental sustainability in the transportation sector.

The charging infrastructure is composed of multiple charging stations, represented in the diagram as "Charging station 1," "Charging station 2," and "Charging station n." This variety in charging stations likely represents different charging speeds, locations, or technologies available to EV users. The inclusion of multiple station types indicates a recognition of diverse user needs and preferences. Some stations may offer rapid charging for users on long trips, while others might provide slower, more economical charging options for overnight or workplace parking. This diversity in charging options enhances the accessibility and convenience of the EV charging network, addressing one of the key concerns in EV adoption - the availability of charging infrastructure. The final component in this ecosystem is the electric vehicles themselves, labeled as "Electric vehicle (Energy consumer)." The diagram shows different vehicle types, acknowledging the range of electric vehicles on the market, from purpose-built EVs to converted traditional vehicle designs. This representation underscores the broad applicability of the charging infrastructure to various EV models and user demographics. The inclusion of different vehicle types also highlights the flexibility of the charging network in accommodating the evolving landscape of electric vehicles.

3.2   Blockchain-Based Approach for Electric Vehicle Charging Network

Figure 2 presents a comprehensive architecture for EV charging network that integrates blockchain technology. This system encompasses various components including energy sources, charging stations, electric vehicles, and a blockchain-based management layer. The architecture illustrates the flow of energy, information, and transactions within the network, showcasing how traditional EV charging infrastructure can be enhanced with blockchain capabilities.

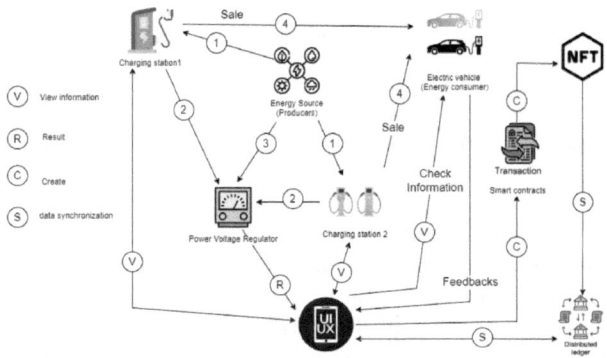

Fig. 2. Blockchain-Integrated Electric Vehicle Charging Network Architecture

The process begins with the energy source (producers) supplying power to the charging stations and the power voltage regulator. This initial step, represents the fundamental energy distribution within the network. Simultaneously, information about this energy supply is sent to the central user interface, likely for monitoring and management purposes. Following the energy distribution, the power voltage regulator adjusts and stabilizes the power supply. This regulated power is then directed to the charging stations (step '2'). This step ensures that the charging stations receive consistent and appropriate power levels for safe and efficient EV charging. The next phase involves the interaction between EVs and charging stations. Arrows labeled '4' show the bidirectional 'Sale' process between charging stations and electric vehicles. This suggests that not only is energy transferred to the vehicles, but there's also a transaction occurring, likely facilitated by the blockchain components of the system.

The central user interface plays a crucial role in this architecture. It receives view information (V) from various components, including charging stations and the power voltage regulator. This interface also checks information from the EVs and receives results (R) from the power voltage regulator. These interactions allow for real-time monitoring and control of the entire system. The blockchain elements of the system are represented by the transaction processing, smart contracts, and distributed ledger components. The process flow shows that transactions are created (C) and then processed through smart contracts. These smart contracts interact with the distributed ledger, facilitating the creation of NFTs. The distributed ledger also engages in data synchronization (S) with the central user interface, ensuring that all blockchain-recorded information is up-to-date and accessible.

4 Evaluation

4.1 EVM-Supported Platform Deployment

In our evaluation of the Electronic Vehicle Charging Payment System, we focus on cross-chain functionality by examining four EVM-supported platforms: Binance Smart Chain (BNB Smart Chain)[1]; Polygon[2]; Fantom[3]; and Celo[4]. The decision to analyze multiple platforms stems from the need to identify the most suitable environment for implementing and managing EV charging payments in a blockchain context. Each platform offers unique characteristics and trade-offs, which can significantly impact the efficiency and cost-effectiveness of payment processes in the EV charging ecosystem.

By analyzing several platforms, we aim to provide a comprehensive understanding of how different blockchain environments handle EV charging-related transactions. This comparative approach allows us to assess the strengths and limitations of each platform, ultimately guiding users and developers towards the most appropriate choice for their specific needs in the EV charging payment domain. Our analysis centers on three primary methods crucial to EV charging payment systems on blockchain: transaction creation, NFT minting, and NFT transfer. These operations represent key processes in the lifecycle of digital assets related to EV charging, from initial setup to ownership transfer. By examining these methods across different platforms, we can gauge the overall performance and suitability of each blockchain for EV charging payment tasks.

To conduct a thorough evaluation, we analyze several critical factors that influence the performance and cost-effectiveness of blockchain operations. These factors include transaction fees, gas limits, and gas prices. Transaction fees are particularly important as they directly affect the cost of performing EV charging-related operations on the blockchain. Gas prices, which can fluctuate based on network demand, play a significant role in determining the overall cost of transactions. It's worth noting that while burn fees are a factor in some blockchain ecosystems, particularly BNB and MATIC (Polygon), we have chosen not to include this in our analysis. For this evaluation, we collected the price data of the cryptocurrencies in June 2024 to ensure cost comparisons.

---

[1] https://github.com/bnb-chain/whitepaper/blob/master/WHITEPAPER.md.
[2] https://polygon.technology/lightpaper-polygon.pdf.
[3] https://whitepaper.io/document/438/fantom-whitepaper.
[4] https://celo.org/papers/whitepaper.

4.2   Transaction Fee

Table 1. Transaction fee

	Contract Creation	Create NFT	Transfer NFT
BNB Smart Chain	0.0273134 BNB ($13.91)	0.00109162 BNB ($0.56)	0.00057003 BNB ($0.29)
Fantom	0.00957754 FTM ($0.00)	0.000405167 FTM ($0.00)	0.0002380105 FTM ($0.00)
Polygon	0.006840710032835408 MATIC($0.01)	0.000289405001852192 MATIC($0.00)	0.000170007501088048 MATIC($0.00)
Celo	0.007097844 CELO ($0.003)	0.0002840812 CELO ($0.000)	0.0001554878 CELO ($0.000)

The analysis of transaction fees across the four EVM-supported platforms, as presented in Table 1, reveals significant variations in cost structure for EV charging payment operations. These differences can substantially impact the choice of platform for implementing blockchain-based EV charging payment solutions. BNB Smart Chain exhibits the highest transaction fees among the four platforms. Contract creation on BNB Smart Chain costs 0.0273134 BNB, equivalent to approximately $13.91, which is notably higher than the other networks. NFT creation and transfer operations on BNB Smart Chain are also more expensive, at 0.00109162 BNB ($0.56) and 0.00057003 BNB ($0.29) respectively. These higher fees could potentially deter users from utilizing BNB Smart Chain for frequent EV charging-related transactions, especially in scenarios involving numerous small-value operations. In contrast, Fantom demonstrates remarkably low transaction fees across all three operations. The costs for contract creation (0.00957754 FTM), NFT creation (0.000405167 FTM), and NFT transfer (0.0002380105 FTM) on Fantom are negligible when converted to USD, all rounding to $0.00. This cost-effectiveness could make Fantom an attractive option for users looking to minimize transaction expenses, particularly for high-volume EV charging payment tasks.

Polygon presents a middle ground in terms of transaction fees. While its fees are higher than Fantom's, they remain very low when converted to USD. Contract creation on Polygon costs 0.006840710032835408 MATIC ($0.01), with NFT creation and transfer fees being even lower at 0.000289405001852192 MATIC and 0.000170007501088048 MATIC respectively, both rounding to $0.00 in USD. This balance of low fees and widespread adoption could make Polygon a practical choice for many EV charging payment applications. Celo's fee structure is similar to Polygon's in terms of USD conversion, with all operations costing less than a cent. Contract creation on Celo costs 0.007097844 CELO ($0.003), NFT creation 0.0002840812 CELO, and NFT transfer 0.0001554878 CELO, with the latter two rounding to $0.000 in USD. This fee structure positions Celo as another cost-effective option for EV charging payment systems on the blockchain.

4.3   Gas Limit

The analysis of gas limits across the four EVM-supported platforms, as shown in Table 2, reveals interesting patterns in resource allocation for EV charging

Table 2. Gas limit

	Contract Creation	Create NFT	Transfer NFT
BNB Smart Chain	2,731,340	109,162	72,003
Fantom	2,736,440	115,762	72,803
Polygon	2,736,284	115,762	72,803
Celo	3,548,922	142,040	85,673

payment operations. These gas limits play a crucial role in determining the computational resources available for executing smart contracts and transactions on these blockchain networks. For contract creation, we observe that BNB Smart Chain, Fantom, and Polygon have relatively similar gas limits, ranging from 2,731,340 to 2,736,440 units. This similarity suggests a comparable approach to resource allocation for complex operations like deploying new smart contracts related to EV charging payment systems. However, Celo stands out with a significantly higher gas limit of 3,548,922 units for contract creation. This higher limit on Celo could potentially allow for more complex or feature-rich smart contracts to be deployed, which might be beneficial for sophisticated EV charging payment systems that require extensive computational resources. When it comes to creating NFTs, which could represent digital assets in EV charging scenarios such as charging station ownership or user credits, we see more variation among the platforms. BNB Smart Chain has the lowest gas limit at 109,162 units, while Fantom and Polygon both allocate 115,762 units. Celo again provides the highest gas limit at 142,040 units. These differences could impact the complexity and features of NFTs that can be minted on each platform, potentially affecting the richness of metadata or additional functionalities that can be incorporated into EV charging-related tokens. For NFT transfers, which might represent ownership changes of EV charging assets or the transfer of charging credits between users, the gas limits are more consistent across platforms, with slight variations. BNB Smart Chain has the lowest limit at 72,003 units, while Fantom and Polygon both allocate 72,803 units. Celo maintains its trend of higher limits with 85,673 units for NFT transfers. These differences, while less pronounced than in other operations, could still affect the efficiency and potential additional features of NFT transfers on each platform in the context of EV charging payments.

The consistently higher gas limits on Celo across all three operations suggest that this platform may be more accommodating to complex or resource-intensive operations in EV charging payment systems. This could be advantageous for implementing advanced features or handling large-scale EV charging networks with complex payment structures. However, it's important to note that higher gas limits don't necessarily translate to better performance or lower costs, as other factors like network congestion and gas prices also play significant roles. The similarities in gas limits between Fantom and Polygon for NFT creation and transfer operations indicate that these platforms may offer comparable capabilities for standard EV charging payment tasks. BNB Smart Chain's slightly lower limits might necessitate more efficient smart contract design to ensure operations fit within the allocated gas limits, which could be a consideration for developers implementing EV charging payment systems on this platform.

4.4 Gas Price

The analysis of gas prices across the four EVM-supported platforms, as presented in Table 3, reveals significant variations in the cost structure for executing EV charging payment operations on these blockchains. Gas prices play a crucial role in determining the overall transaction costs and can greatly influence the economic viability of implementing EV charging payment systems on different networks. BNB Smart Chain demonstrates the highest gas price among the four platforms, with a consistent rate of 0.00000001 BNB (10 Gwei) across all three operations: contract creation, NFT creation, and NFT transfer. This uniformity in gas price simplifies cost calculations for users but also means that BNB Smart Chain maintains relatively higher transaction costs compared to the other networks examined. The higher gas price on BNB Smart Chain could potentially impact the frequency and scale of EV charging-related transactions, especially for operations involving numerous small-value payments or frequent updates to charging station statuses. Fantom offers a significantly lower gas price at 0.0000000035 FTM (3.5 Gwei) for all three operations. This lower gas price could make Fantom an attractive option for users looking to minimize transaction costs in their EV charging payment processes. The reduced costs might enable more frequent transactions or the handling of larger volumes of charging sessions without incurring prohibitive fees. However, it's important to note that the actual cost in fiat currency would depend on the current exchange rate.

Polygon presents a slightly more complex gas price structure, with minor variations across operations. For contract creation, the gas price is 0.00000000250000 0012 MATIC (2.500000012 Gwei), while for NFT creation and transfer, it's 0.000000002500000016 MATIC (2.500000016 Gwei). These prices are lower than both BNB Smart Chain and Fantom, potentially making Polygon a cost-effective choice for EV charging payment tasks. The slight difference in gas price between

Table 3. Gas Price

	Contract Creation	Create NFT	Transfer NFT
BNB Smart Chain	0.00000001 BNB (10 Gwei)	0.00000001 BNB (10 Gwei)	0.00000001 BNB (10 Gwei)
Fantom	0.0000000035 FTM (3.5 Gwei)	0.0000000035 FTM (3.5 Gwei)	0.0000000035 FTM (3.5 Gwei)
Polygon	0.000000002500000012 MATIC (2.500000012 Gwei)	0.000000002500000016 MATIC (2.500000016 Gwei)	0.000000002500000016 MATIC (2.500000016 Gwei)
Celo	0.0000000026 CELO (Max Fee per Gas: 2.7 Gwei)	0.0000000026 CELO (Max Fee per Gas: 2.7 Gwei)	0.0000000026 CELO (Max Fee per Gas: 2.7 Gwei)

contract creation and NFT operations on Polygon is minimal and likely wouldn't significantly impact overall costs for most EV charging use cases. Celo employs a unique approach with its gas pricing mechanism. It uses a consistent price of 0.0000000026 CELO across all operations, but specifies this as a "Max Fee per Gas" of 2.7 Gwei. This structure suggests that Celo implements a form of dynamic gas pricing, where the actual gas price might fluctuate below this maximum value depending on network conditions. This approach could potentially offer users more predictable maximum costs while allowing for lower fees during periods of reduced network congestion, which could be beneficial for EV charging systems that experience varying levels of activity throughout the day.

5 Conclusion

Our comparative analysis of Binance Smart Chain, Polygon, Fantom, and Celo for EV charging payment systems reveals significant variations in performance and cost-effectiveness across these platforms. Each blockchain network presents distinct advantages and challenges in terms of transaction costs, resource allocation, and overall efficiency for EV charging-related operations. The study highlights the importance of carefully considering platform characteristics when implementing blockchain-based EV charging payment systems. Factors such as transaction fees, gas limits, and gas prices play crucial roles in determining the economic viability and operational efficiency of these systems, particularly for different scales and types of charging networks.

References

1. Ahmed, M.A., Kim, Y.C.: Energy trading with electric vehicles in smart campus parking lots. Appl. Sci. (2018)
2. Al-Awami, A., Sortomme, E.: Coordinating vehicle-to-grid services with energy trading. IEEE Trans. Smart Grid (2012)
3. Al-Sorour, A., et al.: Investigation of electric vehicles contributions in an optimized peer-to-peer energy trading system. IEEE Access (2023)
4. Alvaro-Hermana, R., Fraile-Ardanuy, J., Zufiria, P., Knapen, L., Janssens, D.: Peer to peer energy trading with electric vehicles. IEEE Intell. Transp. Syst. Mag. (2016)
5. Baza, M., et al.: Privacy-preserving blockchain-based energy trading schemes for electric vehicles. IEEE Trans. Veh. Technol. (2021)
6. Chen, X., Zhang, X.: Secure electricity trading and incentive contract model for electric vehicle based on energy blockchain. IEEE Access (2019)
7. Chen, Y.W., Chang, J.M.: Fair demand response with electric vehicles for the cloud based energy management service. IEEE Trans. Smart Grid (2018)
8. Ha, X.S., Le, H.T., Metoui, N., Duong-Trung, N.: Dem-COD: novel access-control-based cash on delivery mechanism for decentralized marketplace. In: 2020 IEEE 19th International Conference on Trust, Security and Privacy in Computing and Communications (TrustCom), pp. 71–78. IEEE (2020)
9. Iqbal, A., Rajasekaran, A., Nikhil, G.S., Azees, M.: A secure and decentralized blockchain based EV energy trading model using smart contract in V2G network. IEEE Access. IEEE (2021)

10. Le, H.T., et al.: Introducing multi shippers mechanism for decentralized cash on delivery system. Int. J. Adv. Comput. Sci. Appl. **10**(6) (2019)
11. Le, N.T.T., et al.: Assuring non-fraudulent transactions in cash on delivery by introducing double smart contracts. Int. J. Adv. Comput. Sci. Appl. **10**(5), 677–684 (2019)
12. Liang, Y., Wang, Z., Abdallah, A.B.: V2GNET: robust blockchain-based energy trading method and implementation in vehicle-to-grid network. IEEE Access (2022)
13. Luo, L., et al.: Blockchain-enabled two-way auction mechanism for electricity trading in internet of electric vehicles. IEEE Internet Things J. (2021)
14. Sadiq, A., et al.: Blockchain based data and energy trading in internet of electric vehicles. IEEE Access (2021)
15. Son, H.X., et al.: Towards a mechanism for protecting seller's interest of cash on delivery by using smart contract in hyperledger. Int. J. Adv. Comput. Sci. Appl. **10**(4) (2019)
16. Wang, Y.S., et al.: A fast and secured vehicle-to-vehicle energy trading based on blockchain consensus in the internet of electric vehicles. IEEE Trans. Veh. Technol. (2023)

Using M5Stack Core 2 ESP32 to Raise Children's Awareness About Cyber Security

Yeslam Al-Saggaf[✉] and Alan Ibbett

Charles Sturt University, Wagga Wagga, NSW 2678, Australia
yalsaggaf@csu.edu.au

Abstract. The majority of Australian children aged between 14–18 have a smartphone. Children at this age are concerned more with sharing information with their friends than with protecting their privacy. For this reason, they tend to leave their smartphone's default privacy settings on making it possible for anyone to discover their movements. This project aimed at raising children's awareness about the security issues associated with their smartphones. M5Stack Core 2 ESP32 devices programmed to detect Bluetooth and WI-FI signals were installed around two high school campuses in Australia to capture traffic within their range. Children were then informed of the presence of these network sensors in their campuses, during a cyber safety lesson in which they were shown how to modify their smartphone privacy settings to prevent their smartphones from sharing information about them without their knowledge. Samples of data extracted from the network sensors before and after the delivery of the cyber safety lesson were compared to find out if the children in these two schools changed their smartphone settings to stop their sensitive information from escaping from their smartphones. The outcome of the analysis of the before and after data showed that the volume of traffic captured from smartphones after the cyber safety lesson was significantly less than the volume of traffic captured before the cyber safety lesson, suggesting children must have benefited from the lesson.

Keywords: M5Stack · Network Sensor · Smartphones · Children · Privacy · Cyber Security · Cyber Safety

1 Introduction and Related Work

Children's desire, in some cases pressure, to be online and available 24/7, is making them less risk averse [1]. While evidence from the literature suggests that children do care about their privacy [1], due to pressure to conform to what their friends are doing [2], children tend to neglect properly configuring their smartphone's privacy settings [3]. For this reason, children tend to let their phones share all kinds of personal information about them such as their full names, their current locations, and the times they are in those locations [3]. But in taking this cavalier approach to their cyber security, children place their cyber safety at risk [3]. Using their real names on their phones, leaving their Bluetooth and Wi-Fi and their locations on all the time [3] coupled with other risky online

M. Al-kfairy et al. (Eds.): SocialSec 2024, LNCS 15565, pp. 79–85, 2025.
https://doi.org/10.1007/978-981-96-3774-4_5

behaviour such as joining public Wi-Fis, receiving files from strangers via Bluetooth, and accepting social media friendship requests from unknown users without hesitation [4], can make them vulnerable to grooming, stalking, and sextortion [5]. In the 2022–2023 financial year, the Australian Centre to Counter Child Exploitations received 40,232 reports of cases of child exploitation. These statistics indicate the danger to children is real.

Privacy and security go hand in hand [6]. Privacy is the expression of the value 'security' [7]. Sensitive information escaping from smartphones without users' knowledge can threaten their security [3]. Sar and Al-Saggaf [8] found that most social media platforms leverage the information that social media users unintentionally share to track them. If not configured properly, smartphones' leakage of users' sensitive information can facilitate the tracking of smartphone users [3]. The time and location information that smartphones' Bluetooth and WiFi sensors disclose, if not switched off, can be security-threatening especially if users use their real names on their smartphones [3].

To raise children's awareness about the risks associated with their smartphone sharing of their sensitive information and to train them on how to modify their smartphones' privacy settings to prevent this unwanted information sharing, eight sets of M5Stack Core 2 ESP32 devices were programmed to detect Bluetooth and WI-FI signals and installed around two high school campuses in Australia. Each of the two schools had four sets of these eight M5Stack Core 2 ESP32. Two sets of these devices were placed at two different locations within each school. Following this step, the research team delivered a 'hands-on' cyber safety lesson at each school that showed the students how smartphones share sensitive information, how anyone can easily capture and record sensitive information shared by smartphones, and how students can manage their smartphones to prevent them from sharing sensitive information. Specifically, the cyber safety lesson showed students how to turn off their Bluetooth, how to switch off their Wi-Fi, how to change their Bluetooth name and how to switch off their location services. A few weeks following the cyber safety lesson, the devices were disconnected and donated to the two schools after extracting the data from them. This project builds on Ibbett and Al-Saggaf's [3] project in which the researchers used a Distributed Sensor Network (DSN) implementing Raspberry Pi computers connected to each other through a network controller node (LoRa Gateway) to capture Bluetooth and Wi-Fi traffic in a high school campus. The idea behind this project, and the previous one, is to find out if children will modify their smartphones' privacy settings when shown the ease with which these cheap M5Stack Core 2 ESP32 devices can reveal identifying information about smartphone users. A before and after the cyber safety lesson t-test was run on the data from the M5Stack Core 2 ESP32 devices to see if the cyber safety lesson had an impact on children's attitudes toward protecting their privacy.

2   The Research Project

This project aimed at raising children's awareness about the security risks associated with smartphones' leakage of their sensitive information. The project was run in seven high schools in Australia after receiving Ethics approval from the authors' University Human Research Ethics Committee (HREC) and has been endorsed by the NSW Department of Education Cyber Security Assessment Team. The children are aged between 14 and 18. The reason for selecting this age group is because in Australia children aged 14 or above can consent to participation in research studies with the help of their parents and caregivers. The project involved the delivery of a 'hands-on' cyber safety lesson to show the children in the seven high schools how smartphones share sensitive information, how anyone can easily capture and record sensitive information shared by smartphones, and how students can manage their smartphones to prevent them from sharing sensitive information. The cyber safety lesson showed children how to turn off their Bluetooth, how to switch off their Wi-Fi, how to change their Bluetooth name and how to switch off their location services. The project also involved conducting a survey to gauge children's knowledge of the security issues associated with smartphones and discover their attitudes towards these issues and the level of concern about them. This paper is not concerned with the findings from the survey. The paper is concerned with the findings from the M5Stack Core 2 ESP32 devices, which were installed in two schools to find out if children did indeed modify their smartphones' privacy settings following their attendance of the cyber safety lesson. Before the start of the cyber safety lesson, the children were informed about the presence of these devices on their school grounds. Eight sets of M5Stack Core 2 ESP32 devices programmed to detect Bluetooth and WI-FI signals within their range were installed in two schools of these seven schools. Four sets of M5Stack Core 2 ESP32 devices were placed on each of the two schools' campuses. In one school, the devices were placed in the Library (two devices) and in the Canteen (two devices); in the other school, the devices were placed in the Library and the Computer Lab. The reason the devices were placed at these locations, i.e., the library, canteen, and computer lab, is because they are most frequented by students. The devices captured data leaked from smartphones that crossed the devices' detection area for a period of a few weeks. The volume of data captured by the devices prior to the cyber safety lesson was used as the baseline for the usual activity at that location. The traffic captured by the devices before the cyber safety lesson was compared against the traffic captured after the cyber safety lesson. If the comparison revealed that the volume of traffic captured by the installed devices from the smartphones within their vicinity after the cyber safety lesson was significantly less than the traffic captured before the cyber safety lesson, it may indicate that the children must have modified their smartphone privacy settings to prevent their sensitive information from escaping from their smartphones. This would suggest that the cyber safety lesson must have had a positive effect on the children's attitudes towards cyber safety. The following sections provide more details about the M5Stack Core 2 ESP32 as network sensors and the results of the research project.

3   The M5Stack Core 2 ESP32 as a Network Sensor

The M5Stack Core 2 ESP32 is a low-cost, intelligible to configure, and easy to stack device. In this project, the device was configured as a network sensor to detect Wi-Fi and Bluetooth signals. The device is based on the M5Stack CORE 2 ESP32 IoT Development Kit. The M5Stack Core 2 ESP32-D0WDQ6-V3 features two core Xtensa® 32-bit 240MHz LX6 processors and a 16 MB Flash and 8MB PSRAM, as well as a TYPE-C USB interface for software download, serial communication, and charging. The device comes with built-in M-Bus Socket and Pins, Bluetooth/Wi-Fi, a 2.0-in. integrated touch screen, speaker, power indicator, vibration motor, RTC, I2S amplifier, power button, reset button, PDM microphone, and a 6-axis IMU. The size of the M5Stack CORE 2 ESP32 IoT Development Kit is 54 × 54 × 16 mm. The device also comes with a 390 mAh @ 3.7 V Lithium Battery but when testing revealed the 390 mAh @ 3.7 V battery was insufficient for the purpose of continuous detection of Wi-Fi and Bluetooth signals, it was replaced with an M5Stack battery charger (M5GO BOTTOM2), which features 500 mAh LiPo battery (High Capacity Lithium Polymer battery). A Wall Mount AC Adapter, a USB-C to USB-C cable, and a 32 GB memory card were inserted into the M5Stack device to enable it to function as a sensor. The M5Stack sensor's total cost was 159.65 Australian dollars.

The M5Stack has a built-in SD card slot that supports a wide variety of SD cards. The M5Stack sensor's microSD card stored the SQLite database, where sensor logs are recorded, and a simple text-based ini file. The ini file allowed the sensor to be customised before it was deployed in the field. The settings in the ini file included the sensor name, what it should log (WiFi, Bluetooth or both) and the latitude and longitude of where the sensor is deployed. This was useful as the sensor in this project was deployed in a fixed location, with no GPS module installed. The sensor was programmed in Arduino. The code included functions that could read information from the memory card, detect Wi-Fi or Bluetooth signals (or both), log the results of the Wi-Fi and Bluetooth scans into the SQLite database, as well as enable the user to interact with the M5Stack sensor through programable buttons (via the integrated touch screen) and a serial command menu (via a serial port). Upon compiling and running the sketch in Arduino, the program is serially encoded into the M5Stack device. The code developed for this project is available for download from GitHub. A series of tests were performed to verify that the M5Stack sensor operated in accordance with the project's requirements. Based on the results of these tests, the M5Stack sensor was launched in this research project that aimed at educating children about what their devices are sharing about them without their knowledge. The inclusion of the programable buttons and the serial command menu made interacting with the M5Stack sensor a straightforward task. The ability to stack additional components into the M5Stack, such as (in this project) the M5GO BOTTOM2, makes this device versatile.

The research tasks associated with the use of M5Stack Core 2 ESP32 as network sensors proceeded as follows: First, data that escaped from children's smartphones was captured by each network sensor in its fixed location and stored in the microSD card that stored the SQLite database. Second, the collected network traffic from the stationed network sensors was extracted from the SQLite databases after removing the microSD cards from the network sensors and inserting them into the researcher's laptop. WiFi data was separated from Bluetooth data. This paper focuses only on the data from Bluetooth. Third, the data from each network sensor in each location for each school was combined and preprocessed using SQL queries and classified as either before the cyber safety lesson or after the cyber safety lesson. The SQL queries executed against each SQLite database ensured that only devices that had an obvious Bluetooth name were extracted. Fourth, the collected data was verified by observing the volume of traffic during weekends and school holidays, to make sure the data from all network sensors was valid. Fifth, independent t-tests [9] of the before and after combined data were run for each school after the test of normality of the data was performed and a normal distribution was observed.

4   Results

4.1   School One: Smartphones with an Identifiable Bluetooth Name

The analysis of the sample data from this school focused on Bluetooth names that were identifiable as known smartphone devices (eg. iPhone, Android, Galaxy, etc.). The network sensors captured data every 60 s. But the dataset was constructed, using SQL queries, by taking snapshots of data captured by these network sensors every 30 min. SQL queries were run against the dataset to ensure that each snapshot of the data contained distinct identifiable smartphone devices. The dataset from School One contained 33 snapshots of data before the cyber safety lesson was delivered to students ($M = 2.39$, $SD = 1.368$) and 673 snapshots of data after the cyber safety lesson was delivered to students ($M = 1.71$, $SD = 1.088$). The Levene's Test for Equality of Variances showed a *p-value* of less than 0.015, which is significant. Thus, the result of the t-test with equal variances not assumed was used. The result from the independent t-test that was run on the before and after samples of data [t (34.013) = 2.834, p = 0.008] was statistically significant indicating a drop in the volume of identifiable smartphones pre and post-cyber safety lesson (the Mean Difference [Before – After = 0.685). Thus, in the case of this school, the cyber safety lesson must have had a positive impact on children's attitudes to cyber safety. However, an Eta-squared revealed that only 1.7% of the variance was explained, so further research is needed to investigate these findings.

4.2   School Two: Smartphones with an Identifiable Bluetooth Name

The analysis of the sample data from this school also focused on Bluetooth names that were identifiable as known smartphone devices (eg. iPhone, Android, Galaxy, etc.). The dataset from this school is also based on snapshots of data captured by the network sensors every 30 min. In a process identical to the one followed when creating School One's dataset, each snapshot of the data contained distinct identifiable smartphone devices. The dataset from School Two contained 81 snapshots of data before the cyber safety lesson was delivered to students ($M = 3.31$, $SD = 1.966$) and 857 snapshots of data after the cyber safety lesson was delivered to students ($M = 2.34$, $SD = 1.52$). The Levene's Test for Equality of Variances showed a *p-value* of less than 0.001, which is significant. Thus, the result of the t-test with equal variances not assumed was used. The outcome of an independent t-test of the before and after samples of data [t (89.263) = 4.3, p < 0.001] was statistically significant indicating a significant decrease in the volume of identifiable smartphones pre-cyber safety lesson and post-cyber safety lesson (the Mean Difference [Before – After = 0.966]). Therefore, in the case of School Two, the cyber safety lesson must have influenced children's attitudes towards cyber safety. However, an Eta-squared revealed that only 2.9% of the variance was explained, so again further research is needed to interrogate these findings.

5 Conclusion

Using M5Stack Core 2 ESP32 as network sensors, this study captured network traffic, specifically Bluetooth and WI-FI signals, at two high schools in Australia and then compared the volume of traffic before and after a cyber safety lesson was delivered to the children in these two schools. The cyber safety lesson showed children how to turn off their Bluetooth, how to switch off their Wi-Fi, how to change their Bluetooth name and how to switch off their location services. In the case of both schools, the study found that the network traffic captured after the cyber safety lesson was significantly less than the network traffic captured before the cyber safety lesson. Observing the volume of traffic during weekends and school holidays provided assurance that the collected data from all network sensors was reliably captured. The significant drop in the volume of traffic after the cyber safety lessons confirmed the effectiveness of the cyber safety lessons. The findings from the two schools suggest that the cyber safety lesson must have triggered a behavioural transformation. That is, the children in the two schools must have modified their smartphone privacy settings to prevent leakage of their sensitive information. It should be noted that the findings of this study are specific to the two schools and should not be generalised to the wider Australian population. Given the small sample size, only two schools in this project were involved, further research is needed to confirm these findings. Children neglect to properly configure their smartphone's privacy settings letting their phones share all kinds of personal information about them such as their full names, their current locations, and the times they are in those locations. This can make it easy for anyone to create a profile about their movements over time. Children also join public Wi-Fi networks, exchange files with strangers via Bluetooth, and accept social media friend requests without hesitation. These behaviours can put them at risk of falling victim to cybercriminals. The findings of this study show that when children were shown how to manage their smartphone's privacy settings, they took steps to prevent the leakage of their sensitive information. The findings of this study can inform future children's awareness-raising campaigns about cyber safety.

Acknowledgment. This project was funded through the Australian eSafety Commissioner's Online Safety Grants Program.

References

1. Livingstone, S., Stoilova, M., Nandagiri, R.: Children's data and privacy online: growing up in a digital age: an evidence review. London School of Economics and Political Science, Department of Media and Communications, London, UK (2019). https://eprints.lse.ac.uk/101283/1/Livingstone_childrens_data_and_privacy_online_evidence_review_published.pdf
2. Livingstone, S., Kirwil, L., Ponte, C., Staksrud, E.: In their own words: what bothers children online? Eur. J. Commun. **29**(3), 271–288 (2014). https://doi.org/10.1177/0267323114521045
3. Ibbett, A., Al-Saggaf, Y.: Using a distributed sensor network to educate children about IoT leakage of sensitive information. In: Bravo, J., Ochoa, S., Favela, J. (eds.) UCAmI 2022. LNCS, vol. 594, pp. 505–510. Springer, Cham (2022). https://doi.org/10.1007/978-3-031-21333-5_50
4. Ibbett, A.: An Examination of Real-World Data Leakage from IoT Devices, Doctor of Information Technology Thesis Charles Sturt University (2022)

5. Al-Saggaf, Y.: An exploratory study of attitudes towards privacy in social media and the threat of blackmail: the views of a group of Saudi women. Electron. J. Inf. Syst. Dev. Ctries. **75**(7), 1–16 (2016)
6. Al-Saggaf, Y., Islam, Z.: Data mining and privacy of social network sites' users: implications of the data mining problem. Sci. Eng. Ethics **21**(4), 941–966 (2015)
7. Moor, J.: Towards a theory of privacy in the information age. Comput. Soc. **27**, 27–32 (1997)
8. Sar, R.K., Al-Saggaf, Y.: Propagation of unintentionally shared information and online tracking. First Monday **18**(6) (2013). https://doi.org/10.5210%2Ffm.v18i6.4349. Accessed 3 June 2013
9. Sawalha, G., Taj, I., Shoufan, A.: Analyzing student prompts and their effect on ChatGPT's performance. Cogent Educ. **11**(1) (2024). https://doi.org/10.1080/2331186X.2024.2397200

Machine Learning and Intelligent Systems

ELITE: Efficient and Secure Machine Learning for Intelligent Perception in Smart Road Infrastructure

Swathi Kumar Vembu[1]([✉]) [iD], Trupil Limbasiya[2] [iD],
and Anupam Chattopadhyay[1] [iD]

[1] Nanyang Technological University, 50 Nanyang Ave, Singapore 639798, Singapore
swathkv@gmail.com
[2] Desay SV Automotive Singapore Pte Ltd, International Business Park,
Singapore 609935, Singapore

Abstract. In the realm of Connected and Autonomous Vehicles
(CAVs), securing Deep Neural Networks (DNNs) poses a critical challenge, particularly in ensuring confidentiality and integrity amidst potential attacks and unauthorized access. This paper presents ELITE, a
distributed approach enhancing security and computational efficiency
for V2X applications. ELITE partitions DNNs used in Roadside Units
(RSUs) between the RSU (edge device) equipped with a Hardware
Security Module (HSM) and the cloud, with specific layers processed
within a Trusted Execution Environment (TEE). By leveraging public-
key encryption protocols, ELITE facilitates secure model distribution
and inference. Real-time integrity verification is conducted with the
Zymkey HSM at the RSU while selective processing on the *AWS Nitro
Enclave* offers enhanced security. Experimental results show that ELITE
reduces inference time by 45.73% compared to solely cloud-based processing while maintaining high accuracy with the correct encryption key. This
distributed approach balances security and efficiency, mitigating risks of
unauthorized access and preserving model integrity within DNN-enabled
V2X roadside services.

Keywords: Deep Neural Networks · Connected and Autonomous
Vehicles · Trusted Execution Environment · Privacy-Preserving
Machine Learning

1 Introduction

Connected and Autonomous Vehicles (CAVs) are smart mobility devices
equipped with sophisticated sensors, network components, and cutting-edge
technologies that enable them to process data and communicate with their
surroundings while capable of operating without direct human intervention [1].
CAVs are utilized across transportation, logistics, public safety, and urban plan-
ning. Their automatic navigation and real-time data exchange with various vehicular devices enhance safety, efficiency, and mobility in Intelligent Transportation

M. Al-kfairy et al. (Eds.): SocialSec 2024, LNCS 15565, pp. 89–106, 2025.
https://doi.org/10.1007/978-981-96-3774-4_6

Systems (ITS). They facilitate applications like ride-sharing, freight and logistics, fleet management, and public transit, leveraging Vehicle-to-Everything (V2X) technology [2]. The widespread adoption of CAVs is reshaping society, and revolutionizing transportation by mitigating traffic congestion and environmental pollution through collaboration among multiple heterogeneous road users [3]. They enhance road safety, provide more mobility options, and contribute to the development of smart cities with interconnected infrastructures.

Machine Learning (ML) and sensor fusion technologies have greatly improved vehicle capabilities, enabling better perception, decision-making, and safe navigation. They predict maintenance needs, adapt to new situations, and enhance system performance and efficiency in transportation networks [4]. However, cyber threats on such systems and sensor limitations can lead to erosion of public trust and financial losses [5]. There has been a significant increase ($\approx 50\%$) in vehicle recalls attributed to issues with Advanced Driver Assistance Systems (ADAS) [6]. Deep Neural Networks (DNNs) analyze V2X systems, as displayed in Fig. 1, to enhance situational awareness and decision-making, enhancing road safety and traffic efficiency. Automated services at Roadside Units (RSUs), supported by classification models, improve real-time decision-making and navigation, ensuring safer and more efficient transportation [7].

Challenges in Advanced V2X Service: Deploying classification models for evolving services presents cybersecurity concerns like sensor manipulation, model alteration, and unauthorized access. These issues could enable malicious actors to execute stealing attacks on classification models, undermining their integrity and functionality [8]. Consequently, ensuring model confidentiality is critical to prevent illegal access and alteration. Defending model integrity is vital for maintaining the reliability and safety of ADAS in real-time vehicular applications. Maintaining data privacy is essential to safeguard sensitive information collected by CAVs [9]. Neglecting these measures could erode user trust and raise concerns regarding security, privacy, and safety in the transition to CAVs, despite their societal benefits.

Limitations in Integrating Security: Despite advancements in encryption and storage, security challenges persist for DNNs in V2X. Post-decryption, models remain vulnerable to unauthorized access and manipulation. Even securely stored models are at risk if accessed by unauthorized parties, potentially leading to manipulation or distribution. Secure enclaves, such as TrustZone, serve as local roots of trust in automotive applications, managing security for Electronic Control Units (ECUs). These platforms offer data encryption, segregate critical software from infotainment systems, and support remote attestation for enhanced safety [10].

Our Contributions: This paper tackles security and efficiency challenges in V2X systems by using Trusted Execution Environments (TEEs) and Hardware Security Modules (HSMs). Key contributions include:

- **ELITE:** Method to protect DNNs within a TEE for sensitive DNN inference tasks, ensuring privacy and integrity. HSM manages secure key operations, preventing unauthorized access and tampering. Additionally, strategic DNN partitioning between cloud and edge devices enhances both security and performance.

- **Performance Evaluations:** Experiments validate ELITE's security with 128-bit symmetric encryption. Improved latency and resource efficiency are demonstrated for real-time inference tasks distributed between cloud and edge.

The paper proceeds as follows: Sect. 2 provides background on secure DNN approaches. Section 3 introduces ELITE and includes its security analysis. Section 4 discusses experimental setup and results, and Sect. 5 concludes the work, also presenting future directions in this domain.

2   Background

This section discusses the system architecture and related methodologies.

2.1   System Architecture

ELITE ensures secure real-time DNN inference in V2X networks by utilizing HSMs and cloud-based secure enclaves. This distributed architecture balances computational efficiency and security, safeguarding the DNN model from unauthorized access and tampering. Vehicles equipped with varying computational capabilities collect raw sensor data, which undergoes pre-processing before being fed into the partitioned DNN model for inference. The DNN partitioning strategically divides the model into layers executed on the RSU, with an HSM, while other layers are processed within a secure enclave in the cloud. The HSM stores encryption keys, performs real-time integrity verification, and executes partial inference on the RSU. Meanwhile, the secure enclave provides a TEE for the remaining inference tasks in the cloud. This integration of HSMs and secure enclaves ensures the confidentiality and integrity of the DNN model, protecting it from unauthorized access, distribution, and replication within the V2X network. For a visual representation of the data flow in the V2X network, refer to Fig. 1.

Addressing the distinct challenges of V2X communications in CAVs, ELITE strategically focuses on applications where real-time processing, while critical, can tolerate minimal delays. This includes scenarios like traffic flow management and predictive maintenance where an additional inference time (overhead) is acceptable. Although some V2X use cases, such as object detection for immediate collision avoidance, demand zero-latency responses, our deployment on RSUs is tailored for functions where this slight delay is inconsequential compared to the overall enhancements in decision-making accuracy and security. ELITE significantly bolsters security by secure model distribution and reduces inference latency compared to conventional cloud-only systems, making it optimally suited for specific V2X applications. This approach not only establishes

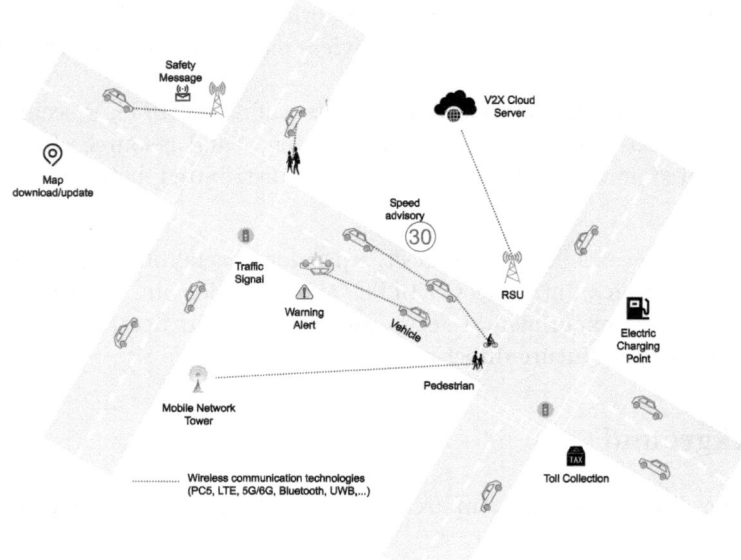

Fig. 1. Relevant information delivery services in the V2X environment, where different vehicles share relevant information with each other for improved road safety using advanced technologies

a robust foundation for future advancements in DNN-enabled roadside services but also demonstrates how ELITE's principles of DNN partitioning and cryptographic key management can be adapted to improve security and efficiency in varied edge/cloud architectures across multiple domains [11].

Scalability within the ELITE framework is effectively managed through our utilization of cloud services. As the deployment of RSUs expands, AWS infrastructure, engineered to dynamically scale based on load-ensures that increased demand is met without any performance degradation [12]. The decryption times, as detailed in our experiments shown in Table 1, demonstrate only a minimal overhead added to the processing times, confirming the system's scalability and efficiency in processing high volumes of data across an expanding network of RSUs.

2.2   Related Works

Various techniques have been explored to enhance the security of DNNs. Watermarking methods embed unique identifiers into DNNs, enabling traceability and detection of unauthorized copies [13]. However, these techniques can be susceptible to removal or alteration by adversaries, compromising their effectiveness in deterring intellectual property theft [14]. Additionally, while watermarking provides traceability, it does not prevent unauthorized distribution. Model owners can employ obfuscation methods to obscure the internal workings of DNNs, thwarting reverse engineering attempts [15]. Despite their potential to enhance model security, obfuscation may impede model interpretability and optimization, posing challenges for performance tuning and debugging. Encryption-based techniques prevent unauthorized usage by encrypting DNN parameters [16]. However, current solutions often rely on local, symmetric-key encryption, which can be vulnerable to side-channel attacks. Privacy-Preserving Deep Learning (PPDL) techniques, such as homomorphic encryption [17], allow computations on encrypted data without decrypting it, thereby preserving privacy. However, integrating homomorphic encryption into DNNs introduces significant computational overhead and complexity [18]. Hardware-based TEEs, such as Intel SGX, facilitate secure DNN inference on Intel processors [19]. Implementing secure DNN inference with TEEs enhances the trustworthiness of DNNs by safeguarding data confidentiality and integrity. However, this approach introduces overhead in memory and computation due to encryption, decryption, and enclave management, impacting performance and resource utilization in DNN inference. Additionally, hardware-based TEE solutions entail significant costs and may not directly address pressing challenges in real-world applications.

Recent research has focused on enhancing security across the V2X processing pipeline, incorporating intrusion detection systems to thwart malicious activities [20]. This is crucial for maintaining data integrity and confidentiality in V2X environments, which are vital for safe autonomous driving. However, there is a notable gap in addressing specific needs, such as robust encryption, and challenges like real-time responsiveness and defense against attacks, in securing DNN-based modeling within V2X. To address these issues, new investigations are exploring tailored approaches for securing V2X data using DNNs, with a focus on privacy-preserving models and defense against attacks [21,22]. Yet, there is still a scarcity of research on securing DNN models themselves. Despite these promising developments, challenges persist in effectively integrating DNN protection mechanisms within the dynamic and resource-constrained V2X ecosystem. Balancing security and privacy requirements with real-time performance considerations, alongside the diverse computational capabilities of V2X components, underscores the complexity of this endeavor. Moreover, ensuring seamless interoperability and scalability across heterogeneous V2X deployments remains a significant challenge.

3   Proposed Approach

This section introduces the key concepts and the innovative methodology along with the security implications.

3.1   Preliminaries

ELITE ensures secure DNN inference in V2X systems with the following assumptions. We assume *access to cloud-based TEEs*, such as AWS Nitro Enclaves [23], which provide isolated environments for sensitive computations. We also consider a *secure infrastructure utilizing the Transport Layer Security (TLS) protocol* [24] between the RSU, Trusted Authority (TA), and the cloud, protecting data transmission from eavesdropping or tampering. Additionally, we assume that the RSUs are deployed by the TA with *sufficient computational resources* to perform DNN inference tasks. These assumptions pave the way for ELITE to enhance security and optimize performance in V2X DNN inference.

The core principles driving ELITE are outlined below.

- **Partitioning** in the context of DNNs, involves breaking down large models into smaller components. This approach is crucial for optimizing inference tasks, especially in resource-constrained environments like V2X systems. By partitioning DNN models, specific segments can be allocated to different computational resources, such as edge devices or cloud servers, allowing for efficient execution and reducing latency. Additionally, partitioning enhances security by limiting the exposure of sensitive model details and facilitating controlled access to various components of the network architecture.
- **Public Key Infrastructure (PKI)** plays a crucial role in establishing secure communication channels within V2X networks. PKI provides the creation, distribution, and management of keys, which are essential for authenticating entities and encrypting data transmissions. By employing PKI, V2X systems can authenticate participants, verify data integrity, and mitigate the risks associated with unauthorized access and data manipulation.
- **TEEs and Enclaves** such as Intel SGX [25], AMD SEV [26], and cloud-based enclaves like AWS Nitro Enclaves [23], provide isolated execution environments for sensitive computations. These secure enclaves protect critical assets, such as DNN models and cryptographic keys, from unauthorized access and tampering. By leveraging TEEs and enclaves, ELITE ensures the confidentiality and integrity of DNN inference tasks, even in untrusted or semi-trusted environments.
- **HSMs** are hardware devices designed to safeguard cryptographic keys and perform secure cryptographic operations. By integrating HSMs into ELITE, we enhance the security posture of V2X networks, protecting against threats such as key compromise and unauthorized access. Although HSMs have occasionally faced challenges from sophisticated attacks, they continue to set the industry benchmark for secure cryptographic operations. Thus, integrating HSMs into RSUs significantly enhances their defense. The HSMs used in the work is the Zymbit Zymkey HSM [27].

3.2   Proposed Mechanism: ELITE

This subsection details our secure and efficient DNN inference mechanism for the V2X domain, leveraging cloud-based TEEs and DNN partitioning. Our approach adopts a layer-based partitioning method, initially distributing the model equally between the cloud and edge. Subsequent experiments explore alternative partitioning strategies to enhance performance. Secure key management ensures the protection of cryptographic keys, while the model distribution process securely shares the models. The secure inference procedure safeguards privacy during predictions. The detailed description of *Secure Key Management and Model Distribution* and *Secure Inference Procedure* are given as below.

Secure Key Management and Model Distribution

1. Key Generation and Exchange: The client (RSU) generates a cryptographic key pair (P_k, S_k), where P_k is the public key and S_k is the private key. The S_k is securely locked by the HSM. The cloud enclave generates another key pair (EP_k, ES_k), where EP_k is the enclave's public key and ES_k is its private key. The client and enclave securely transmit their public key (P_k, EP_k) to the server.
2. Model Partitioning, Encryption, and Distribution: The server generates a Neural Network key (N_k) used to encrypt the DNN and partitions the DNN into two parts: M_1 and M_2. The server then encrypts M_1 and M_2 with N_k. The server distributes the encrypted M_1 directly to the cloud enclave and M_2 to the client.
3. Key Encryption and Distribution: The server encrypts N_k twice: once with client's P_k and once with enclave's EP_k. The server sends N_k encrypted with P_k to the client and N_k encrypted with EP_k to the enclave.

Secure Inference Procedure

1. Data Transmission and Enclave-side Inference: The cloud enclave decrypts N_k using its private key (ES_k). Using the decrypted N_k, the enclave decrypts and performs inference for M_1 using the data received from the client.
2. Inference Result Transmission: The enclave securely transmits the inference results back to the client.
3. Client-side Inference: The client decrypts N_k using its private key S_k, which is locked by the HSM. The encrypted model remains in the memory at all times. To perform inference, the client decrypts N_k to decrypt M_2 and performs inference locally using results from M_1. After decryption, the model is temporarily stored in the memory. After inference, the client promptly removes the decrypted model from memory to ensure secure storage.

This secure and efficient mechanism utilizes secure key management, model partitioning, and trusted execution enclaves to achieve privacy-preserving inference and optimize resource utilization for DNNs in V2X communication. A detailed illustration of this process is provided in Fig. 2.

3.3   Security Analysis

We discuss a detailed evaluation of ELITE in order to understand its robustness in different security properties.

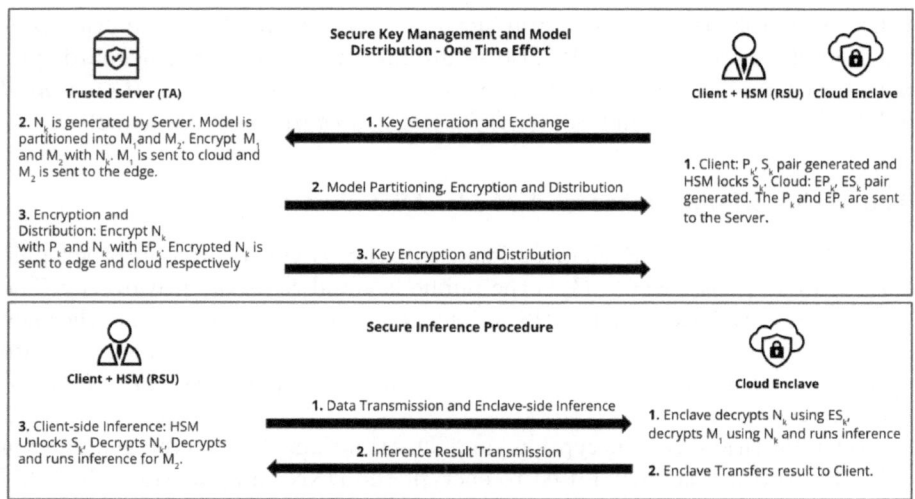

Fig. 2. The description of the proposed mechanism, ELITE, for preventing unauthorized usage and copying of Neural Networks in V2X Systems

Confidential Computing Measures: Our security framework ensures protection for sensitive components and extends coverage to semi-trusted RSUs, reducing risks related to illegal model distribution. By leveraging HSMs and TEEs, we secure keys, control model access, and safeguard inference processes, limiting access and thwarting potential threats. For instance, [28], proposes an efficient inference mechanism using TEEs to enhance data and model confidentiality. Lightweight, keyed model obfuscation schemes [15] further enhance defense against model stealing attacks, particularly in Neural Processing Units (NPUs) used for DNN model execution. These efforts underscore the importance of robust security measures, as implemented in our framework, in protecting intellectual property and sensitive data in distributed computing environments.

Access Control and Integrity Protection: Our security measures, such as encryption and secure storage (e.g., enclaves, HSMs), protect our models and ensure their integrity. Authorized entities possess the necessary keys for access, minimizing the risk of unauthorized retrieval or tampering. This approach, as described by [16], ensures that only authorized users can utilize the model, providing robust protection against unauthorized usage.

Partitioning Strategy: In the event of a breach in security measures like HSM or TEE, our partitioning strategy adds complexity to model retrieval. By distributing model layers, we introduce a higher level of intricacy into the system. The interdependence among various layers of the model significantly complicates the task of adversaries attempting to replicate its full functionality with access to only a portion of the architecture and weights. For instance, [29], explores the challenges of reconstructing raw data from intermediate layer outputs, shedding light on the complexity of the problem. Furthermore, studies investigating the relationship between privacy and intermediate results of DNNs reinforce the effectiveness of partitioning strategies in enhancing privacy protection [30].

Security Strengths and Robustness of ELITE: ELITE employs robust security measures including key generation, encryption, and decryption. These operations utilize Rivest, Shamir, Adleman (RSA [31]) with key sizes of 1024 bits, 2048 bits, and 4096 bits, Elliptic Curve Cryptography (ECC [32]) with a key size of 256 bits, and Kyber [33] with key sizes of 512 to 1024 bits. Additionally, S-Box AES [34] encryption with 128-bit keys is integrated into ELITE for security operations. RSA, ECC, or Kyber can be combined with S-Box AES to enhance security. The minimum security strength of ELITE is 128-bit symmetric security, achievable with ECC-256 and AES-128. ELITE can further enhance security strengths by implementing larger key sizes.

Acknowledging the importance of rigorous analysis, we propose conducting a formal security proof as vital follow-up work. We intend to employ tools like Scyther [35], as detailed by [36] in their work on Model Checking Security Protocols. This will allow us to perform a detailed formal evaluation of the ELITE system, enhancing the robustness and validity of our security claims.

4   Performance Evaluation

This section outlines the experimental setup used to assess the efficacy of ELITE for secure inference in V2X systems.

4.1   Experimental Setup

In our experiment, the **cloud enclave** utilized an AWS EC2 instance of type m6a.xlarge [37] running on Amazon Linux. This instance configuration provided 4 vCPUs and 16 GiB of memory, equipped with AWS Nitro Enclave [23] functionality for hardware-based isolation. The enclave was initiated with a dedicated key pair to bolster security. This environment serves as the trusted space for model inference and key management in the cloud. The **Edge Device** used is a Raspberry Pi (RPI) 4 Model B [38] for local data processing and communication with the cloud enclave. A Zymkey **HSM** [27] is attached to an RPI for secure key management, ensuring that the raw keys and models remain protected and inaccessible to the semi-trusted RSU to prevent meaningful data and the system from potential attacks by adversaries [39,40].

Cloud Enclave Setup: ELITE utilizes AWS Nitro Enclaves [23] to provide a secure environment. This involves deploying an EC2 instance with stringent security configurations and precise rules for inbound and outbound communication between the enclave, trusted authority, and edge device. These measures ensure that all communication strictly adheres to trusted pathways, effectively preventing unauthorized access. Importantly, Nitro Enclaves restrict interactions solely to a secure virtual socket that connects with the EC2 parent instance. This isolation from external connections guarantees the integrity and confidentiality of the enclave's operations. We operate under the assumption that edge devices communicate with a single enclave instance, emphasizing architectural simplicity and security. A Docker image is created to encapsulate communication protocols, inference processes, and dependencies. This image serves as the foundation for generating the enclave image file (.EIF) using the nitro-cli build-enclave command. This approach ensures that the enclave operates within a self-contained environment, safeguarded against external threats. Subsequently, the enclave is initiated via the nitro-cli run-enclave command, establishing a tamper-proof enclave.

4.2   Experimental Design

The experiment comprises two phases: initial setup and inference. Before proceeding to inference, we establish communication by distributing encrypted model partitions to both the cloud and the edge device. Key exchange mechanisms are configured, and encrypted keys are employed to ensure communication security. The core experiment addresses a basic classification problem using the MNIST dataset [41], utilizing a standard CNN Network compromising 2 convolutional layers, 2 max pool layers, and 2 fully connected layers totaling 46,566 parameters. We compare three scenarios to evaluate the overhead involved in setting up communication protocols for secure model deployment.

Initial Setup

- Scenario 1: Establish communication for model transmission between the server and edge device without involving any keys or encryption. This scenario excludes key generation, encryption, partitioning, and cloud involvement.
- Scenario 2: Include key exchange and model encryption in the setup of Scenario 1.
- Scenario 3: Partition the model into two parts for parallel communication with both the cloud and the edge device, in addition to key exchange and model encryption.

Inference

- Scenario 1: Perform inference without partitioning or encryption/decryption.
- Scenario 2: Decrypt and perform inference on the edge device.
- Scenario 3: Decrypt and perform inference on the edge device and the cloud within a secure enclave.

To ensure statistical significance and reduce variability in performance results, each scenario under both the initial setup and inference was tested in five separate trials. The average outcome for the initial setup and inference times was calculated from these five trials. Any identified outliers were analyzed individually to verify that they were not caused by experimental errors. Additionally, accuracy was assessed across all trials to ensure its reliability.

4.3   Experimental Results

Initial Setup

- Scenario 1: Without involving any keys or encryption, it took 8.22 s to establish communication for model transmission between the server and the edge.
- Scenario 2: Adding key exchange and model encryption in the second scenario, increased the setup time slightly to 9.21 s.
- Scenario 3: Introducing partitioning and involving the cloud resulted in a setup time of 8.74 s, a marginal increase of less than 0.5 s compared to Scenario 1.

Inference

- Scenario 1: Without employing partitioning or encryption, the inference time was 0.53 s.
- Scenario 2: Decrypting using HSM and conducting inference on the edge device increased the time to 2.49 s.
- Scenario 3: Decryption and inference occurred on both the edge device and the cloud within a secure enclave, resulting in a time of 3.21 s.

Our findings indicate that partitioning the model and simultaneously setting up communication with both the cloud and edge device, as demonstrated in Scenario 3, provides a strategic advantage in minimizing overhead. Moreover, the results suggest that while encryption and key exchange introduce additional steps, their impact on overall setup time remains relatively minimal, with an observed increase of only around 1 s in Scenario 2 and less than 0.5 s in Scenario 3. This highlights the feasibility and efficiency of incorporating encryption and key exchange mechanisms in secure model deployment protocols. Additionally, we conducted three distinct scenarios to analyze the inference process results as shown in Fig. 3.

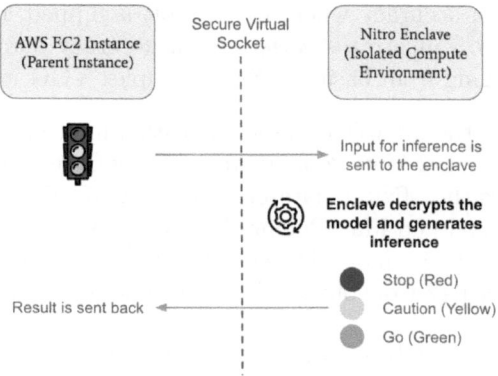

Fig. 3. Inference Process in the cloud

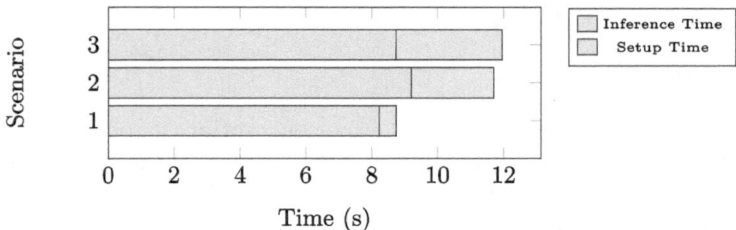

Fig. 4. Overhead for the Base Experiment: Comparison of Setup and Inference Times in different scenarios

Despite the overhead observed between Scenarios 1 and 3, it is crucial to note that Scenario 3 offers significantly enhanced security measures compared to the previous approaches. While Scenario 3 introduces an additional <1-s overhead compared to Scenario 2, the substantial increase in security makes it the most preferable option. Conversely, Scenario 1, despite its efficiency, lacks any security measures, rendering the model vulnerable. Scenario 2 enhances security to some extent, but Scenario 3 stands out for its robust security measures, despite a slight increase in overhead. Figure 4 highlights the overhead comparison.

In the context of CAVs, the deployment of deep learning models on RSUs serves critical applications such as traffic flow management. Here, an additional inference time (small overhead as seen above) is acceptable, particularly in scenarios where timely, but not instantaneous, responses are sufficient. For example, in predictive analytics for vehicle maintenance or traffic condition forecasts, this delay is negligible relative to the benefits of enhanced decision-making accuracy and improved safety measures provided by the deep learning models.

4.4   Extended Analysis

The initial experiment demonstrates the functionality of encryption [16], showcasing maintained accuracy when using the correct key. However, there is a significant decline in accuracy when just one bit is flipped, resembling random classification. Figure 5 illustrates variations in accuracy across different model configurations, ranging from basic CNNs to complex VGG models.

- Model 1: Utilizes the MNIST dataset [41] with a model architecture comprising 2 Convolutional, 2 Max Pooling, and 2 Fully Connected layers.
- Model 2: Utilizes the MNIST dataset with the VGG16 model [42], consisting of 13 Convolutional and Max Pooling layers and 3 Fully Connected layers.
- Model 3: Utilizes the Fashion-MNIST [43] dataset with the same model architecture as Model 1 (2 Convolutional, 2 Max Pooling, and 2 Fully Connected layers).
- Model 4: Utilizes the CIFAR-10 [44] dataset with a model architecture comprising 4 Convolutional, 2 Max Pooling, and 2 Fully Connected layers.

– Model 5: Utilizes the CIFAR-100 [45] dataset with the same model architecture as Model 4 (4 Convolutional, 2 Max Pooling, and 2 Fully Connected layers).

It is observed that with the correct key, there is no drop in accuracy, indicating that encryption does not impair the model's performance. Additionally, we analyze the impact of model sizes on encryption and decryption times, summarized in Table 1 to assess their effects.

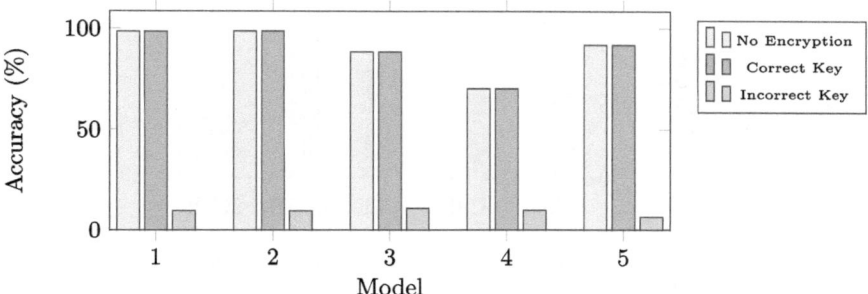

Fig. 5. Encryption Accuracies: Accuracy of different models (basic CNNs to VGG) with the correct key and incorrect key

Table 1. Encryption and Decryption Results for Different Number of Parameters and Layers

No. of Parameters	No. of Layers	Encryption Time	Decryption and Inference Time
46,566	9	0.042 s	0.064 s
581,270	11	0.485 s	0.540 s
4,154,116	11	2.889 s	3.161 s
37,703,106	25	30.011 s	33.202 s

We tested ELITE's compatibility with public key algorithms, such as RSA [31], ECC [32], and Kyber [33] across various key sizes, finding effective performance with minimal overhead for all protocols and sizes. Larger key sizes incurred a one-time setup time of approximately 0.2 s for data exchange, while quantum-based algorithms had slightly longer setup times (up to 1.5 s) depending on the key size, without impacting inference overhead.

Analyzing the effect of distributed partitioning on overhead, inference time was measured across various configurations involving both cloud and edge setups. With nine layers (including input, output, and dropout) distributed, the fastest inference time (2.49 s) occurred when all layers were on the edge device, although compromising security. Conversely, processing all layers in the cloud took the longest time (4.92 s), highlighting the benefit of workload distribution. Experimental results depicting different partitioning strategies between the cloud and edge device are illustrated in Fig. 6. Varying partitioning strategies demonstrated a trade-off between security and efficiency. A balanced approach was achieved (2.67 s) with two layers in the cloud and seven at the edge, representing a 45.73% reduction in time compared to all-cloud processing.

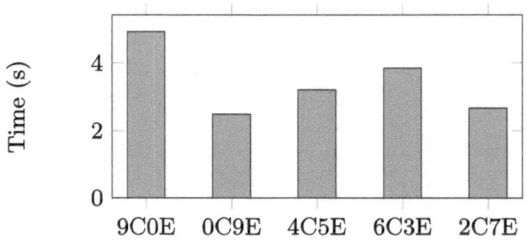

Fig. 6. Time for various Partitioning Strategies between Cloud and Edge C: No. of layers in Cloud and E: No. of layers in Edge

Table 2 compares our study with existing research on DNN protection and distribution, focusing on performance, security, and efficiency. The claims in the table address model privacy, data privacy, and model security. Model privacy aims to prevent reverse-engineering a DNN's architecture and parameters, while data privacy seeks to protect sensitive training data. Model security safeguards against adversarial attacks that can lead to incorrect inferences. Our approach, ELITE, leverages distributed partitioning using HSM and secure enclaves and balances accuracy and relatively fast inference time. This efficiency surpasses other methods, which, while achieving higher accuracy (due to hyperparameters, or model structure) or similar levels of security, often come with longer inference times.

Additionally, comparing edge-based secure execution environments like Arm TrustZone [46] with cloud-based solutions highlights various cost and performance considerations. While edge devices may have higher initial costs, they significantly reduce latency by processing data locally, ensuring secure processing with TEEs and potentially lower long-term expenses. Our review extends to frameworks like [47], which securely executes deep learning inference on edge devices using TrustZone, maintaining model integrity and accuracy. Conversely, EC2 instances offer powerful processing capabilities and scalability, with costs varying based on usage. Future work can explore substituting the cloud enclave with an Arm TrustZone based on model capabilities, providing a comprehensive analysis of the trade-offs between these approaches.

Table 2. Benchmarking with Prior Works

Reference	Claim	Architecture	Accuracy (%)	Inference Time (s)
ELITE (*this work*)	Model Privacy and Security	2C, 2MP, 2FC	98.58	2.67
[48]	Data and Model Privacy	2C, 2MP, 2FC	99	3.58
[49]	Data Privacy	C, 2MP, 1FC	99.21	11
[50]	Model Performance	Resnet-18	99.74	54.2
[47]	Model Privacy	10C layers	–	30.26

5   Conclusions and Future Works

ELITE offers a secure DNN-based solution to address the unique challenges posed by V2X environments. By leveraging a combination of HSMs and Secure Enclaves, ELITE achieves a balance between computational efficiency and security. The implementation results demonstrate the significance of key management in maintaining high inference accuracy, while incorrect keys render the model ineffective. Furthermore, our analysis of different partition distribution strategies highlights the importance of dispersing layers across the edge and cloud to achieve enhanced performance. This research enhances smart road infrastructure security and efficiency for widespread CAV adoption. It ensures the integrity and confidentiality of DNNs in real-world deployments. In comparison with state-of-the-art solutions, our approach improves inference times while maintaining accuracy and enhancing system security. Future research can explore designing solutions for different vehicular system-on-chips to enhance efficiency. Additionally, investigating the use of hardware-based TEEs as substitutes for cloud enclaves can be effective.

Acknowledgement. This work is supported by Nanyang Technological University (NTU)-Desay SV Research Program under Grant 2018-0980.

References

1. Sun, X., Yu, F.R., Zhang, P.: A survey on cyber-security of connected and autonomous vehicles (CAVs). IEEE Trans. Intell. Transp. Syst. **23**(7), 6240–6259 (2021)
2. Strulak-Wójcikiewicz, R., Wagner, N.: Exploring opportunities of using the sharing economy in sustainable urban freight transport. Sustain. Urban Areas **68**, 102778 (2021)
3. Tran, T.T.M., Parker, C., Tomitsch, M.: Scoping out the scalability issues of autonomous vehicle-pedestrian interaction. In: Proceedings of the 15th International Conference on Automotive User Interfaces and Interactive Vehicular Applications, pp. 167–177. Association for Computing Machinery (2023)
4. Soori, M., Arezoo, B., Dastres, R.: Artificial intelligence, machine learning and deep learning in advanced robotics, a review. Cogn. Robot. **3**, 54–70 (2023)

5. Cui, J., Liew, L.S., Sabaliauskaite, G., Zhou, F.: A review on safety failures, security attacks, and available countermeasures for autonomous vehicles. Ad Hoc Netw. **90**, 101823 (2019)

6. U. D. of Transportation: NHTSA recalls by manufacturer (2024). https://datahub.transportation.gov/stories/s/NHTSA-Recalls-by-Manufacturer/38mw-dp8u/. Accessed Apr 2024

7. Cui, C., et al.: A survey on multimodal large language models for autonomous driving. In: Proceedings of the IEEE/CVF Winter Conference on Applications of Computer Vision, pp. 958–979 (2023)

8. Shen, Y., He, X., Han, Y., Zhang, Y.: Model stealing attacks against inductive graph neural networks. In: 2022 IEEE Symposium on Security and Privacy (SP), pp. 1175–1192. IEEE (2022)

9. Nouri, A., Cabrero-Daniel, B., Törner, F., Sivencrona, H., Berger, C.: Engineering safety requirements for autonomous driving with large language models, *arXiv preprint* arXiv:2403.16289 (2024)

10. Scopelliti, G., et al.: End-to-end security for distributed event-driven enclave applications on heterogeneous tees. ACM Trans. Priv. Secur. **26**(3), 1–46 (2023)

11. Zheng, W., Deng, R., Chen, W., Popa, R.A., Panda, A., Stoica, I.: Cerebro: a platform for {Multi-Party} cryptographic collaborative learning. In: 30th USENIX Security Symposium (USENIX Security 2021), pp. 2723–2740 (2021)

12. Srivastava, A., Ragab, A., Balasubramaniam, M., Ranganathan, S.: Achieve four times higher ML inference throughput at three times lower cost per inference with amazon EC2 G5 instances for NLP and CV PyTorch models (2022). https://aws.amazon.com/blogs/machine-learning/achieve-four-times-higher-ml-inference-throughput-at-three-times-lower-cost-per-inference-with-amazon-ec2-g5-instances-for-nlp-and-cv-pytorch-models/

13. Bansal, A., et al.: Certified neural network watermarks with randomized smoothing. In: International Conference on Machine Learning, pp. 1450–1465. PMLR (2022)

14. Aiken, W., Kim, H., Woo, S., Ryoo, J.: Neural network laundering: removing black-box backdoor watermarks from deep neural networks. Comput. Secur. **106**, 102277 (2021)

15. Goldstein, B.F., Patil, V.C., Ferreira, V.C., Nery, A.S., França, F.M., Kundu, S.: Preventing DNN model IP theft via hardware obfuscation. IEEE J. Emerg. Sel. Top. Circ. Syst. **11**(2), 267–277 (2021)

16. Alam, M., Saha, S., Mukhopadhyay, D., Kundu, S.: NN-Lock: a lightweight authorization to prevent IP threats of deep learning models. ACM J. Emerg. Technol. Comput. Syst. **18**(3), 1–19 (2022)

17. Marcano, N.J.H., Moller, M., Hansen, S., Jacobsen, R.H.: On fully homomorphic encryption for privacy-preserving deep learning. In: IEEE Globecom Workshops, pp. 1–6. IEEE (2019)

18. Gupta, S., Cammarota, R., Šimunić, T.: MemFHE: end-to-end computing with fully homomorphic encryption in memory. ACM Trans. Embed. Comput. Syst. **23**(2), 1–23 (2024)

19. Lee, T.,et al.: Occlumency: privacy-preserving remote deep-learning inference using SGX. In: The 25th Annual International Conference on Mobile Computing and Networking, pp. 1–17 (2019)

20. Selamnia, A., Brik, B., Senouci, S.M., Boualouache, A., Hossain, S.: Edge computing-enabled intrusion detection for C-V2X networks using federated learning. In: GLOBECOM 2022-2022 IEEE Global Communications Conference, pp. 2080–2085. IEEE (2022)

21. Chen, J., Li, K., Philip, S.Y.: Privacy-preserving deep learning model for decentralized VANETs using fully homomorphic encryption and blockchain. IEEE Trans. Intell. Transp. Syst. **23**(8), 11 633–11 642 (2021)
22. Yao, Y., Zhao, J., Li, Z., Cheng, X., Wu, L.: Jamming and eavesdropping defense scheme based on deep reinforcement learning in autonomous vehicle networks. IEEE Trans. Inf. Forensics Secur. **18**, 1211–1224 (2023)
23. Amazon: AWS nitro enclaves (2024). https://aws.amazon.com/ec2/nitro/nitro-enclaves/
24. Limbasiya, T., Das, D.: SearchCom: vehicular cloud-based secure and energy-efficient communication and searching system for smart transportation. In: Proceedings of the 21st International Conference on Distributed Computing and Networking, pp. 1–10 (2020)
25. Intel: Reduce the attack surface around your data to unlock new opportunities (2024). https://www.intel.com/content/www/us/en/products/docs/accelerator-engines/software-guard-extensions.html
26. AMD: AMD secure encrypted virtualization (SEV) (2024). https://www.amd.com/en/developer/sev.html
27. ZYMBIT: ZYMKEY4 plug-in security module for Raspberry PI (2024). https://www.zymbit.com/zymkey/
28. Liu, R., Garcia, L., Liu, Z., Ou, B., Srivastava, M.: SecDeep: secure and performant on-device deep learning inference framework for mobile and IoT devices. In: Proceedings of the International Conference on Internet-of-Things Design and Implementation, pp. 67–79 (2021)
29. Tuor, T., Wang, S., Leung, K.K., Ko, B.J.: Understanding information leakage of distributed inference with deep neural networks: overview of information theoretic approach and initial results. In: Ground/Air Multisensor Interoperability, Integration, and Networking for Persistent ISR IX, vol. 10635, pp. 129–136 (2018)
30. Chaopeng, G., Zhengqing, L., Jie, S.: A privacy protection approach in edge-computing based on maximized DNN partition strategy with energy saving. J. Cloud Comput. **12**(1), 29 (2023)
31. Rivest, R.L., Shamir, A., Adleman, L.: A method for obtaining digital signatures and public-key cryptosystems. Commun. ACM **21**(2), 120–126 (1978)
32. Hankerson, D., Menezes, A.: Elliptic curve cryptography. In: Jajodia, S., Samarati, P., Yung, M. (eds.) Encyclopedia of Cryptography, Security and Privacy, pp. 1–2. Springer, Heidelberg (2021). https://doi.org/10.1007/978-3-642-27739-9
33. Avanzi, R., et al.: Crystals-Kyber algorithm specifications and supporting documentation. NIST PQC Round **2**(4), 1–43 (2019)
34. N. I. of Standards and Technology: Advanced encryption standard (AES) (2001). https://nvlpubs.nist.gov/nistpubs/FIPS/NIST.FIPS.197.pdf. Accessed Apr 2024
35. Cremers, C.J.F.: The Scyther tool: verification, falsification, and analysis of security protocols. In: Gupta, A., Malik, S. (eds.) CAV 2008. LNCS, vol. 5123, pp. 414–418. Springer, Heidelberg (2008). https://doi.org/10.1007/978-3-540-70545-1_38
36. Basin, D., Cremers, C., Meadows, C.: Model checking security protocols. In: Handbook of Model Checking, pp. 727–762. Springer, Cham (2018). https://doi.org/10.1007/978-3-319-10575-8_22
37. AWS: Amazon EC2 m6a instances (2024). https://aws.amazon.com/ec2/instance-types/m6a/
38. Raspberry PI: Raspberry PI 4 tech specs (2024). https://www.raspberrypi.com/products/raspberry-pi-4-model-b/specifications/

39. Islami, L., Fischer-Hübner, S., Papadimitratos, P.: Capturing drivers' privacy preferences for intelligent transportation systems: an intercultural perspective. Comput. Secur. **123**, 102913 (2022)
40. Eryonucu, C., Papadimitratos, P.: Security and privacy for mobile crowdsensing: Improving user relevance and privacy. In: Katsikas, S., et al. (eds.) ESORICS 2023. LNCS, vol. 14398, pp. 474–493. Springer, Cham (2023). https://doi.org/10.1007/978-3-031-54204-6_28
41. Deng, L.: The MNIST database of handwritten digit images for machine learning research. IEEE Signal Process. Mag. **29**(6), 141–142 (2012)
42. Simonyan, K., Zisserman, A.: Very deep convolutional networks for large-scale image recognition. In: Proceedings of the International Conference on Learning Representations (ICLR) (2015). https://arxiv.org/abs/1409.1556
43. Xiao, H., Rasul, K., Vollgraf, R.: Fashion-MNIST: a novel image dataset for benchmarking machine learning algorithms (2017). http://arxiv.org/abs/1708.07747
44. Krizhevsky, A., Nair, V., Hinton, G.: CIFAR-10 (Canadian Institute for Advanced Research). http://www.cs.toronto.edu/~kriz/cifar.html
45. Krizhevsky, A., Nair, V., Hinton, G.: CIFAR-100 (Canadian Institute for Advanced Research). http://www.cs.toronto.edu/~kriz/cifar.html
46. Arm: Trustzone for cortex-M: system-wide security for IoT devices (2024). https://www.arm.com/technologies/trustzone-for-cortex-m
47. Islam, M.S., Zamani, M., Kim, C.H., Khan, L., Hamlen, K.W.: Confidential execution of deep learning inference at the untrusted edge with arm trustzone. In: Proceedings of the Thirteenth ACM Conference on Data and Application Security and Privacy, pp. 153–164 (2023)
48. Liu, J., Juuti, M., Lu, Y., Asokan, N.: Oblivious neural network predictions via minionn transformations. In: Proceedings of the 2017 ACM SIGSAC conference on computer and communications security, pp. 619–631 (2017)
49. Wang, Y., Liang, X., Hei, X., Ji, W., Zhu, L.: Deep learning data privacy protection based on homomorphic encryption in AIoT. Mob. Inf. Syst. **2021**, 1–11 (2021)
50. Zhang, T., Li, Z., Chen, Y., Lam, K.-Y., Zhao, J.: Edge-cloud cooperation for DNN inference via reinforcement learning and supervised learning. In: IEEE International Conferences on Internet of Things (iThings), pp. 77–84. IEEE (2022)

Gamma Sampling for Intrusion Detection with Imbalanced Data

Firuz Kamalov[1] , Rohan Mitra[2] , and Hana Sulieman[3]([✉])

[1] Department of Electrical Engineering, Canadian University Dubai, Dubai, UAE
firuz@cud.ac.ae
[2] Department of Computer Science and Engineering, American University of Sharjah, Sharjah, UAE
b00085023@alumni.aus.edu
[3] Department of Mathematics and Statistics, American University of Sharjah, Sharjah, UAE
hsulieman@aus.edu

Abstract. Recent advances in artificial intelligence have prompted the use of machine learning methods in network security. In this paper, we address the issue of imbalanced data that is often present in network security datasets used in machine learning. We propose an oversampling method based on the Gamma distribution to balance the data prior to training. The results on several imbalanced datasets show the potential of the proposed method as a viable tool to build intrusion detection systems based on artificial intelligence. The accompanying code for the study is available on Github.

Keywords: intrusion detection · machine learning · imbalanced data · sampling · Gamma distribution

1 Introduction

In recent years, the field of network security has witnessed a significant transformation with the integration of artificial intelligence (AI) and machine learning (ML) techniques. As cyber threats continue to evolve in complexity and frequency, traditional rule-based security systems have proven insufficient in detecting and mitigating novel attacks. This has led to increased interest in leveraging AI and ML algorithms to enhance intrusion detection systems (IDS) and other network security applications.

However, the implementation of ML methods in network security faces a critical challenge: the inherent imbalance in security datasets. In real-world scenarios, network traffic data typically contains a disproportionate number of normal instances compared to malicious ones. This imbalance can significantly impact the performance of ML models, as they tend to favor the majority class, potentially overlooking the minority class that often represents the attacks or anomalies of interest.

The issue of imbalanced data is particularly problematic in the context of intrusion detection, where the ability to accurately identify rare but critical security events is

The financial support by the American University of Sharjah through the Faculty Research Grant FRG22-C-S60 is acknowledged.

crucial. Traditional machine learning algorithms often struggle with such skewed distributions, leading to suboptimal performance in real-world applications. This limitation has spurred research into various data balancing techniques to improve the efficacy of ML-based security solutions.

In this paper, we address the challenge of imbalanced data in network security datasets and propose an oversampling method based on the Gamma distribution. Our approach aims to create a more balanced dataset prior to training, thereby enhancing the ability of ML models to detect both common and rare security events accurately. Unlike other existing methods such as synthetic minority over-sampling technique (SMOTE), the Gamma distribution yields more realistic samples by targeting areas near the existing minority samples. The proposed method is tested extensively across different imbalance ratios and classifiers. Our experimental results over multiple imbalanced datasets demonstrate that the proposed method holds significant promise as an effective approach for developing AI-powered intrusion detection systems.

The remainder of this paper is organized as follows. We first provide a brief overview of existing literature in the field of imbalanced data in ML, particularly in the context of network security. We then describe our proposed Gamma distribution-based oversampling method in detail, including its theoretical foundations and implementation. Subsequently, we present the results of our experiments on several imbalanced network security datasets, demonstrating the effectiveness of our approach compared to existing methods. Finally, we discuss the implications of our findings and outline potential directions for future research in this area.

By addressing the critical issue of data imbalance, this study contributes to the ongoing efforts to improve the reliability and effectiveness of AI-driven intrusion detection systems, ultimately enhancing the overall security posture of modern networks.

2 Literature

The rapid evolution of ML has led to its widespread adoption across various fields, with notable success in intrusion detection systems (IDS). A comprehensive evaluation of IDS-applicable ML techniques, including support vector machines (SVM), random forests (RF), extreme learning machines (ELM), and adversarial techniques has been considered in several studies [4, 14, 30]. Empirical evidence suggested ELM's superiority, although ML-based IDS have shown varying degrees of efficacy. Cloud computing security has received growing attention of the researchers [25]. It was examined in [13], addressing both anomaly identification and attack classification. The researchers utilized deep learning methods to achieve R values over 0.95 [13]. In [19], a boosting-based feature selection method was employed to reduce data dimensionality. Subsequently, diverse ML algorithms were applied to the condensed dataset, demonstrating the feature selection technique's ability to enhance detection rates up to 90.85%. An innovative strategy focusing on optimizing model training size was introduced in [16]. This approach successfully minimized computational time while maintaining a 99% detection accuracy. The study in [9] proposed a hybrid method for intrusion information detection, integrating Elman neural networks with SVM. This combined approach yielded detection rates ranging from 87.3% to 100%. Data preprocessing based on a combination of oversampling via SMOTE and feature selection via XGBoost was proposed in [28] to improve classification while ensuring dependebality of the system. An ensemble method based on RF, Gradient Boosting (GB), Adaboost, XGBoost, bagging, and simple stacking was proposed in [15]. A deep learning model designed for intrusion detection in IoT systems was proposed in [2]. The authors propose a 4-layer multi-layer perceptron system as a communication protocol-independent system.

The challenge of imbalanced datasets has been explored in various domains such as healthcare, financial fraud detection, and others. However, its impact on intrusion detection systems remains largely unexplored [5]. Two primary strategies exist for addressing data imbalance: data manipulation [29] and cost-adjusted learning [11,20]. The former involves altering class proportions by either augmenting minority samples or reducing majority instances, with the augmentation method generally considered more effective [10]. Cost-adjusted learning, conversely, modifies the error function to penalize misclassifications of minority samples more heavily. Among data manipulation techniques, synthetic minority over-sampling technique (SMOTE) stands out as a widely-adopted approach. SMOTE generates new data points through stochastic linear interpolation between existing neighboring samples [6,8]. Numerous researchers have proposed enhancements to the original SMOTE algorithm to boost its performance [3,24]. While SMOTE is based on uniform density sampling of the synthetic points, other methods have been introduced based on different probability densities such as the Gamma distribution [17]. Recent advancements in AI have led to the development of generative methods utilizing trained neural networks capable of synthesizing novel samples from latent representations [7]. An ensemble approach based on the kernel density estimation was proposed in [18], where the authors used a collection of decision trees trained on oversampled data. More recently, a hybrid approach combining transfer learning together with active sampling, was proposed in [21] to deal with static and real-time data. Oversampling in the regime of noisy data was proposed in [22].

3   Gamma-Based Oversampling

Our proposed method addresses the class imbalance problem in network security datasets by generating synthetic data points for the minority class using the Gamma distribution. This approach creates new points along the line connecting existing neighboring points from the minority class, effectively increasing its representation in the dataset. The proposed method extends the technique introduced in [17] to include parameter tuning and categorical features.

The Gamma distribution's probability density function is defined by the following equation:

$$f(x; k, \theta) = \frac{x^{k-1}e^{-\frac{x}{\theta}}}{\Gamma(k)\theta^k}, \tag{1}$$

where $\Gamma(z) = \int_0^\infty x^{z-1}e^{-x}\,dx$ represents the Gamma function. The distribution is characterized by two key parameters: k, the shape parameter, and θ, the scale parameter. The shape parameter k influences the distribution's form, with higher values of k resulting in a more symmetrical distribution. Conversely, the scale parameter θ affects the distribution's spread, with larger values of θ leading to a more stretched-out distribution.

In addition, the Gamma distribution encompasses several important special cases. For instance, when $k = 1$, the Gamma distribution reduces to the exponential distribution. Similarly, the chi-squared distribution is another notable special case of the Gamma distribution. The Gamma-based sampling procedure enables the new points to lie in close proximity of the existing minority points. It is a desirable characteristic in the case of high dimensional and non-convex data. In addition, it provides a greater range of possible locations for the new sample than the traditional techniques such as SMOTE.

The process for generating synthetic points, with respect to numerical features, using the Gamma distribution consists of the following steps:

1. Point Selection: Begin by randomly selecting a point $x_1 \in \mathbf{R}^m$ in the minority class. Then, choose x_2 as the nearest point of x_1 within the minority class.
2. Direction Vector Calculation: Compute a normalized direction vector u between the two selected points:

$$u = \frac{x_2 - x_1}{\|x_2 - x_1\|}.$$

3. Gamma Distribution Sampling: Draw a random value t from the Gamma distribution with shape parameter k and scale parameter θ:

$$t \sim \text{Gamma}(k, \theta)$$

4. Mode Calculation: Calculate the mode of the Gamma distribution:

$$\text{mode} = (k - 1) \cdot \theta$$

5. Synthetic Point Generation: Finally, generate the new synthetic point z using the formula:

$$z = x_1 + (t - \text{mode}) \cdot u$$

The algorithm presented above is designed only for numerical columns, and not for categorical columns. Treating categorical columns as continuous may lead to invalid values being produced for those variables. Hence, we ammend this algorithm and use the above algorithm only for numerical variables, while assigning the final synthetic data point z to have the same values of any categorical variables as x_1. Assigning the categorical variables to be the same as x_1 is influenced by the fact that z will be numerically closer to x_1 and hence would likely have the same categorical variables.

In Fig. 1, we illustrate the Gamma distribution for a pair of minority points in $\mathbf{R}^2$. Given the initial minority point at $(3, 2)$ and a neighboring point at $(6, 5)$, we scale and orient the base Gamma distribution accordingly. Thus, the new minority points sampled by the gamma distribution will be more likely to generated near the initial point $(3, 2)$ and in the direction of the neighboring point at $(6, 5)$.

We adopted a systematic approach to identify the optimal shape and scale parameters for the Gamma distribution to be used in oversampling. This process involves

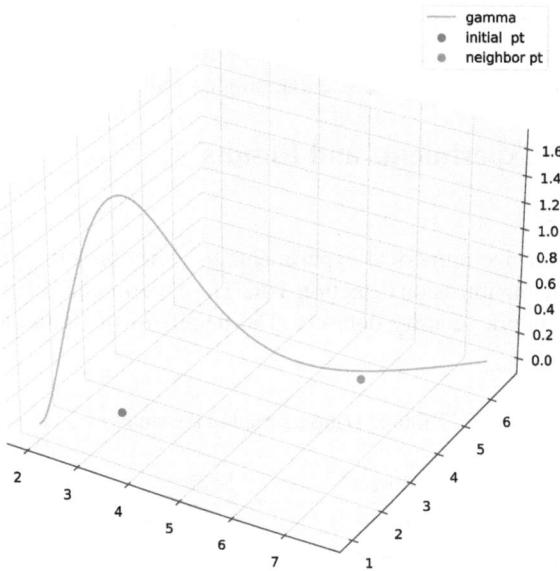

Fig. 1. Given a minority point at $(3, 2)$ and a neighboring point at $(6, 5)$ the base gamma distribution is scaled and oriented accordingly.

defining a range of values for k $(2, 3, 5, 7, 9)$ and θ $(0.5, 1, 2)$. Then, for each combination of k and θ, we split the dataset into stratified training and validation sets, apply the oversampling procedure to the training data, train a Random Forest classifier on the oversampled dataset, evaluate the trained model on the validation set, and identify the optimal parameter combination using the macro average F1 score. By employing this method, we can generate synthetic samples that effectively balance the class distribution while maintaining the intrinsic characteristics of the minority class, aiming to improve the performance of ML models on imbalanced network security datasets and potentially enhancing the accuracy and reliability of intrusion detection systems.

The Gamma method is particularly well-suited for intrusion detection because of the inherent nature of network security data, which often exhibits severe class imbalance, with normal traffic vastly outnumbering malicious instances. Intrusion detection requires models that can effectively identify rare, critical security events such as attacks or anomalies. Traditional oversampling techniques like SMOTE may generate synthetic points that do not adequately represent the true structure of the minority class, especially in highly non-linear and complex feature spaces typical of network data.

The Gamma method, by generating new synthetic points near existing minority instances using a probabilistic distribution, allows for more realistic and meaningful sample generation. This helps in preserving the underlying patterns of the minority class, improving the ability of machine learning models to recognize subtle anomalies or attack behaviors that might otherwise be overlooked. Additionally, the Gamma method's ability to handle high-dimensional spaces and non-convex data structures makes it particularly advantageous for network intrusion detection, where the relationships between features are often complex and not easily captured by simpler oversampling techniques. This targeted approach ensures that intrusion detection models remain sensitive to rare but dangerous events, enhancing overall detection accuracy.

4 Numerical Experiments and Results

4.1 Methodology

We performed extensive numerical experiments to verify the effectiveness of Gamma sampling for balancing intrusion detection data. The experiments were carried our based on three major network security datasets. The details of the datasets are provided in Table 1.

Table 1. Datasets used in the study.

Name	Features	Size	Target	Source
Kaggle	39, mixed	25,192	binary	UCI repository [27]
AWS	69, numerical	6,798,163	binary	Canadian Institute for Cybersecurity [26]
IoV	10, numerical	1,408,219	binary/multi-class	Canadian Institute for Cybersecurity [23]

Several ML algorithms were trained and tested before and after data balancing to measure the impact of Gamma sampling. The details of the algorithms are presented in Table 2.

Table 2. Machine learning algorithms used in the study.

Name	Settings
Logistic Regression	$penalty = L2, C = 1.0$
Multi-Layer Perceptron	$num\_hidden\_layers = 2, hidden\_layer\_sizes = (100, 100), activation = ReLU$
AdaBoost	$n\_estimators = 50, learning\_rate = 1$
Random Forest	$n\_estimators = 100$
Gradient Boosting	$n\_estimators = 100, learning\_rate = 1.0, max\_depth = 1$
K-Nearest Neighbors	$n\_neighbors = 5$

To obtain a comprehensive analysis, we considered a range of imbalance ratios. To this end, we artificially sampled the minority class data to obtain the necessary imbalance ratios for the experiment. In addition, since most of the ML algorithms performed well on the original datasets, we divided the data into smaller subsets to better observe the effect of the sampling procedure on the classification accuracy.

The performance of the ML models was measured in terms of macro average precision, recall, and F1 scores. The macro average is an unweighted average of scores on each class. Then, the difference between the scores before and after applying Gamma sampling is calculated.

The summary of the methodology for the experiments is provided below:

1. Divide each of the three main datasets into 10 equal-size and stratified subsets
2. For each subset, select the fraction of minority points to obtain the desired imbalance ratio
3. Train and test each ML classifier on the imbalanced dataset
4. Use Gamma sampling on the minority class to achieve a balanced dataset (including finding the optimal shape and scale parameters)
5. Train and test each ML classifier on the balanced dataset
6. Calculate the difference in macro average precision, recall, and F1-score between the balanced and imbalanced datasets

The accompanying code containing the methodology and the numerical experiments related to the study is publicly available on Github [12].

4.2 Results

In this section, we present the results of the empirical evaluation of Gamma sampling for balancing intrusion detection datasets.

Amazon Web Services (AWS). We begin our empirical evaluation with the AWS dataset. The original dataset includes seven different attack scenarios: Brute-force, Heartbleed, Botnet, DoS, DDoS, Web attacks, and infiltration of the network from inside. We converted the target variable into a binary class by labelling all the attack instances as malicious and normal traffic as benign. Further details about the dataset are presented in Table 1.

The data was divided into 10 equal subsets and the difference in the performance of the ML models before and after balancing was recorded. The final results are presented as the average scores over 10 subsets.

As shown in Fig. 2, Gamma sampling improves F1 scores for Logistic Regression and Gradient Boosting models. The improvement is valid across the range of imbalance ratios. At the same time, balancing does not affect the remaining models. Indeed, the remaining models achieve near perfect scores on the imbalanced data so there is no room for improvement after balancing. The precision scores shown in Fig. 3 reflect the F1 scores discussed previously. Data balancing produces huge precision gains for Gradient Boosting especially at the lower imbalance ratio values. As the imbalance ratio increases the benefits of balancing decline. It is explained by the fact that the ML models are able to achieve near perfect accuracy on this dataset even in the imbalanced regime.

As shown in Fig. 4, balancing produces huge gains in recall for Logistic Regression especially at low imbalance ratio values, while the gains Gradient Boosting are less prominent.

Kaggle. The Kaggle dataset is the classic intrusion detection dataset that was presented in KDD-99. It is based on raw TCP/IP dump data for a network from simulating a typical US Air Force LAN. The class variable is binary. Further details about the dataset

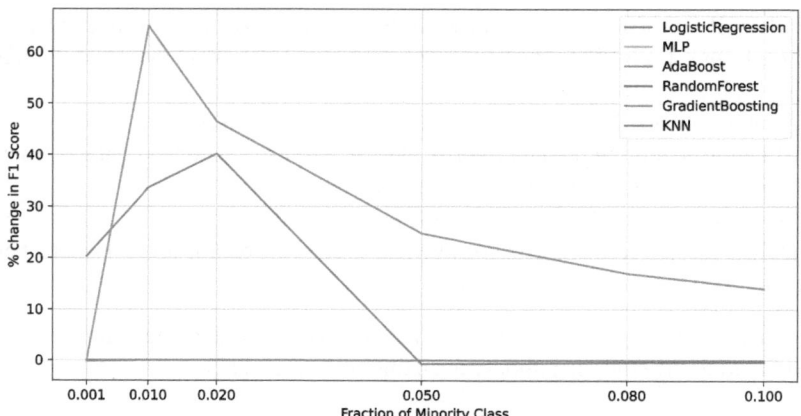

Fig. 2. AWS F1 scores.

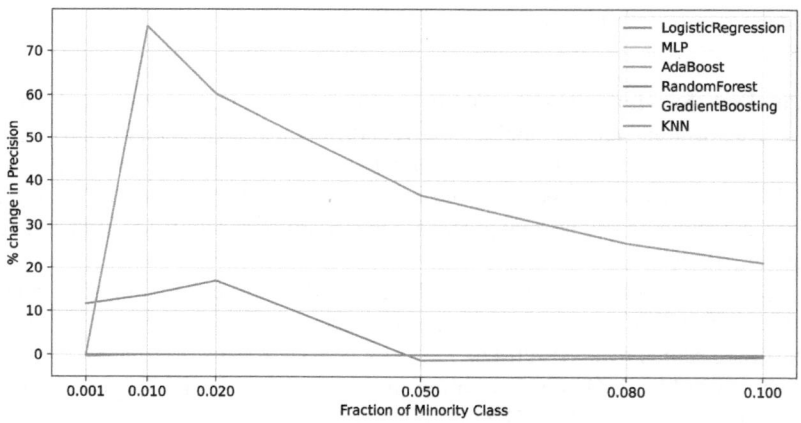

Fig. 3. AWS Precision scores.

are presented in Table 1. We apply the same procedure as in the AWS dataset to perform the numerical experiments on the Kaggle data.

As shown in Fig. 5, the balancing procedure provides a marked improvement in F1 scores for almost all ML models at the imbalance ratio 0.01. The effect of balancing gradually diminishes as the imbalance ratio increases. Data balancing provides a significant enhancement to Gradient Boosting, while it reduces the F1 score for Logistic Regression.

The precision scores presented in Fig. 6 support the results in F1 scores. There is an improvement in precision for all models at the ratio 0.01 followed by drop at 0.02. While the precision improves as the imbalance ratio increases, it is evident that sampling has a detrimental effect on the overall precision.

The recall scores shown in Fig. 7 diverge from F1 and precision scores discussed above. In particular, the recall scores improve significantly after balancing especially

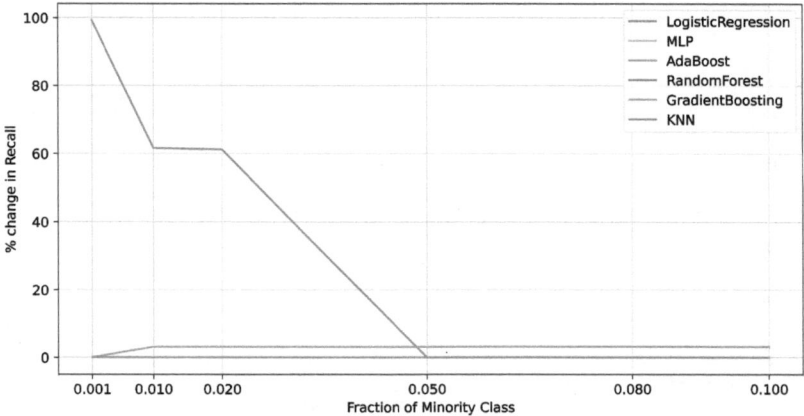

Fig. 4. AWS Recall scores.

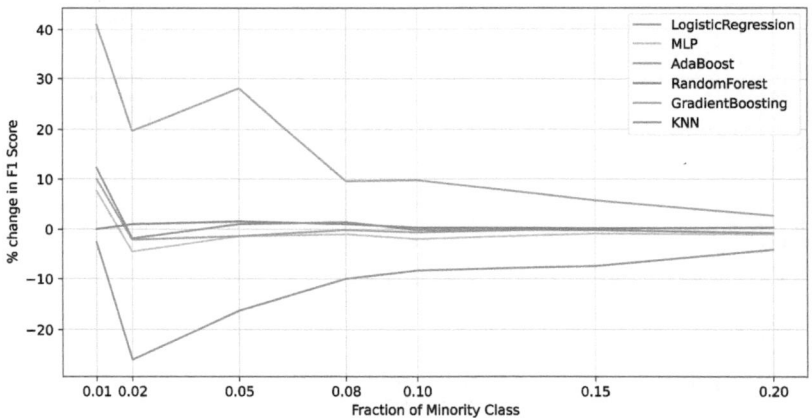

Fig. 5. Kaggle F1 scores.

at the low imbalance ratio values. In particular, KNN and Gradient Boosting achieve significantly higher recall scores due to balancing.

Internet of Vehicles (IoV). The IoV dataset aims to simulate network attacks on a Ford car. In particular, the datasets contains DoS and Spoofing attacks. The Spoofing attacks are further categorized as Gas, SW, Speed, and RPM. The class variable is converted to binary by labeling all the attacks with a common label. Further details about the dataset are presented in Table 1.

As shown in Fig. 8, the balancing procedure does not play a significant role in the performance of the models in terms of the F1 score. The main reason for this phenomenon is the near perfect performance of the ML models on imbalanced data. Indeed, despite reducing the size of the original data by splitting it into 10 subsets and applying

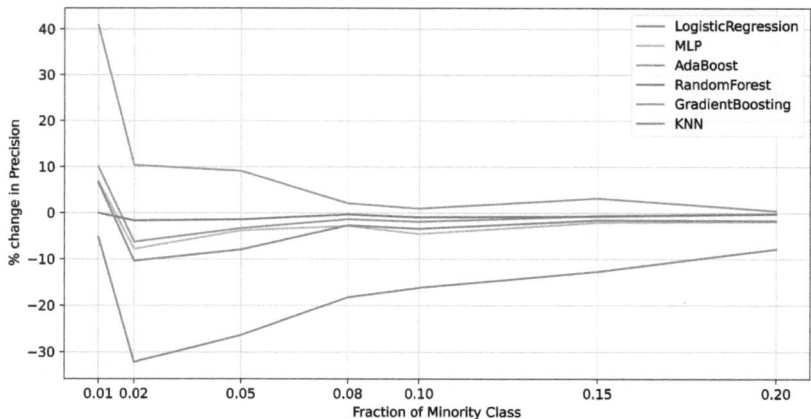

Fig. 6. Kaggle Precision scores.

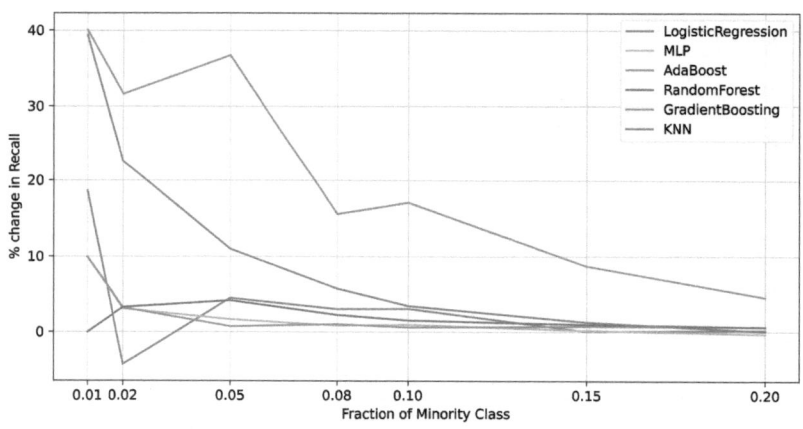

Fig. 7. Kaggle Recall scores.

extreme imbalance ratios, ML models are able to achieve over 99% accuracy. Therefore, there is no room for improvement after the balancing procedure. The only model that experienced a significant impact of balancing is Logistic Regression. Balancing reduced the performance of the model at low imbalance ratios and improved the performance at higher ratios.

Similar to F1 scores, the precision scores shown in Fig. 9, reveal the lack of impact of balancing on the performance of ML models. As mentioned, above the models achieve near perfect accuracy on imbalanced data leaving little room for improvement after balancing. We note that balancing reduced the precision of Logistic Regression.

The recall scores shown in Fig. 10 tell a similar story as above. The only exception is Logistic Regression whose recall improved dramatically due to balancing. The improvement is valid across the range of imbalance ratios but especially at the lower values.

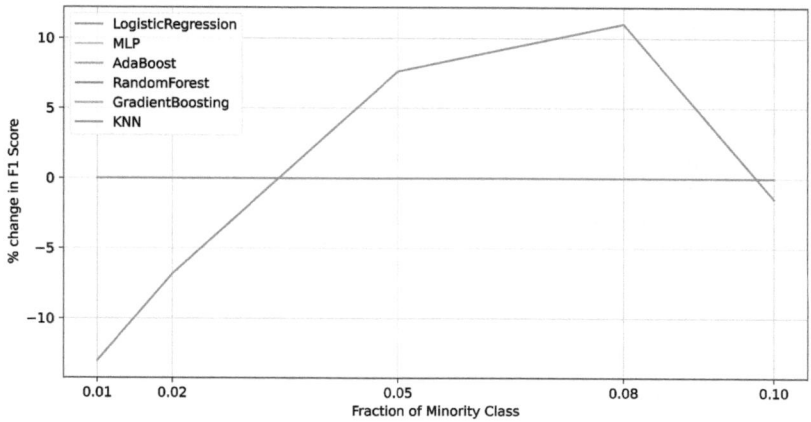

Fig. 8. IoV F1 scores.

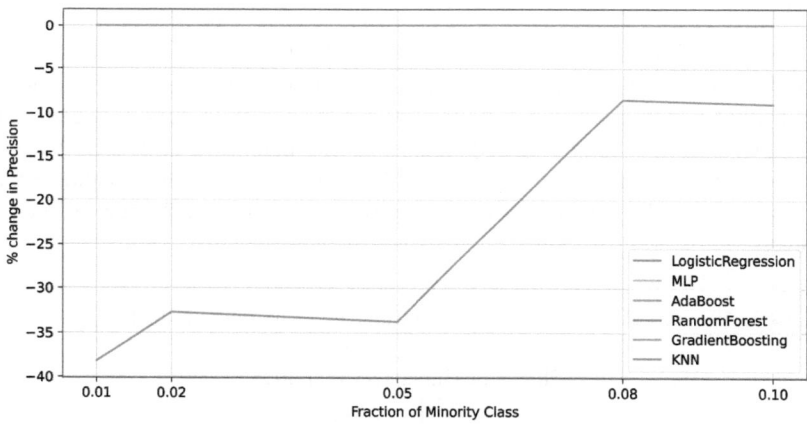

Fig. 9. IoV Precision scores.

4.3 Benchmarking

To further evaluate our proposed Gamma method, we compared its performance against two well-known sampling techniques, SMOTE and ROS, to address class imbalance in datasets. Advanced methods like GAN-based techniques were considered but could not be applied due to the extreme class imbalance and insufficient minority instances, which caused training failures. We measured the effectiveness of each method by calculating the change in the average F1 score for various class ratios, before and after applying the balancing techniques. This was done across multiple classifiers, with the average performance for each class ratio presented for two datasets: Kaggle and IoV.

The results presented in Tables 3 and 4 show that the Gamma method outperforms SMOTE and ROS in several cases, particularly when the class imbalance is most extreme. On the Kaggle dataset, Gamma consistently improved F1 scores, especially

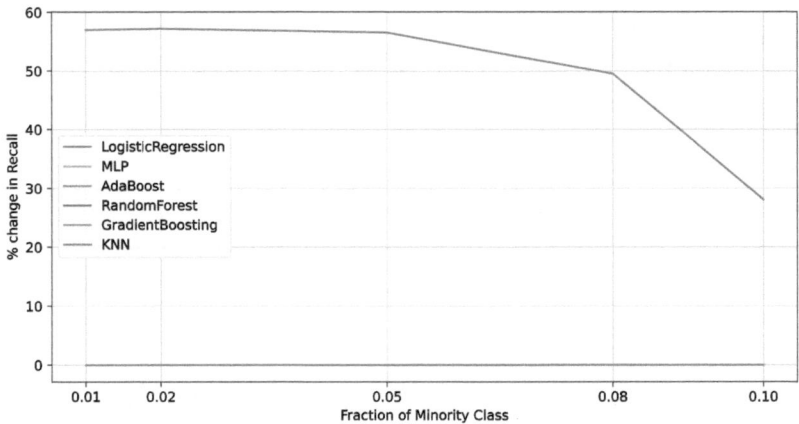

Fig. 10. IoV Recall scores.

at a class ratio of 0.01, where it achieved a significant increase of 0.04 compared to a drop of -0.06 with SMOTE. In contrast, ROS showed moderate improvements but lagged behind Gamma. On the IoV dataset, while the differences between methods were smaller, Gamma still performed on par or better than SMOTE and ROS across all class ratios. These findings demonstrate that Gamma is a robust and adaptable method for dealing with class imbalance, performing well across different datasets and imbalance levels.

Table 3. Average change in F1 scores before and after sampling for the Kaggle dataset.

Class ratio	Gamma	SMOTE	ROS
0.01	0.04	–0.06	0.02
0.02	–0.03	–0.16	0.03
0.05	0.02	0.02	0.00
0.10	0.00	0.02	0.01

4.4   Discussion

It was a challenge to measure the effectiveness of the Gamma sampling procedure given a near perfect performance of the ML models on imbalanced data. to address this issue we reduced the size of the original dataset by dividing it into 10 subsets. Furthermore, we reduced the imbalance ratio to make it harder for classifiers to learn from the minority class. Despite limiting the amount of training data and significantly reducing the number of minority points, the ML models continued to achieve high accuracy scores. Nevertheless, we were able to discern several patterns regarding the effectiveness of the sampling procedure on intrusion detection data.

Table 4. Average change in F1 scores before and after sampling for the IoV dataset.

Class ratio	Gamma	SMOTE	ROS
0.01	–0.01	–0.01	–0.01
0.02	0.00	–0.01	–0.01
0.05	0.01	0.01	0.01
0.10	0.00	0.00	0.00

Gamma-based balancing was particularly impactful on Logistic Regression and Gradient Boosting. It had mixed effects on Logistic Regression -performing well on the AWS dataset and poorly on the Kaggle and IoV dateasets. On the other hand, data balancing showed a consistent and significant positive effect on Gradient Boosting across all three datasets.

The varying performance of the Gamma method across different classifiers likely stems from how each model handles imbalanced data. Algorithms like Gradient Boosting, which focus on difficult-to-classify instances, may better utilize the synthetic data generated by Gamma, leading to consistent improvements. In contrast, simpler models like Logistic Regression may not benefit as much, particularly when the data is complex or contains important categorical features. Additionally, the diminishing effect of Gamma balancing at higher imbalance ratios can be explained by the efficiency of certain classifiers, which may already achieve strong performance, leaving little room for further improvement. The method's ability to handle categorical variables effectively was especially useful in datasets like those used for intrusion detection.

In general, Gamma balancing had a positive effect on intrusion detection data at low imbalance ratios. The effect of the balancing diminished as the imbalance ratio increased. This is mainly explained by the efficiency of the ML algorithms in classifying imbalanced dataset. As a result, there was little room for improvement after balancing.

Additionally, the proposed method to extend the Gamma distribution based synthetic data creation to accommodate categorical variables works well as seen with the improvements on the Kaggle dataset. Assigning the categorical variable of the new datapoint to be the same as the first point considered allows this method to be used in a variety of methods. Most importantly, it is particularly useful in intrusion detection datasets that often contain categorical features such as: The different services (UDP,TCP), different flags (FIN, SYN, ACK), the direction of travel, etc. Finally, results show that Gamma balancing has the biggest impact on the recall scores. It helps improve the recall efficiency across different dataset.

5   Conclusion

In this study, we proposed a Gamma distribution-based oversampling method to address the challenge of imbalanced data in network security datasets. Our extensive numerical experiments across three major datasets-AWS, Kaggle, and IoV-demonstrated that this approach can significantly enhance the performance of machine learning models, particularly in improving recall scores. Notably, Gradient Boosting consistently showed significant performance improvements, highlighting the potential of combining this classifier with Gamma sampling for effective intrusion detection.

While the performance impact varied across different models and datasets, the overall results indicate that Gamma-based oversampling effectively improves the detection of rare security events, which are critical in network security. These findings underscore the importance of addressing data imbalance in developing reliable AI-driven intrusion detection systems. Future research could further refine this approach and explore its application in other domains facing similar challenges.

References

1. Abdulganiyu, O.H., Ait Tchakoucht, T., Saheed, Y.K.: A systematic literature review for network intrusion detection system (IDS). Int. J. Inf. Secur. **22**(5), 1125–1162 (2023)
2. Awajan, A.: A novel deep learning-based intrusion detection system for IOT networks. Computers **12**(2), 34 (2023)
3. Bao, Y., Yang, S.: Two novel SMOTE methods for solving imbalanced classification problems. IEEE Access **11**, 5816–5823 (2023)
4. Kavin, S., Mohan, S.K., Karthick, V.I., Sudar, K.M.: Performance comparison of support vector machine, random forest, and extreme learning machine for intrusion detection. IEEE, Special Section on Survivability Strategies for Emerging Wireless Networks (2018)
5. Liu, A., Cheng, L., Yu, C.: SASMOTE: a self-attention oversampling method for imbalanced CSI fingerprints in indoor positioning systems. Sensors **22**(15), 5677 (2022)
6. Chawla, N.V., Bowyer, K.W., Hall, L.O., Kegelmeyer, W.P.: SMOTE: synthetic minority over-sampling technique. J. Artifi. Intell. Res. **16**, 321–357 (2002)
7. Ding, H., et al.: RVGAN-TL: a generative adversarial networks and transfer learning-based hybrid approach for imbalanced data classification. Inf. Sci. **629**, 184–203 (2023)
8. Elreedy, D., Atiya, A.F., Kamalov, F.: A theoretical distribution analysis of synthetic minority oversampling technique (SMOTE) for imbalanced learning. Mach. Learn. 1-21 (2023)
9. Fang, W., Tan, X., Wilbur, D.: Application of intrusion detection technology in network safety based on machine learning. Saf. Sci. **124**, 104604 (2020)
10. Fu, Y., Du, Y., Cao, Z., Li, Q., Xiang, W.: A deep learning model for network intrusion detection with imbalanced data. Electronics **11**(6), 898 (2022)
11. Fu, S., Tian, Y., Tang, J., Liu, X.: Cost-sensitive learning with modified Stein loss function. Neurocomputing **525**, 57–75 (2023)
12. Github repository. Gamma Balancer (2024). https://github.com/ro1406/GammaBalancer
13. Hasimi, L., Zavantis, D., Shakshuki, E., Yasar, A.: Cloud computing security and deep learning: an ANN approach. Proc. Comput. Sci. **231**, 40–47 (2024)
14. He, K., Kim, D.D., Asghar, M.R.: Adversarial machine learning for network intrusion detection systems: a comprehensive survey. IEEE Commun. Surv. Tutorials **25**(1), 538–566 (2023)
15. Hossain, M.A., Islam, M.S.: Ensuring network security with a robust intrusion detection system using ensemble-based machine learning. Array **19**, 100306 (2023)
16. Injadat, M., Moubayed, A., Nassif, A.B., Shami, A.: Multi-stage optimized machine learning framework for network intrusion detection. IEEE Trans. Netw. Serv. Manag. (2020)
17. Kamalov, F., Denisov, D.: Gamma distribution-based sampling for imbalanced data. Knowl.-Based Syst. **207**, 106368 (2020)
18. Kamalov, F., Moussa, S., Avante Reyes, J.: KDE-based ensemble learning for imbalanced data. Electronics **11**(17), 2703 (2022)

19. Kasongo, S.M., Sun, Y.: Performance analysis of intrusion detection systems using a feature selection method on the UNSW-NB15 dataset. J. Big Data **7**(1), 1–20 (2020). https://doi.org/10.1186/s40537-020-00379-6
20. Kumaravel, A., Vijayan, T.: Comparing cost sensitive classifiers by the false-positive to false-negative ratio in diagnostic studies. Expert Syst. Appl. **227**, 120303 (2023)
21. Liu, Y., et al.: Imbalanced data classification: using transfer learning and active sampling. Eng. Appli. Artifi. Intell. **117**, 105621 (2023)
22. Liu, Y., Liu, Y., Bruce, X.B., Zhong, S., Hu, Z.: Noise-robust oversampling for imbalanced data classification. Pattern Recogn. **133**, 109008 (2023)
23. Neto, E.C.P., et al.: CICIoV2024: advancing realistic IDS approaches against DoS and spoofing attack in IoV CAN bus. Internet of Things **26**, 101209 (2024)
24. Nguyen, T., Mengersen, K., Sous, D., Liquet, B.: SMOTE-CD: SMOTE for compositional data. PLoS ONE **18**(6), e0287705 (2023)
25. Nizamudeen, S.M.T.: Intelligent intrusion detection framework for multi-clouds-IoT environment using swarm-based deep learning classifier. J. Cloud Comput. **12**(1), 134 (2023)
26. Sharafaldin, I., Habibi Lashkari, A., Ghorbani, A.A.: Toward generating a new intrusion detection dataset and intrusion traffic characterization. In: International Conference on Information Systems Security and Privacy (2018)
27. Stolfo, S., Fan, W., Lee, W., Prodromidis, A., Chan, P.: KDD Cup 1999 Data. UCI Mach. Learn. Repository (1999). https://doi.org/10.24432/C51C7N
28. Talukder, M.A., et al.: A dependable hybrid machine learning model for network intrusion detection. J. Inform. Sec. Appli. **72**, 103405 (2023)
29. Thabtah, F., Hammoud, S., Kamalov, F., Gonsalves, A.: Data imbalance in classification: experimental evaluation. Inf. Sci. **513**, 429–441 (2020)
30. Zhang, C., Jia, D., Wang, L., Wang, W., Liu, F., Yang, A.: Comparative research on network intrusion detection methods based on machine learning. Comput. Sec. **121**, 102861 (2022)

SmartAudit: Smart Contract Vulnerability Detection Using Transfer Learning

Ankur Jain⬤ and Somanath Tripathy(✉)⬤

Department of Computer Science and Engineering, Indian Institute of Technology
Patna, Patna, India
{ankur_2221cs19,som}@iitp.ac.in

Abstract. Ethereum being a dominant player in decentralized finance, invites a vast number of smart contracts annually. Though smart contracts play a crucial role in developing decentralized applications that are safe, secure, and efficient, Ethereum lost a huge amount due to various attacks caused by different vulnerabilities within the smart contracts. Therefore, it is crucial to audit the reliability of smart contracts before their deployment. This paper proposes *SmartAudit* which identifies whether the smart contract is vulnerable. *SmartAudit* employs BERT (Bidirectional Encoder Representations from Transformers) to identify vulnerabilities in unseen smart contracts. It utilizes optimized opcode sequences derived from a pruned control flow graph as input. The results show that *SmartAudit* significantly improves accuracy, precision, recall and F1-score compared to the state-of-the-art models.

Keywords: Blockchain · Smart Contract · Deep Learning · Vulnerabilities

1 Introduction

The immutable nature inherent in blockchain technology has accelerated the emergence of a wide array of applications, with prominent examples like Bitcoin illustrating its transformative impact [21]. Furthermore, the rise of decentralized applications (DApps), comprising executable smart contracts embedded within blockchain blocks, has significantly expanded the versatility of blockchain ecosystems [28]. These smart contracts, typically written in languages such as Solidity, possess distinctive features such as open-source licensing, native cryptocurrency support, decentralized consensus mechanisms, and resilience against single points of failure [24]. The proliferation of DApps underscores their increasing importance, with thousands now operational across various blockchain platforms, spanning industries from gaming and social networking to financial services [29]. This trend highlights their growing role in transforming traditional sectors and enabling novel applications in a decentralized, secure manner.

In recent years, smart contracts have evolved beyond simple monetary transactions to facilitate decentralized sharing of digital assets. This expansion has

M. Al-kfairy et al. (Eds.): SocialSec 2024, LNCS 15565, pp. 122–137, 2025.
https://doi.org/10.1007/978-981-96-3774-4_8

empowered individual developers to create and deploy new contracts. However, these contracts are susceptible to potential vulnerabilities, presenting opportunities for attackers to exploit weaknesses embedded within the code. This has resulted in numerous attacks on smart contracts, leading to substantial financial losses and reputational damages in recent years as mentioned in Table 1. These attacks exploit vulnerabilities inherent in the code to manipulate contract behavior, siphon funds, or disrupt operations, underscoring the critical need for robust security measures [3] thorough auditing processes to mitigate risks associated with smart contract vulnerabilities. The infamous Reentrancy attack, exemplified by The DAO Hack in 2016 [18], resulted in a staggering loss of $60 million worth of Ethereum at the time. Similarly, the Parity Multisig Wallet Hack in 2017 exploited an Integer Overflow vulnerability, leading to a loss of $32 million [1]. Denial-of-Service (DoS) attacks, such as the one experienced by CryptoKitties in 2017, caused network congestion, although the monetary loss was not quantified [9]. Furthermore, the DeFi Lender bZx Hack in 2019 exploited Unchecked External Calls, resulting in a loss of $1 million [11]. Access Control Issues were at the forefront of the Lendf.me Hack in 2020, culminating in a substantial loss of $25.1 million [23]. These incidents underscore the critical importance of addressing vulnerabilities in smart contracts to enhance the security and resilience of blockchain-based systems. Therefore, identifying vulnerabilities in Ethereum smart contracts is essential for ensuring the security and reliability of blockchain-based systems.

Table 1. List of attacks in Ethereum smart contract

Vulnerability	Attack Example	Year	Loss (USD Est.)
[18] Reentrancy	The DAO Hack	2016	$60 Million (ETH at the time)
[1] Integer Overflow	Parity Multisig Wallet Hack	2017	$32 Million
[9] Denial-of-Service (DoS)	CryptoKitties	2017	N/A (Network Congestion)
[11] Unchecked External Calls	DeFi Lender bZx Hack	2019	$1 Million
[23] Access Control Issues	Lendf.me Hack	2020	$25.1 Million

As smart contracts gain popularity in applications such as decentralized finance (DeFi) and non-fungible tokens (NFTs), the risk of exploiting vulnerabilities within these contracts has become a significant concern. To address this issue, advanced techniques like integrating deep learning with smart contract code offer a promising approach for vulnerability detection [15]. In this paper, we have developed a novel mechanism aimed at enhancing the precision and effectiveness of vulnerability detection by directly analyzing the compiled bytecode. Bytecode analysis is crucial because it provides an accurate and immutable representation of the smart contract's operational logic. This approach improves security audits by eliminating discrepancies between the source code and its compiled form. By focusing on the actual code executed on the blockchain, our method ensures a thorough examination of potential vulnerabilities. In summary, our contribution to this paper can be outlined as follows:

- We introduce a novel mechanism *SmartAudit* that integrates deep learning with bytecode analysis for detecting vulnerabilities in smart contracts.
- We collected a significant dataset of 7,017 smart contracts from the Ethereum mainnet, each meticulously annotated over more than 10 vulnerabilities. Further, Optimized Control-Flow Graphs (CFGs) generated corresponding to each smart contract opcodes to enhance the efficiency.
- Design a binary classification model based on BERT (Bidirectional Encoder Representations from Transformers) by utilizing reduced set of opcode sequences for classify whether smart contract is vulnerable.

2   Background

2.1   Smart Contract Program

In the Ethereum blockchain, a smart contract acts as a self-governing program residing at a specific address within the distributed ledger [5]. This code segment contains a series of interconnected functions and related data values, enabling the automated and trustless execution of predetermined actions [22]. By enabling these autonomous operations, smart contracts form the foundation for decentralized applications (dApps) running on the Ethereum network [27].

Solidity: Solidity is a high-level programming language specifically tailored for developing smart contracts that run on the Ethereum blockchain. It empowers developers to construct secure and autonomous applications (dApps) by providing them with the necessary tools to define the functionalities and behaviour of these contracts [6].

Bytecode: EVM bytecode forms the core representation of smart contract code, specifically designed for execution by the Ethereum Virtual Machine (EVM). Visually, it appears as a lengthy sequence of hexadecimal numbers, often starting with "**0x606040520060...**". Functioning similarly to assembly language, EVM bytecode acts as a stack-based bytecode language. This bytecode is generated through the compilation process, transforming high-level programming languages like Solidity into a machine-readable format that the EVM can directly interpret and execute [28].

Opcodes: The Ethereum Virtual Machine (EVM) relies on a set of pre-defined instructions called opcodes to perform operations. These opcodes act as the building blocks for smart contract execution. Each opcode corresponds to a specific action the EVM can understand. For instance, the bytecode sequence "0x606040520060..." begins with the opcode "0x60," which translates to "PUSH1" in the EVM instruction set. Similar to "PUSH1," there exist numerous PUSH opcodes, each handling data of varying sizes. Additionally, there are opcodes for various operations within the Ethereum ecosystem, like "0x52" which translates to "MSTORE". This particular opcode retrieves two elements from the stack, performs their addition, and then pushes the resulting sum back onto the stack. It's important to note that the number of elements manipulated by each opcode can vary depending on the specific instruction being executed.

Vulnerabilities of Smart Contract: Ethereum smart contracts have become a frequent target for cyberattacks, leading to substantial financial losses in recent years. Several well-documented vulnerabilities that affects these contracts, including Reentrancy, Denial-of-Service attacks, and Integer Overflow/Underflow. In our proposed *SmartAudit* model, we focus on mitigating particular ten well-known vulnerabilities as mentioned in the Table 2. A significant challenge in developing *SmartAudit* lies in the creation of a labelled dataset encompassing various vulnerabilities. To address this obstacle, we leverage an existing tools such as Oyente [17] and Mythril [20].

2.2   Control-Flow Graph

A Control-Flow graph (CFG) visualizes smart contract code as a directed graph. In this graph, each vertex (node) represents a basic block, which is a sequence of bytecode instructions that execute sequentially without interruptions from jumps (like loops or conditional statements). Edges within the CFG depict the permissible flow of execution between these basic blocks. This graphical representation offers significant advantages for code analysis compared to traditional linear code views. By capturing the essential semantic structure of the smart contract, CFGs enable a more comprehensive understanding of the program's behaviour.

2.3   Bidirectional Encoder Representations from Transformers

BERT (Bidirectional Encoder Representations from Transformers) stands as a groundbreaking natural language processing (NLP) model developed by Google AI [8]. This powerful model leverages the transformer architecture, allowing it to understand the intricacies of language by considering the context of both surrounding and preceding words. BERT's capability to analyze text in a bidirectional manner has resulted in exceptional performance across various NLP tasks, including sentiment analysis, question answering, and text classification.

3   Related Works

Securing smart contracts is crucial due to their inherent immutability and the potential financial losses they can incur if compromised. Machine learning (ML) and deep learning (DL) techniques have emerged as promising tools for automated vulnerability detection in smart contracts. This section delves into several notable works that have laid the groundwork for advancements in this field, while also highlighting ongoing challenges.

Traditional approaches to detecting vulnerabilities in smart contracts typically involve static and dynamic analysis methods. Kushwaha et al. [16] compiled a list of tools that utilize static analysis techniques, including source code and bytecode analysis, along with dynamic analysis techniques like control flow analysis during the execution of smart contracts.

Oyente [17] and Osiris [25] use a technique called static analysis to quickly examine numerous contracts, often within seconds. This makes them perfect for checking a lot of contracts at once, but there's a catch. They focus on finding common patterns that might indicate weaknesses, similar to a guard checking for obvious signs of trouble. While they're great at catching basic problems, they might miss more cleverly hidden vulnerabilities.

For a more thorough investigation, we have Mythril [20] and Securify [26]. These tools are like detectives meticulously examining every detail of a crime scene. They use a powerful technique called symbolic execution, which allows them to explore all possible ways a smart contract could run. This helps them uncover a wider range of vulnerabilities, including sneaky attacks that try to exploit the contract multiple times (Reentrancy exploits) or cause math mistakes (integer overflows) that could steal user funds. However, this extra scrutiny takes time, with each contract analysis potentially taking several minutes compared to the lightning-fast speed of static analysis tools. Another contender in the security arena is Manticore [19]. Think of it as a detective with a supercomputer at their disposal. Manticore combines symbolic execution with real-world data to find even the most devious vulnerabilities. While its capabilities are remarkable, the analysis process can be considerably time-consuming, occasionally extending to as much as 24 min per contract. [13] proposes a novel method that integrates features from both contract source code and opcodes to enhance vulnerability detection. These foundational works collectively illustrate the ongoing evolution of smart contract vulnerability detection. They also showcase the potential need for ML and DL techniques in the field of vulnerability detection but also highlight the remaining challenges. As the field progresses, it is crucial to integrate diverse methodologies, such as combining static and dynamic analysis with powerful learning algorithms. Additionally, refining feature extraction techniques and developing models that can learn and adapt to the ever-changing threat landscape are critical for robust vulnerability detection in smart contracts. In the given Table 2, a comparison is drawn between models such as Oyente, Mythril, Securify and CSCO with our model, *SmartAudit*.

4   The Proposed Smart Contract Vulnerability Detection Technique

In this section, we propose *SmartAudit*, a smart contract vulnerability detection technique, various components of which is as shown in Fig. 1. To detect the vulnerability, a large dataset of smart contracts solidity source codes are

Table 2. Comparison of *SmartAudit* with various vulnerability tools.

S. No.	Vulnerability	Model			
		Oyente	Mythril	Securify	(Our Work) SmartAudit
1	Reentrancy with Ether	✓	✓	✓	✓
2	Uninitialized State	✓	×	✓	✓
3	Suicidal	×	✓	×	✓
4	Shadowing State	✓	✓	✓	✓
5	Unchecked Transfer	✓	×	✓	✓
6	tx.origin	×	✓	✓	✓
7	Divide-Multiply Precedence	✓	✓	×	✓
8	Unstored Return	×	✓	✓	✓
9	Return Without Check	×	✓	×	✓
10	Uninitialised Local Variable	✓	✓	✓	✓

✓: Corresponding tool can detect that vulnerability, ×: Not Considering that vulnerability

collected, and labelled over 10 distinct vulnerabilities. During the preprocessing, Opcodes are extracted corresponding to each smart contract solidity source code. The Opcode to Control-Flow Graph (Op2CFG) component constructs the Control-Flow Graph (CFG) for each smart contract by utilizing opcodes. The Vulnerability Detector then employs the nodes of the CFG, generates tokens, and pre-trains them using the BERT model to classify each smart contract.

4.1 Smart Contract Data Preprocessing

Data preprocessing is essential for refining raw contract code by resolving issues like code formatting and data inconsistencies. To perform this task, we created a dataset containing bytecodes from smart contracts for our vulnerability detection model. This dataset serves as a foundation for training our model to identify vulnerabilities effectively.

Data Collection: For our dataset creation, we depended on two primary platforms: Etherscan [4] and Infura [14]. Etherscan acts as a block explorer for the Ethereum mainnet, allowing us to initially gather nearly ten thousand real-world smart contract addresses. Subsequently, we utilized the Infura API to acquire the bytecodes associated with these addresses. This procedure resulted in establishing our dataset, comprising ten thousand bytecodes. This dataset serves as the cornerstone for our subsequent analysis and model training. In essence, we utilized Etherscan to identify real-world smart contract addresses and then utilized Infura to retrieve the corresponding bytecode data for further examination and processing.

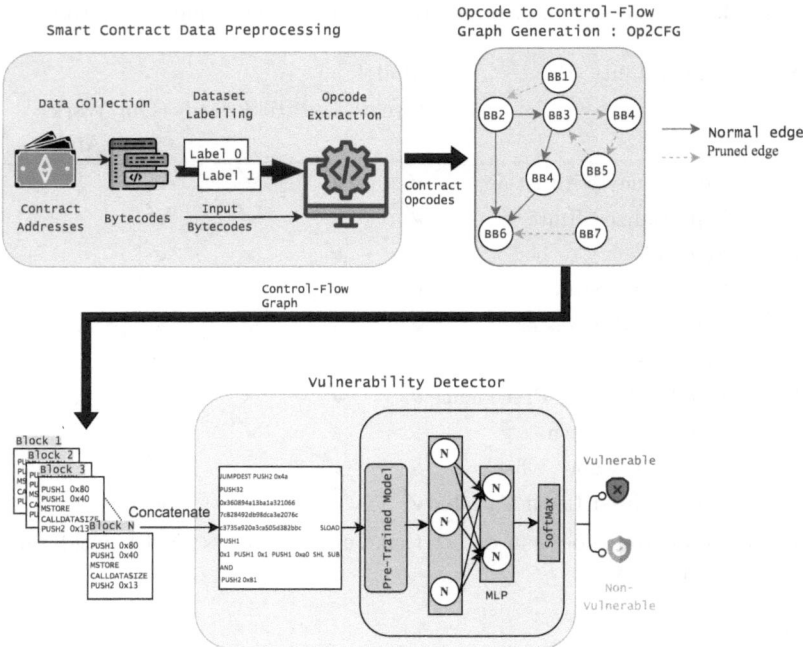

Fig. 1. Overview Design of *SmartAudit*

Data Labeling: To accurately label our dataset, we employed a combination of static analysis tools, specifically Oyente [17] and Mythril [20], to detect the presence of 10 well-known vulnerabilities in smart contracts as shown in Table 3. These tools were chosen for their effectiveness in identifying specific classes of vulnerabilities, such as reentrancy and integer overflows. However, we acknowledge that both tools have limitations; they are designed to detect certain vulnerabilities and may miss or incorrectly label others. We encountered challenges with the availability of the source code for all ten thousand smart contract addresses initially collected. Consequently, our dataset was reduced to 7017 entries that had accessible Solidity source code for labelling purposes.

To address the limitations of relying solely on Oyente and Mythril, we cross-validated the results with manual checks and supplemented the dataset using insights from other relevant tools and research findings. This multi-step labelling process ensures a more comprehensive and reliable set of labels for training, mitigating potential inaccuracies from relying on these tools. This approach improves the robustness of our dataset, allowing our model to detect vulnerabilities more accurately during evaluation.

Opcode Extraction: Opcode extraction stands as a vital component within the data preprocessing phase. It involves retrieving the opcodes, which represent individual instructions within the bytecode of smart contracts. These opcodes serve as fundamental building blocks essential for analyzing the Control-Flow

Table 3. Various vulnerabilities within smart contracts and related information.

S. No.	Vulnerability	Description	Labelling Tool	Occurance
1	Reentrancy with Ether	Using the fallback function to re-execute a function before modifying the state variable (recursive call attack); Reentrancy without involving Ether transactions is not typically reported	Mythril	39
2	Uninitialised State	Local storage variables are inadequately initialized, potentially leading to unexpected storage references within the contract	Oyente	56
3	Suicidal	The selfdestruct instruction initiated by any account without restriction.	Mythril	49
4	*Shadowing State	State variables that are defined in multiple instances both within the contract and within specific functions.	Mythril	52
5	*Unchecked Transfer	The result of an external transfer or transfer From call is not verified.	Oyente	262
6	*tx.origin	The protection mechanism based on tx.origin for authorization can be exploited by a malicious contract in the event that a genuine user engages with the malicious contract.	Mythril	19
7	*Divide-Multiply Precedence	The imprecise order of arithmetic operations, as division could result in truncation.	Oyente	176
8	*Unstored Return	The outcome of an external call is not retained within a local or state variable.	Mythril	2427
9	*Return Without Check	If the return value of a send operation isn't checked, any failed sends could result in a locked Ether.	Mythril	68
10	*Uninitialised Local Variable	When local variables are uninitialized, sending Ether to them can result in the loss of that Ether.	Oyente	114
		Total number of non-vulnerable contracts		3262

$*$: Theoretical vulnerabilities

of any smart contract program. By extracting opcodes, we gain insight into the specific operations and functionalities encoded within the smart contract. This process enables a deeper understanding of how the contract functions at the bytecode level, facilitating subsequent analyses aimed at identifying potential vulnerabilities or assessing the contract's behavior and structure. Essentially, opcode extraction forms a foundational step in comprehensively examining the intricacies of smart contract code, laying the groundwork for further analysis and evaluation.

Understanding the structure of a smart contract is essential for effective analysis [28]. To gain deeper insight into this structure, we've devised a method to generate Control-Flow graphs (CFGs) for each contract, rather than simply examining a list of code fragments. CFGs provide visual representations of how the code within a contract flows and executes. In our *SmartAudit* model, the Op2CFG component plays a pivotal role. This component utilizes the opcodes extracted earlier to construct a CFG. Specifically, it focuses on opcodes such as

JUMP, JUMPI, and JUMPDEST, which dictate the flow of execution within Ethereum smart contracts. By employing CFGs, we can analyze the structure of contracts more comprehensively, identifying potential issues and vulnerabilities with greater clarity.

Control-Flow Graph Generation: We provided the opcodes extracted from input bytecodes corresponding to specific smart contract addresses; these opcodes then break down into opcode sequences representing various graph nodes(or basic blocks), providing a clearer understanding of its operation. This understanding is key for ensuring the contract functions as intended and is secure.

Control-Flow Graph (CFG) Optimization: In our optimization process for Ethereum smart contract Control-Flow graphs (CFGs), we implemented three distinct graph pruning techniques to enhance code efficiency and improve security.

1. **Isolated Node Elimination**: This technique involves identifying and removing nodes (basic blocks) within the CFG that are unreachable or never executed during contract execution. Such nodes could include functions that are never called or conditional branches that are always evaluated as false. Specifically, we target nodes with no edges as these nodes contribute little or nothing to the contract's functionality.
2. **Nodes Inline**: In this method, we identify consecutive nodes within the CFG where both the in-degree and out-degree are equal to 1. These nodes represent sequences of instructions with no branching or merging. By merging the opcode instructions of such nodes, we effectively reduce the total number of nodes in the CFG, simplifying the computational complexity of analyzing the contract's Control-Flow.
3. **Multi-node Loop Unrolling**: This technique focuses on identifying loops within the CFG that span multiple nodes. By merging the instruction opcodes of nodes within these loops and combining their in-degree and out-degree nodes, we streamline the execution flow of looped sections in the contract. This not only optimizes the code for efficiency but also enhances security by reducing the potential for vulnerabilities related to complex loop structures.

Overall, these graph pruning techniques are instrumental in optimizing Ethereum smart contract CFGs, leading to improved code efficiency and strengthened security posture against potential vulnerabilities and exploits.

4.2 Vulnerability Detector

Once the Optimized Control-Flow graphs are collected for each smart contract, Opcode sequences of each block are concatenated to generate a feature vectors that will act as input to BERT model.

Vulnerability Classification: After extracting feature vectors from the pre-processed smart contract code, the model progresses to the training phase for vulnerability classification. This phase adopts a dual approach, combining the strengths of a pre-trained BERT model and a Multilayer Perceptron (MLP).

The pre-trained BERT model is employed for feature analysis. Trained on a vast corpus of code data, BERT is well-equipped to capture intricate contextual relationships and pinpoint key features within the feature vectors. This gives the classifier a deep understanding of the underlying semantics of the code, enabling it to go beyond surface-level patterns.

The second component, the Multilayer Perceptron (MLP), functions as an advanced analytical engine. The rich feature representations produced by BERT are fed into the MLP, where they pass through its layered architecture. Each layer applies non-linear transformations, gradually extracting more complex feature combinations and higher-order relationships that suggest potential vulnerabilities. In binary classification, the MLP's ability to learn intricate patterns within the feature space is particularly beneficial, as it excels at differentiating between two classes-in this case, vulnerable and benign smart contracts. By progressively refining feature distinctions, the MLP enhances classification accuracy, ensuring reliable detection of vulnerabilities.

Model Training: Our system uses a pre-trained technique called BERT to understand the code better. BERT is like a super translator that's been trained on massive amounts of text data. BERT can take the code as a sequence of opcode instructions and turn it into a more meaningful format that our system can understand [8]. This pre-training step makes our system work faster and more accurately. Moreover, as BERT is already so good at understanding language, we do not need as much specific code data to train it for our particular task compared to starting from scratch as suggested in [12].

The first part of our system (the input module) takes a cleaned-up version of the smart contract code. Imagine the code as a series of instructions, broken down into smaller chunks. The system then turns these chunks into a special format the computer can understand, kind of like translating a language. It uses a tool called an *Auto-tokeniser* to perform this task. Next, the system creates a special code for each chunk and the entire block of instructions. To understand these codes better, it uses three different tools (embedding layers) that add extra information, like labels and details [2]. Finally, it combines all this extra information for each chunk into one big code, like putting all the puzzle pieces together. This big code represents the entire smart contract code for the system to analyze.

After the code is transformed, It is passed through the pre-trained BERT model. BERT is like an advanced code reader that can understand the meaning of each part of the code about the whole thing. It assigns a special code (embedding) to each chunk of code, capturing the important details and how they connect. The output from BERT is a tensor with dimensions (None, 40, 768), representing 40 tokens with 768-dimensional embeddings. Regardless of the code's length, BERT always gives a fixed-size output summarising the most important information [7]. It goes through a series of layers that help extract even more information and identify patterns. These layers use special functions (ReLU [10] and dropout) to improve accuracy and prevent the system from memorizing specific examples instead of learning the general concept. Finally, the code is fed into a final layer that gives a score indicating how likely it is for the smart contract to be vulnerable. This score helps determine if the contract has weaknesses that could be exploited.

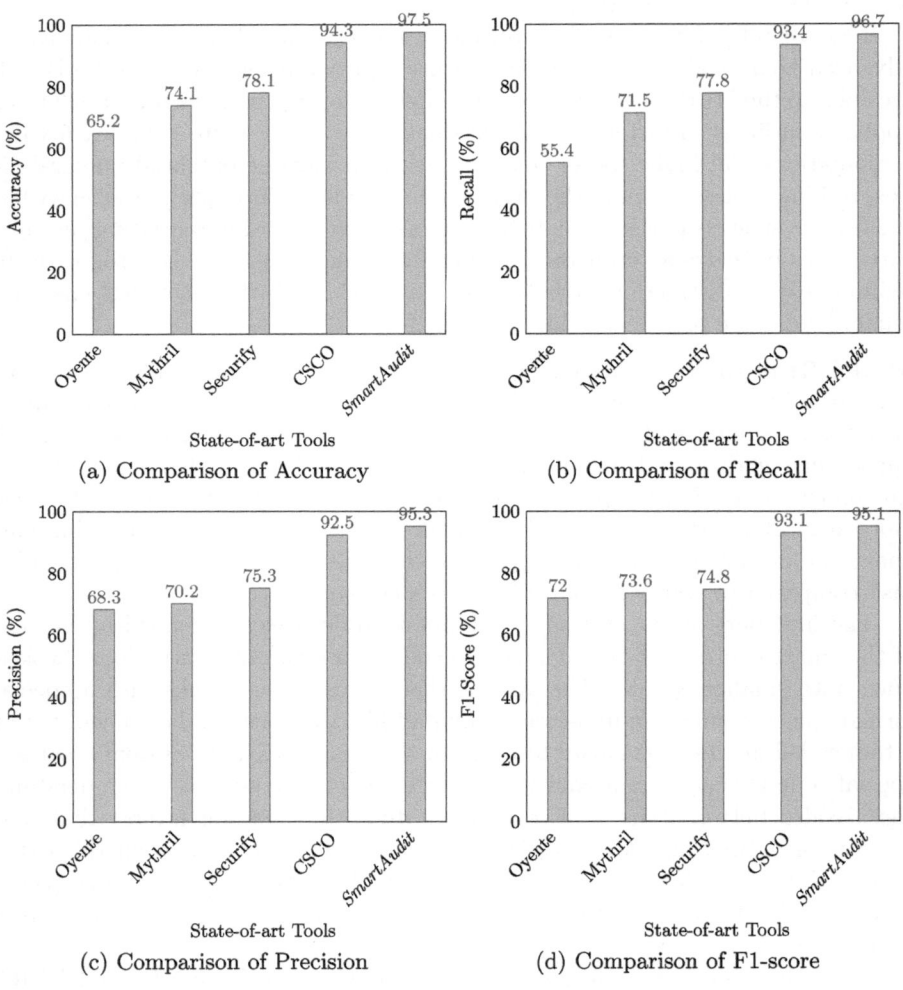

(a) Comparison of Accuracy

(b) Comparison of Recall

(c) Comparison of Precision

(d) Comparison of F1-score

Fig. 2. Performance comparison with different state-of-art Tools

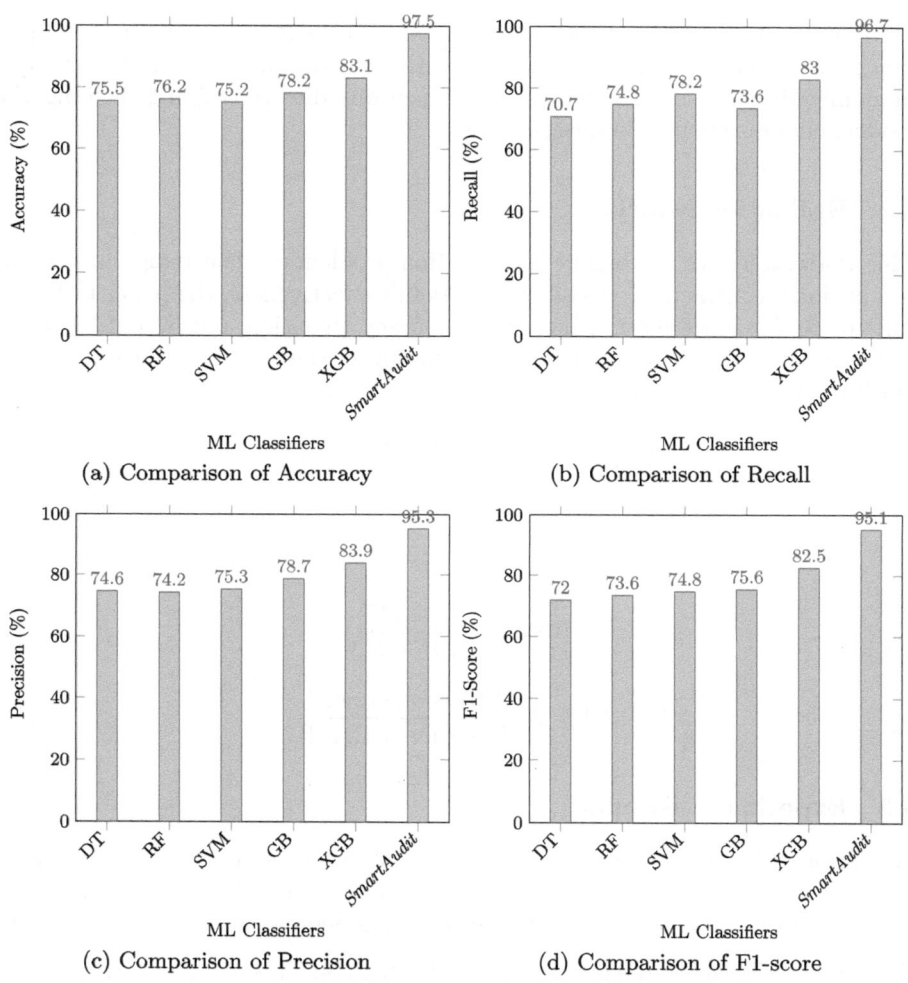

Fig. 3. Performance Comparison with various ML Classifiers

5   Experiment Evaluation

This section analyzes the performance of *SmartAudit*. We present the training and testing setup, evaluation metrics, and model results in this section.

5.1   Experiment System Setup

We implemented our proposed model and all baseline models using Python's deep learning framework: Python3.10 and TensorFlow-CUDA. Additionally, we utilized the Scikit-learn library for complementary machine-learning tasks. To accelerate training, we executed the experiments on a multi-GPU hybrid cluster equipped with a powerful Nvidia GeForce GTX 1080Ti GPU.

To prevent overfitting during training, we used the ReLU [10] activation function and applied dropout regularization with a 0.1 dropout rate. This technique randomly drops a certain percentage of neurons during training, helping the model generalize better to unseen data.

5.2   Evaluation Matrix

This work addresses the binary classification problem of identifying vulnerabilities in smart contracts. To assess *SmartAudit*'s effectiveness, the paper utilizes a suite of performance metrics including accuracy, precision, recall, and F1-score. These metrics offer a comprehensive evaluation of the model's ability to distinguish between vulnerable and non-vulnerable contracts.

$$\text{Accuracy} = \frac{TP + TN}{TP + TN + FP + FN} \tag{1}$$

$$\text{Precision} = \frac{TP}{TP + FP} \tag{2}$$

$$\text{Recall} = \frac{TP}{TP + FN} \tag{3}$$

$$F1 = 2 \cdot \frac{\text{Precision} \cdot \text{Recall}}{\text{Precision} + \text{Recall}} \tag{4}$$

5.3   Experiment Results

We performed two different experiments to analyse the performance of our model *SmartAudit*. We compared *SmartAudit* with four state-of-the-art models in the first experiment and with five different ML classifiers in the second experiment.

Comparing Results with State-of-Art Models: This research compares the proposed model with the state-of-the-art models for detecting vulnerable smart contracts such as Oyente [17], Mythril [20], Securify [26] and CSCO [13]. The comparison of *SmartAudit* with state-of-the-art models is shown in Table 4.We compare our proposed approach as shown in Fig 2. From this result, We can infer that the performance of *SmartAudit* is showing significantly better results. Our model is more accurate, and precision is high for vulnerability detection in smart contracts, indicating its efficacy in identifying potential security flaws with greater reliability.

Comparing Results with Machine Learning Classifiers: ML and DL techniques for smart contract vulnerability detection have gained significant traction in recent years. We compare our proposed approach as shown in Fig 3 against established methods like Decision Tree (DT), Random Forests (RF), Support Vector Machines (SVM), Gradient Boosting (GB) and Extreme Gradient Boosting (XGB). Our model shows significant improvement in accuracy i.e., 85.4% as compared to different ML classifiers.

Table 4. Comparison of proposed work with state-of-art existing models

Model	Method	Performance Metrics			
		Accuracy	Recall	Precision	F1-Score
Oyente [17]	SA	65.2	55.4	68.3	72.0
Mythril [20]	SA	74.1	71.5	70.2	73.6
Securify [26]	SA	78.1	77.8	75.3	74.8
CSCO [13]	DL	94.3	93.5	92.5	93.1
(*SmartAudit*) **Our Work**	DL	**97.5**	**96.7**	**95.3**	**95.1**

SA: Static Analysis, DL: Deep Learning

6 Conclusion

In this paper, we proposed *SmartAudit*, a model for detecting vulnerable and non-vulnerable smart contracts with high accuracy. We prepared a dataset of 7,017 smart contracts labeled for over 10 vulnerabilities, generated Control-Flow graphs from opcode sequences, and optimized them using pruning techniques. The opcode sequences were pre-trained using the BERT model, and the performance of SmartAudit was compared against state-of-the-art models and machine learning classifiers. Our model achieved an accuracy of 97.5%, significantly outperforming existing models. For future work, we plan to incorporate sequence-level embedding in Control-Flow graphs and integrate both source code and bytecode for enhanced analysis.

Acknowledgments. We acknowledge the Government of India, Ministry of Electronics and Information Technology, for funding this research under the project ISEA Phase-III.

References

1. The parity wallet hack explained - open zeppelin blog - blog.openzeppelin.com. https://blog.openzeppelin.com/on-the-parity-wallet-multisig-hack-405a8c12e8f7, Accessed 24 April 2024
2. Transformers. https://huggingface.co/google-bert/bert-base-uncased, Accessed 25 April 2024
3. Atzei, N., Bartoletti, M., Cimoli, T.: A survey of attacks on ethereum smart contracts (SoK). In: Maffei, M., Ryan, M. (eds.) POST 2017. LNCS, vol. 10204, pp. 164–186. Springer, Heidelberg (2017). https://doi.org/10.1007/978-3-662-54455-6_8
4. Bhd BSS: ETHERSCAN: Block Explorer and Analytics Platform (2015). https://static.nhtsa.gov/odi/inv/2016/INCLA-PE16007-7876.PDF
5. Buterin, V., et al.: A next-generation smart contract and decentralized application platform. White paper **3**(37), 2–1 (2014)
6. Dannen, C., Dannen, C.: Solidity programming. Introducing Ethereum and Solidity: Foundations of Cryptocurrency and Blockchain Programming for Beginners, pp. 69–88 (2017)

7. Das, S., Singh, A., Saha, S., Maurya, A.: Negative review or complaint? exploring interpretability in financial complaints. IEEE Trans. Comput. Soc. Syst. (2024)

8. Devlin, J., Chang, M.W., Lee, K., Toutanova, K.: Bert: Pre-training of deep bidirectional transformers for language understanding. arXiv preprint arXiv:1810.04805 (2018)

9. Dika, A., Nowostawski, M.: Security vulnerabilities in ethereum smart contracts. In: 2018 IEEE international conference on Internet of Things (iThings) and IEEE green computing and communications (GreenCom) and IEEE cyber, physical and social computing (CPSCom) and IEEE Smart Data (SmartData), pp. 955–962. IEEE (2018)

10. Glorot, X., Bordes, A., Bengio, Y.: Deep sparse rectifier neural networks. In: Proceedings of the Fourteenth International Conference on Artificial Intelligence and Statistics, pp. 315–323. JMLR Workshop and Conference Proceedings (2011)

11. Hacken: 7 Most Common Smart Contract Attacks - Hacken - hacken.io. https://hacken.io/discover/most-common-smart-contract-attacks, Accessed 24 April 2024

12. Howard, J., Ruder, S.: Universal language model fine-tuning for text classification. arXiv preprint arXiv:1801.06146 (2018)

13. Huang, H., Guo, L., Zhao, L., Wang, H., Xu, C., Jiang, S.: Effective combining source code and opcode for accurate vulnerability detection of smart contracts in edge ai systems. Appl. Soft Comput. **158**, 111556 (2024)

14. Inc CS: INFURA: Web Development Platform| IPFS API & Gateway (2024). https://www.infura.io/

15. Jin, L., Cao, Y., Chen, Y., Zhang, D., Campanoni, S.: Exgen: cross-platform, automated exploit generation for smart contract vulnerabilities. IEEE Trans. Dependable Secure Comput. **20**(1), 650–664 (2022)

16. Kushwaha, S.S., Joshi, S., Singh, D., Kaur, M., Lee, H.N.: Ethereum smart contract analysis tools: a systematic review. IEEE Access **10**, 57037–57062 (2022)

17. Luu, L., Chu, D.H., Olickel, H., Saxena, P., Hobor, A.: Making smart contracts smarter. In: Proceedings of the 2016 ACM SIGSAC Conference on Computer and Communications Security, pp. 254–269 (2016)

18. Mehar, M.I., et al.: Understanding a revolutionary and flawed grand experiment in blockchain: the dao attack. J. Cases Inform. Technol. (JCIT) **21**(1), 19–32 (2019)

19. Mossberg, M., et l.: Manticore: a user-friendly symbolic execution framework for binaries and smart contracts. In: 2019 34th IEEE/ACM International Conference on Automated Software Engineering (ASE), pp. 1186–1189. IEEE (2019)

20. Mueller, B.: Smashing ethereum smart contracts for fun and real profit. HITB SECCONF Amsterdam **9**, 54 (2018)

21. Narayanan, A., Bonneau, J., Felten, E., Miller, A., Goldfeder, S.: Bitcoin and cryptocurrency technologies: a comprehensive introduction. Princeton University Press (2016)

22. Queralta, J.P., Keramat, F., Salimi, S., Fu, L., Yu, X., Westerlund, T.: Blockchain and emerging distributed ledger technologies for decentralized multi-robot systems. Current Robot. Rep. **4**(3), 43–54 (2023)

23. Samreen, N.F., Alalfi, M.H.: A survey of security vulnerabilities in ethereum smart contracts. arXiv preprint arXiv:2105.06974 (2021)

24. Szabo, N.: Formalizing and securing relationships on public networks. First monday (1997)

25. Torres, C.F., Schütte, J., State, R.: Osiris: hunting for integer bugs in ethereum smart contracts. In: Proceedings of the 34th Annual Computer Security Applications Conference, pp. 664–676 (2018)

26. Tsankov, P., Dan, A., Drachsler-Cohen, D., Gervais, A., Buenzli, F., Vechev, M.: Securify: practical security analysis of smart contracts. In: Proceedings of the 2018 ACM SIGSAC Conference on Computer and Communications Security, pp. 67–82 (2018)
27. Wang, S., Yuan, Y., Wang, X., Li, J., Qin, R., Wang, F.Y.: An overview of smart contract: architecture, applications, and future trends. In: 2018 IEEE Intelligent Vehicles Symposium (IV), pp. 108–113. IEEE (2018)
28. Wood, G., et al.: Ethereum: a secure decentralised generalised transaction ledger. Ethereum Project Yellow Paper **151**(2014), 1–32 (2014)
29. Zohar, A.: Bitcoin: under the hood. Commun. ACM **58**(9), 104–113 (2015)

FLAIR: A Federated Learning Approach Against Inference Attacks and Risks

Mouad Bouharoun[1(✉)] and Mohammed Erradi[1,2]

[1] Henceforth, Rabat, Morocco
m.bouharoun@henceforth.ma
[2] ENSIAS, Mohammed V University in Rabat, Rabat, Morocco

Abstract. Is there a secure way to share cyber threats knowledge among multiple organisations for a collective defense strategy ? Federated Learning (FL) has been introduced to enable collaboration among multiple organizations. In this paper, we propose a privacy-preserving federated learning approach to share cyber threat intelligence. The distributed nature of FL gives rise to different threats, such as inference attacks, poisoning attacks, and identity theft. In this work, we consider inference attacks, where a malicious subset of participant nodes aim to infer the training data of the victim. The attacker may generate and optimize vectors of features values to infer these data. We suggest a Federated Learning Approach Against Inference Attacks and Risks (FLAIR) where nodes collaboratively train models without a centralized server. We measured the data generated by the attacker against the real data of the target victim, and we show that the accuracy of this inference attack is low. We additionally conducted a set of experiments to test the performance and resilience of FLAIR. We then attended a high performance metrics with an accuracy around eighties.

Keywords: Threat intelligence · Federated learning · Knowledge sharing · Secure aggregation · Privacy-preserving

1 Introduction

Threat intelligence is a discipline based on intelligence techniques, which aims to collect and organize all information related to threats in cyberspace, in order to draw up a portrait of attackers. The knowledge related to those cyber threats includes threat actors, threat indicators, suspicious network activities, etc. This raises the following question: Is there a secure way to share this knowledge among multiple organizations for a collective defense strategy?

Federated Learning (FL) has been introduced to address this question. It's a decentralized approach that enables multiple parties, or "nodes," to collaborate in order to share their knowledge while preserving data privacy. In fact, federated learning is utilized for various applications in cybersecurity (e.g., network intrusion detection [1], securing wireless edge networks [2,16], programmable logic controller (PLC) systems [3], and Internet of Things (IoT) networks [4]).

© The Author(s), under exclusive license to Springer Nature Singapore Pte Ltd. 2025
M. Al-kfairy et al. (Eds.): SocialSec 2024, LNCS 15565, pp. 138–156, 2025.
https://doi.org/10.1007/978-981-96-3774-4_9

FL algorithms perform their computations (local training) on a distributed set of nodes (participants). These computations are done in several rounds until convergence of the global model. In each training round, a central aggregator selects a random subset of nodes that train a model on their local data. Then, nodes send their model parameters to the server, which calculates the aggregated function by averaging incoming updates into a global model [17]. The resulting model is used for the next round. This will hide the node's actual data since it sends only its model parameters. However, there are several issues and attack vectors with the FL approach [13, 18–20] such as: data poisoning, model poisoning, inference attacks, reconstruction attacks, byzantine attacks, evasion attacks, model extraction attacks, and identity theft. Traditional approaches have also a limited capability to handle increased traffic since the server acts as the only coordinator of the exchanges and of the aggregation.

In this work, we address the inference attacks [5, 6] provided by a malicious participant node seeking to infer some feature values from victim training data. We assume that the architecture is provided over a reliable network. Also, the participant nodes that have the same features. In addition, those nodes train the same machine learning model architecture. Concerning the attacker, we assume that it exists among the participant nodes and could have access to the exchanged parameters. We investigate the above assumptions using two neural network models: Long Short-Term Memory (LSTM), and Graph Convolutional Networks (GCN).

This paper makes the following contributions: we propose an approach against inference attacks named Federated Learning Architecture Against Inference Attacks and Risks (FLAIR). The suggested approach is dedicated:

1. To provide high performance metrics at the end of the FL rounds. Thus, the nodes would have a global predictive model based on their federated security data.
2. To be scalable and efficient in terms of communication, even when a novel set of nodes enters on each round. This can be ensured by managing the coordination, training, and aggregation in a peer-to-peer (P2P) manner [36–38].
3. To provide security and privacy-preserving by securely exchanging and aggregating node's model parameters.

We evaluate FLAIR using Netflow datasets (NF-BoT-IoT, NF-ToN-IoT, NF-UNSW-NB15, NF-UQ-NIDS). The obtained results yield several interesting findings. First, we show that even with a large percentage of malicious nodes that target one victim the attack achieves a low accuracy in data reconstruction. Second, we show that we achieve a good balance between performance and security, and the global model may still converge accurately even with the introduction of the secure aggregation method.

The rest of the paper is organized as follows: In Sect. 2, we highlight the components of federated learning and its inner workings. Section 3 presents the system model and the threat model. In Sect. 4, we provide the experimental results. Section 5 presents the related works while highlighting the suggested approach. Finally, in Sect. 6, we present the conclusion.

2   Federated Learning Principle

In federated learning [17], we have a central server $\mathcal{S}$, and a set of nodes U. Each node $u \in U$ holds a private set D_u of training examples and trains local models in parallel. While the central server coordinates the process of exchanges and aggregation (see Fig. 1).

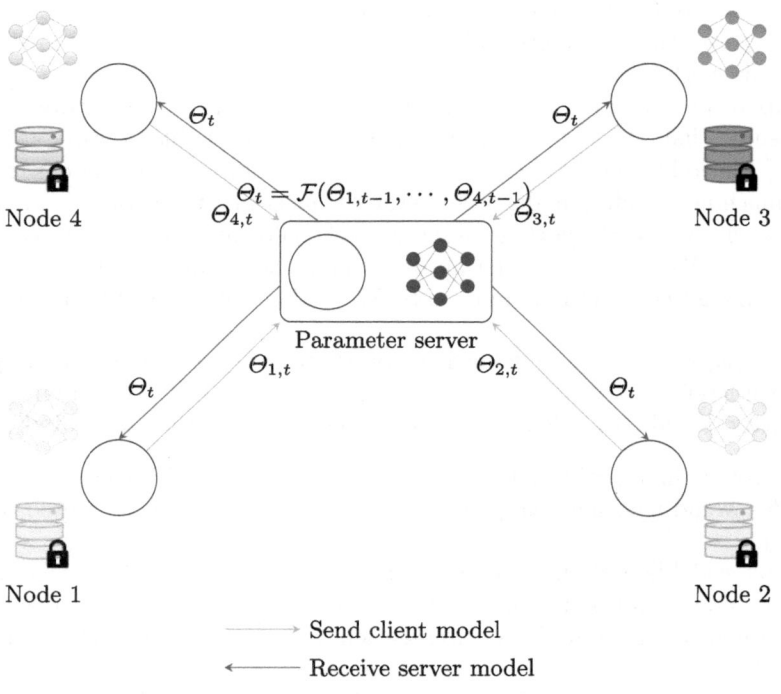

Fig. 1. Federated learning system with 4 nodes and a global coordinator.

In a given round t, the global server selects a subset of nodes U_t in U. It initializes the global model Θ_t, and distributes it over the participating nodes. Then, each node u receives the global model Θ_t, and creates a set of mini-batches from his local training data $D_{u,t} = \{D_{u,t}^{(i)}\}_{i=1}^{|D_{u,t}|}$. Where $|.|$ refers to the *card* operator. Afterward, the node calculates the loss function

$$L_f(D_{u,t}, \Theta_t) = -\frac{1}{|D_{u,t}|} \sum_{i=1}^{|D_{u,t}|} \sum_{j=1}^{C} y_{ij,t} \cdot \log(\hat{y}_{ij,t})$$

where C is the number of classes, $y_{ij,t} \in \{0, 1\}$ indicates whether the class j is the correct classification for the i-th input. $\hat{y}_{ij,t}$ is the predicted probability that the i-th input belongs to class j. Then, the node computes the mini-batch loss gradient $\nabla L_f(D_{tu}, \Theta_t)$ and performs a gradient descent step:

$$\Theta_{u,t} \leftarrow \Theta_t - \eta_u \nabla L_f(D_{tu}, \Theta_t)$$

where η_u is the learning rate (hyper-parameter of u). Each node $u \in U_t$ sends $\Theta_{u,t}$ to the server which in turn calculates the new global model by averaging these updates:

$$\Theta_{t+1} = \sum_{u \in U_t} \alpha_{u,t} \Theta_{u,t}$$

where $\alpha_{u,t} = \frac{|D_{u,t}|}{|D_t|}$, $D_t = \bigcup_{u \in U_t} D_{tu}$ is the mini-batch formed by concatenating all mini-batches of nodes on round t. The result Θ_{t+1} is distributed among the participant nodes to start a new federated learning round $t+1$. This process will be performed for a limited number of rounds until convergence at a given round t_l, where $\|\Theta_{t_l+1} - \Theta_{t_l}\| \leq \epsilon$. The symbol $\| \cdot \|$ denotes the Euclidean norm, and ϵ is a small positive threshold indicating the desired level of convergence.

3   The Proposed Method

3.1   System Model

The goal is to design practical defenses against inference attacks. We will evaluate the defense in a systematic manner to ensure that the attack achieves low accuracy (i.e., high privacy preservation).

The Proposed Approach. We suppose that the proposed system is built upon $|U|$ communicating nodes U. In each round, a sample of nodes U_t of size $n_t = |U_t|$ can participate in the training, each node manages its own local resources (model parameters, data) independently via local hash tables for example. We conserve the same notations as in the previous sections.

Step 1 (Initialization and node setup). Initialize the global model parameters and identify the participating nodes U_t (the selection is done uniformly).

Step 2 (Local training). All participating nodes perform local training and generate the model parameters. We denote by Θ_u the local parameters of u. Node u computes

$$\tilde{\Theta}_{u,t} = \frac{|D_{u,t}|}{|D_t|} \times \Theta_{u,t}.$$

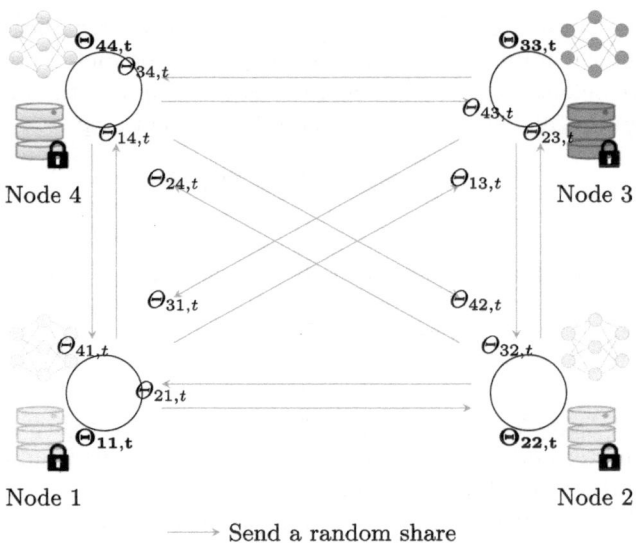

Fig. 2. System model and exchanges flow. The parameters in bold are kept private at each node, while the others are shared.

Step 3 (Model exchange and Secure aggregation). All nodes in U_t split their computed value in this way (lines 10, 11, and 12 in Algorithm 1 show the method for partitioning these values):

$$\begin{cases} \tilde{\Theta}_{1,t} = \tilde{\Theta}_{11,t} + \ldots + \tilde{\Theta}_{1j,t} + \ldots + \tilde{\Theta}_{1n_t,t}, \\ \vdots \\ \tilde{\Theta}_{i,t} = \tilde{\Theta}_{i1,t} + \ldots + \tilde{\Theta}_{ij,t} + \ldots + \tilde{\Theta}_{in_t,t}, \\ \vdots \\ \tilde{\Theta}_{n_t,t} = \tilde{\Theta}_{n_t1,t} + \ldots + \tilde{\Theta}_{n_tj,t} + \ldots + \tilde{\Theta}_{n_tn_t,t}. \end{cases}$$

This generates the following matrix, where the diagonal elements remain private, i.e., $\tilde{\Theta}_{uu,t}$ is never shared by the node u.

$$M = \begin{bmatrix} \tilde{\Theta}_{11,t} & \tilde{\Theta}_{12,t} & \tilde{\Theta}_{13,t} & \cdots & \tilde{\Theta}_{1n_t,t} \\ \tilde{\Theta}_{21,t} & \tilde{\Theta}_{22,t} & \tilde{\Theta}_{23,t} & \cdots & \tilde{\Theta}_{2n_t,t} \\ \tilde{\Theta}_{31,t} & \tilde{\Theta}_{32,t} & \tilde{\Theta}_{33,t} & \cdots & \tilde{\Theta}_{3n_t,t} \\ \vdots & \vdots & \vdots & \ddots & \vdots \\ \tilde{\Theta}_{n_t1,t} & \tilde{\Theta}_{n_t2,t} & \tilde{\Theta}_{n_t3,t} & \cdots & \tilde{\Theta}_{n_tn_t,t} \end{bmatrix}$$

On the other hand, u shares $\tilde{\Theta}_{uv,t}$ with v (see Fig. 2), so we can compute the following values:

$$
\begin{cases}
y_{1,t} = \tilde{\Theta}_{11,t} + \cdots + \tilde{\Theta}_{j1,t} + \cdots + \tilde{\Theta}_{n_t 1,t} \text{ by node } 1 \\
\vdots \\
y_{i,t} = \tilde{\Theta}_{1i,t} + \ldots + \tilde{\Theta}_{ji,t} + \ldots + \tilde{\Theta}_{n_t i,t} \text{ by node } i \\
\vdots \\
y_{n_t,t} = \tilde{\Theta}_{1n_t,t} + \ldots + \tilde{\Theta}_{jn_t,t} + \ldots + \tilde{\Theta}_{n_t n_t,t} \text{ by node } n_t
\end{cases}
$$

Thus, we can compute the sum: $\sum_{i=1}^{n_t} y_{i,t}$. On the other side,

$$
\sum_{i=1}^{n_t} y_{i,t} = \sum_{i=1}^{n_t} \sum_{j=1}^{n_t} \tilde{\Theta}_{ji,t} = \sum_{j=1}^{n_t} \sum_{i=1}^{n_t} \tilde{\Theta}_{ji,t} = \sum_{i=1}^{n_t} \sum_{j=1}^{n_t} \tilde{\Theta}_{ij,t} = \sum_{i=1}^{n_t} \tilde{\Theta}_{i,t} = \sum_{i=1}^{n_t} \alpha_{i,t} \times \Theta_{i,t}
$$

Accordingly, we can compute exactly the sum of model updates by summing the values $y_{i,t}$. In other words, this method hides all information about nodes' individual inputs, except for their sum. When secure aggregation is added to federated learning, the aggregation of model updates is logically performed by the virtual third party induced by the secure multiparty communication. This summation is performed in a collaborative manner by all participating nodes (a fully peer-to-peer network). This method not only enhances the security of the federated learning process but also ensures that the final summation is unbiased. The computed value $\sum_{i=1}^{n_t} y_i$ is the aggregated model. It is used by the nodes for the next federated learning round (see Algorithm 1).

3.2   Threat Model

In federated learning, malicious or curious nodes could exploit the exchanged, and aggregated model parameters to infer sensitive information (see Fig. 3). In this work, our focus is on generative-based inference attacks [9], but it's essential to recognize that various inference techniques exist such as: equality solving inference [8], membership inference [10,12,24,25], and property inference [28,29, 31] etc.

Definition of Inference. Given a federated learning system U, a local model Θ_k of a node k in U, and some training data points $\tau = \{z_1, \ldots, z_n\}$ according to [12], an inference attack on $z \in \tau$ aims to estimate the probability of z belonging to the node k:

$$
S(\Theta_k, z) := P(s_{k,z} = 1 | \Theta_k, z)
$$

Algorithm 1. The proposed approach (FLAIR)

Require: t (round number), U the set of nodes, Θ_{t-1} (global model from round $t-1$),
    η (learning rate)
Ensure: Θ_t (global model for round t)
1: Select the participating nodes U_t from U
2: $n_t \leftarrow card(U_t)$ //Number of participating nodes at rount t
3: **for** each node $u \in U_t$ **do**
4:     // Local training
5:     Initialize $D_{u,t}$ //Local training data of u at round t
6:     split $D_{u,t}$ into mini-batches of equal sizes
7:     **for** each mini-batch b **do**
8:         $\Theta_{u,t} \leftarrow \Theta_{t-1} - \eta\nabla_{\Theta_{t-1}}L(b,\Theta_{t-1})$
9:     **end for**
10:     $\tilde{\Theta}_{u,t} \leftarrow \frac{|D_{u,t}|}{|D_t|} \times \Theta_{u,t}$
11:     //Exchange model parameters
12:     $S\Theta_{u,t} \leftarrow random(\{-\infty, \Theta_{u,t}\}, n_t)$ //choose n_t random vector values from $-\infty$
    to $\Theta_{u,t}$
13:     // This random vector values are objects of same size of model parameters of
    u
14:     $P\Theta_{u,t} \leftarrow [S\Theta_{u,t}[1]] + [S\Theta_{u,t}[i] - S\Theta_{u,t}[i-1]$ for $i = 1 \cdots n_t - 1]$ // A list of
    random partitions of $\Theta_{u,t}$
15:     $P\Theta_{u,t} \leftarrow P\Theta_{u,t} + [\Theta_{u,t} - S\Theta_{u,t}[-1]]$
16:     $\sum_{i=1}^{n_t} P\Theta_{u,t}[i] \leftarrow \Theta_{u,t}$
17:     keep $P\tilde{\Theta}_{u,t}[i_u]$ private //i_u is the index of u
18:     send $\tilde{\Theta}_{u,t}[i_v]$ to each $v \in U_t \setminus \{u\}$
19: **end for**
20: //Model aggregation
21: **for** each node $u \in U_t$ **do**
22:     $y_{u,t} \leftarrow \sum_{i_v=1}^{n_t} \Theta_{u,t}[i_v]$
23: **end for**
24: $\Theta_t \leftarrow \sum_u y_{u,t}$
25: **return** Θ_t

---

where $s_{k,z}$ represents a binary random variable with values 1 if z belong to k and 0 otherwise.

Methodology (Generative-Based Inference Attack). We simulate an inference attack method in which the attacker can be one or many nodes on the federated learning system. The purpose is to reconstruct the corresponding data of a victim v, given the information available to the attacker. We assume that the attacker has access to the model update $\Theta_{v,t}$ of the victim at round t trained using the concatenated mini-batches $D_{v,t}$ of v's data. The adversary can use the vector of predictions from v's model and build a Generative Neural Network model to perform the inference task. In more detail, let $P_v = (P_{v,1}, \ldots, P_{v,n})$

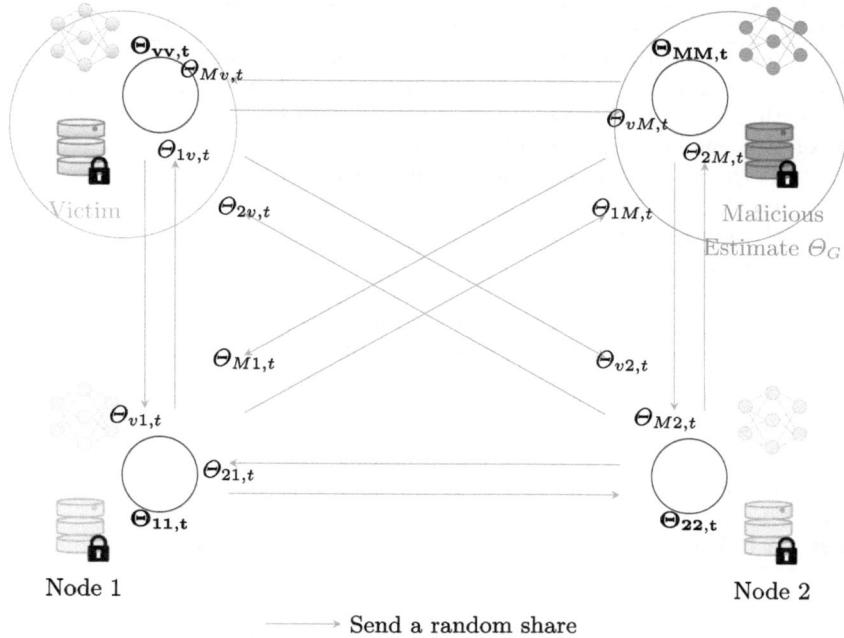

Fig. 3. Inference attack scenario.

be n prediction outputs of n samples $\{x_{v,i}\}_{i=1}^{n}$ of v's data, and d_v number of features of v. The objective of the adversary is to train a generator model Θ_G, such that given some $d_{x,i}$ known feature values of $x_{v,i}$, denoted by the vector $z_{v,i} = (z_{v,i}^{(j)})_{j=1}^{d_v - d_{x,i}}$, of each i-th sample, the generator outputs the corresponding estimation $\hat{x}_{v,i} = \hat{z}_{v,i} \cup z_{v,i}$ of complete feature values. To train the model, the adversary can apply the mini-batch stochastic gradient descent method. The objective function is as follows:

$$\min_{\Theta_G} L = \min_{\Theta_G} \frac{1}{n} \sum_{i=1}^{n} \tfrac{1}{2} \| f_v(f_G(z_{v,i}; \Theta_G); \Theta_v) - P_{v,i} \|^2 + \frac{1}{2} \Lambda \sum_{w \in \mathrm{Params}(\Theta_G)} w^2$$

$f_v(.)$ is the output of v's model providing a list of probabilities for different classes, and $f_G(.)$ is the output of the generator. $\frac{1}{2} \Lambda \sum_{w \in \mathrm{Params}(\Theta_G)} w^2$ is an L_2 regularization term used to prevent the generator from over-fitting and Λ is the regularization strength. This function serves as a measure that the attacker aims to minimize during the training of the generator. The method is to calculate the gradient $\nabla_{\Theta_G} L$ and perform a gradient descent step.

Algorithm 2. Generative-based inference attack methodology

Require: Θ_v : model parameters of v, d_v number of features of v, $P_v = (P_{v,i})_{i=1}^n$ vector of predictions, $\mu, \sigma, \mu', \sigma'$ hyper-parameters, η learning rate, Λ regularization strength, $x_v = \bigcup_i x_{v,i}$ a random set of known feature values

Ensure: Θ_G : model parameters of the generator

1: $\Theta_G \leftarrow \mathcal{N}(\mu, \sigma^2)$ // Initialize generator parameters
2: $n \leftarrow \dim(\mathrm{P_v})$
3: **for** each iteration **do**
4:     **for** $i \leftarrow 1$ to n **do**
5:         $L \leftarrow 0$
6:         $\hat{x}_{v,i} \leftarrow f_G(z_{v,i}; \Theta_G)$ // output of generator
7:         $\hat{P}_{v,i} \leftarrow f_v(\hat{x}_{v,i}; \Theta_v)$ // prediction output
8:         $L \leftarrow L + \frac{1}{n} \times \frac{1}{2} \left\| \hat{P}_{v,i} - P_{v,i} \right\|^2$
9:         $L \leftarrow L + \frac{1}{2} \times \Lambda \sum_{w \in Params(\Theta_G)} w^2$
10:        $\Theta_G \leftarrow \Theta_G - \eta \nabla_{\Theta_G} L$ // gradient descent step
11:    **end for**
12: **end for**
13: **return** trained generator model Θ_G

Algorithm 2 outlines the attack methodology. In each iteration, the adversary generates a random vector for each sample i which he concatenates with its known feature values $z_{v,i}$ to obtain the generated data point $\hat{x}_{v,i}$. The value $\hat{x}_{v,i}$ is fed to v's model to obtain a prediction $\hat{P}_{vi}$. Then, it calculates the loss between $\hat{P}_{v,i}$, and $P_{v,i}$, and tries to optimize it using stochastic gradient descent.

In the next section, we evaluate this inference attack against the proposed FLAIR approach. We measure its accuracy in data reconstruction of the victim. Additionally, we show the performance metrics of FLAIR to enhance threat intelligence knowledge sharing.

4 Experiments

4.1 Datasets

We use eight popular netflow datasets [26]: The datasets NF-BoT-IoT and NF-ToN-IoT are derived from a real-world deployment of IoT infrastructure, attack categories are DoS, Theft, Reconnaissance. Then, NF-UNSW-NB15, and NF-UQ-NIDS that are extracted from a university network. Some of the attacks are fuzzers, backdoors, shellcode. Version 2 datasets (NF-BoT-IoT-v2, NF-UNSW-NB15-v2, NF-ToN-IoT-v2, NF-UQ-NIDS-v2) are expanded versions of the corresponding version 1 with larger numbers of flows. Feature sets and attack categories remain largely the same.

4.2 Models

Long Short-Term Memory (LSTM) [34] is a type of Recurrent Neural Networks (RNN). The model contains basically: an input layer for the netflow data sequence, some hidden layers with equation $h_t = \tanh(W_{ih} \cdot x_t + W_{hh} \cdot h_{t-1} + b_h)$, and an output layer for the classification predictions: The LSTM output equation: $y_t = W_{oh} \cdot h_t + b_o$. Where h_t is the cell state at time t, x_t is the input at time t, $W_i h$, $W_h h$, and $W_o h$ are the weight matrices, b_h and b_o are the bias vectors.

Graph Convolutional Networks (GCN) [21,35] are a type of Neural Networks designed for analyzing graph-structured data. To train a GCN model with the netflow datasets, we model data as a single homogeneous graph based on interconnection between IPs of the traffic flow. The constructed graph can capture neighborhood information between graph entities. Using this construction, we associate to our dataset a graph $\mathcal{G} = (\mathcal{V}, \mathcal{X}, A)$, where $\mathcal{V}$ is the graph entities, $\mathcal{X}$ is a matrix of entities initial feature vectors. A is the adjacency matrix, which is a matrix representation of the adjacency relations between the vertices of the graph. For each graph entity $u \in \mathcal{V}$, we denote x_u as its initial feature vector. We measure edge weights between two entities u, and v in $\mathcal{V}$ using cosine similarity. $cos(x_u, x_v) = \frac{x_u \cdot x_v}{\|x_u\|\|x_v\|}$ Then all graph entities update their feature vectors in an iterative way using the system of equations below:

$$\begin{cases} h_v^{(0)} = x_v \\ h_v^{(l)} = \sigma\left(\frac{1}{|\mathcal{N}(v)|} \sum_{u \in \mathcal{N}(v)} w^{(l-1)} h_u^{(l-1)} + B_{l-1} h_v^{(l-1)}\right) \quad \forall l \in \{1, 2, \ldots, L-1\} \\ z_v = h_v^{(L)} \end{cases}$$

In this system of equations, $h_v^{(0)}$ is the initial embedding vector of v. x_v is the initial feature vector of v. $h_v^{(l)}$ is the embedding of v at layer l. $|\mathcal{N}(v)|$, is the number of neighbors of v. z_v is the final embedding vector of v. This equations highlight a basic approach for aggregating neighborhood information at a given layer. In the objective of constructing a high-order graph entity representation (or embedding vector). The final embedding is fed to a non-linear layer in which we apply an activation function σ to make a prediction.

4.3   Experiments Settings

To conduct the experiments, we have used 4 virtual machines (VMs), each of which is equipped with x86_64, 4 vCPUs, a Genuine Intel Common KVM processor, and 4GB of RAM, running Ubuntu 22.04.2 LTS. VMs communicate via a virtual bridge interface using Ethernet frames. To run local models, we utilize TensorFlow and Keras, and we choose to test two models: Graph Convolutional Network (GCN) and Long Short Term Memory (LSTM).

Each machine holds 2 nodes, which makes a total of 8 candidate nodes to participate in FLAIR training. We use the datasets of the previous section. Each node holds one dataset that remains private at the steps of training and testing (see Table 1).

Table 1. distribution of datasets between nodes.

Node1	NF-BoT-IoT
Node2	NF-UNSW-NB15
Node3	NF-ToN-IoT
Node4	NF-UQ-NIDS
Node5	NF-BoT-IoT-v2
Node6	NF-UNSW-NB15-v2
Node7	NF-ToN-IoT-v2
Node8	NF-UQ-NIDS-v2

4.4   Results Analysis

Performance Evaluation. The first purpose is to evaluate the performance of FLAIR. In other words, how much a given node can make correct predictions on the data of the other nodes. We conduct six experiments with different node sample sizes $|U|$ from 3 to 8. As shown in Figs. 4, and 5, we start attending convergence in most cases in 20 to 50 rounds, using a convergence limit rate $\epsilon = 0.055$. The best metrics are achieved when the sample size is maximal ($|U| = 8$) with average test accuracy (μ test acc = 81.36%), and average false alert rate (μ FAR = 5.26%) when using the GCN model. And average test accuracy (μ test acc = 73.29%), and average false alert rate (μ FAR = 6.46%) when using LSTM model. This showcases the model's ability to perform predictions accurately in distributed data. The experiments show a positive correlation between the size of the sampled nodes $|U|$ and the overall predictive accuracy of FLAIR.

Communication Efficiency. While FLAIR introduces an excessive number of communications its essential to measure μ round-trip time (μ-RTT) to test the communication efficiency. (μ-RTT) is the average time between sending a model update from a node and receiving the aggregated model through all communication rounds.

Lower μ-RTT indicates faster communication. To send and receive model updates, its essential to choose proper serialization techniques to transform the model into a byte series. We chose to test two popular techniques, MSGPack and Pickle in both, GCN and LSTM.

Test Case 1 (usage of GCN). The experiments (Fig 6) show that μ-RTT grows rapidly when the sample size increases. Its normal because of the quadratic complexity introduced by the usage of SMPC (total number of communication per round $t = O(|U|^2)$). In addition, MSGPack appears to be a more suitable serialization method (μ-RTT = 138 ms, when $|U| = 8$) comparing to Pickle (μ-RTT = 161 ms, when $|U| = 8$).

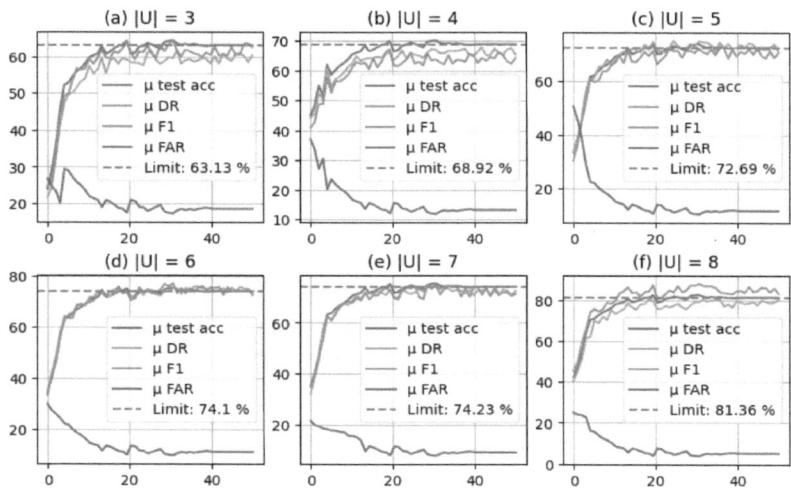

Fig. 4. GCN model experiments with sample size between 3 to 8, and 50 FL rounds

Test Case 2 (usage of LSTM). The experiments show the same results as test case 1 (see Fig. 7). MSGPack achieves best results (μ-RTT = 119 ms, when $|U| = 8$) comparing to Pickle (μ-RTT = 130 ms, when $|U| = 8$).

Indeed, μ-RTT with LSTM is less than its value using GCN. This is due to the topology of GCN, which relies on capturing complex relationships between data points and uses it as additional features to train the model. This method produces a larger update matrix and larger serialized objects.

For a real-world deployment, its essential to choose the best trade-off between communication efficiency and model performance. In our case, $|U| = 6$, and $|U| = 7$: These points seem to offer a good balance between test accuracy and communication efficiency. $|U| = 8$: while this provides high accuracy, the communication cost is higher. Depending on the application and the feasibility of the communication infrastructure, this may or may not be acceptable. To reduce μ-RTT and enhance communication efficiency we can rely on other techniques like model compression [14], or decentralized sampling-based learning [15]. We can resume the findings in the Tables 2 and 3.

Security and Privacy Preservation. To test the resilience of FLAIR against the designed inference attack, we try to infer the remaining unknown feature values through several experiments with different percentage $\%m = \frac{M}{7}$ of malicious nodes. Then, we measured the mean squared error (MSE) between the inferred values and the correct feature values, and attack accuracy (AAC); the number of correctly inferred values divided by all unknown feature values. A resilient FL system requires a large MSE, and a low AAC. The expression of MSE is as follows:

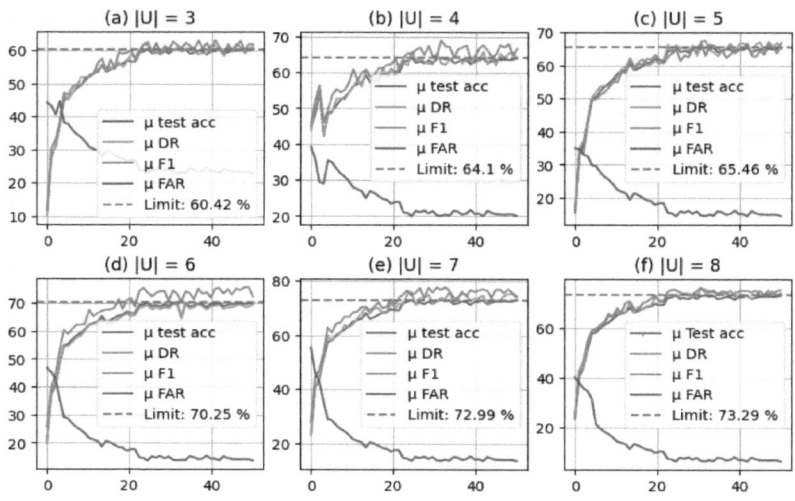

Fig. 5. LSTM model experiments with sample size between 3 to 8, and 50 FL rounds

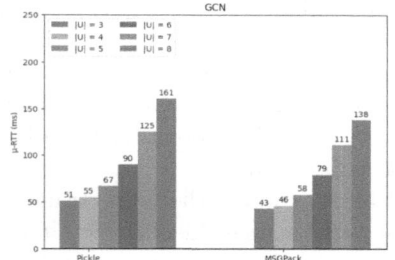

Fig. 6. Average round-trip time in ms per round for different sample sizes and serialization techniques for GCN

Fig. 7. Average round-trip time in ms per round for different sample sizes and serialization techniques for LSTM

Table 2. Performance metrics when training FLAIR with different sample sizes using GCN.

Sample size	μ Test acc	μ DR	μ F1	μ FAR	μ-RTT (MSGPack)	μ-RTT (Pickle)
|U| = 3	63.13 %	60.33 %	62.55 %	18.53 %	43 ms	51 ms
|U| = 4	68.92 %	65.46 %	64.30 %	13.17 %	46 ms	55 ms
|U| = 5	72.69 %	71.23 %	70.79 %	11.59 %	58 ms	67 ms
|U| = 6	74.10 %	72.56 %	72.81 %	11.32 %	79 ms	90 ms
|U| = 7	74.23 %	72.52 %	71.37 %	9.22 %	111 ms	125 ms
|U| = 8	81.36 %	80.19 %	83.20 %	5.26 %	138 ms	161 ms

Table 3. Performance metrics when training FLAIR with different sample sizes using LSTM.

Sample size	μ Test acc	μ DR	μ F1	μ FAR	μ-RTT (MSGPack)	μ-RTT (Pickle)
$|U| = 3$	60.42 %	61.23 %	61.86 %	22.85 %	33 ms	42 ms
$|U| = 4$	64.10 %	63.97 %	66.67 %	20.03 %	37 ms	47 ms
$|U| = 5$	65.46 %	64.95 %	66.86 %	14.57 %	47 ms	58 ms
$|U| = 6$	70.25 %	69.44 %	72.41 %	13.80 %	60 ms	73 ms
$|U| = 7$	72.99 %	73.46 %	74.41 %	13.63 %	92 ms	99 ms
$|U| = 8$	73.29 %	74.28 %	75.55 %	6.46 %	119 ms	130 ms

$$\text{MSE} = \frac{1}{n} \sum_{i=1}^{n} \frac{1}{d_v - d_{x,i}} \sum_{j=1}^{d_v - d_{x,i}} \left\| \hat{z}_{v,i}^{(j)} - z_{v,i}^{(j)} \right\|^2$$

Example (attack scheduling with $M = 1$, $v = $ Node1) Initially, the attacker knows the values depicted in the table (Table 4):

Table 4. Some known and unknown feature values in D_{vt}.

Source IPv4	Source Port	Dest IPv4	Dest Port	L7 Protocol	In Bytes	Out Bytes	flags	P_{vt}
192.168.100.3	.	.	.	.	4992 bytes	.	.	P_{vt}^1
192.168.100.46	.	.	.	.	9545 bytes	.	.	P_{vt}^2

In this case, $z_{v,1} = (192.168.100.3, 4992 \text{ bytes})$, $z_{v,2} = (192.168.100.46, 9545 \text{ bytes})$ and $P_v = (P_v^1, P_v^2)$ where $P_v^1 = [0.17, 0.7, 0.03, 0.1]$, and $P_v^2 = [0.01, 0.07, 0.85, 0.07]$ (because the dataset of node 1 contains 5 classes). The adversary generates random vector values which he concatenates with $z_{v,1}$ and $z_{v,2}$ as follows $V_1 = (192.168.100.3, r_1, r_2, r_3, r_4, 4992, r_5, r_6)$, $V_2 = (192.168.100.46, r_1', r_2', r_3', r_4', 4545, r_5', r_6')$. The generated vectors are fed to v's model. However, the available information for the attacker from v's model is the split value (from secure aggregation) Θ_{vM}. He tries to minimize $\{\text{diff}(f_{vM}(V_1), P_v^1)^2 + \text{diff}(f_{vM}(V_2), P_v^2)^2\}$ in each attack iteration. Where f_{vM} is the output of the model Θ_{vM}. Figures 8, 9 show the evolution of MSE and AAC in this example.

The adversary is unable to infer any unknown feature value from D_{vt} (AAC = 0%). However, MSE decreases per attack epochs to minimize the difference between generated feature values and actual feature values. The value of MSE stabilizes at epoch = 19 with a minimal value of 787.

If There are Multiple Adversaries? When there are $M \geq 2$ adversaries $\{\mathcal{M}_i\}_{i=1}^{M}$, the available information from v's model is $\sum_{i=1}^{M} \Theta_{v\mathcal{M}_i}$. We schedule

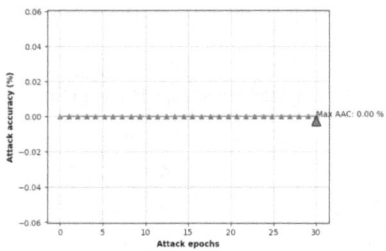
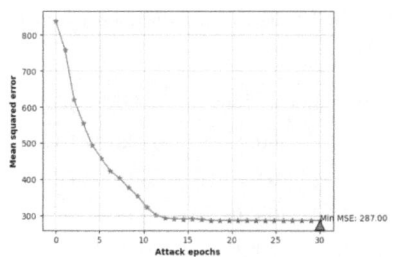

Fig. 8. Measure of AAC per attack epochs ($M = 1$, $v = $ Node1, $|D_{vt}| = 2$, $dim(z_{v,1}) = dim(z_{v,2}) = 2$)

Fig. 9. Measure of MSE per attack epochs (M $= 1$, v $= $ Node1, $|D_{vt}| = 2$, $dim(z_{v,1}) = dim(z_{v,2}) = 2$)

the same attack procedure, and we measure AAC and MSE for different number of adversaries: M $= \{2 \ldots 6\}$ (i.e., m=$\{28.57\% \ldots 85.71\%\}$). As shown in Figs. 10, 11, when the percentage of adversaries m is less than 57.14% they are still unable to reconstruct any information from v's training data. However, when $m = 71.42\%$ at attack iteration 13, the adversaries start inferring correctly some unknown feature values, and the attack reaches a maximal accuracy value AAC $= 9.85\%$. Finally, when $m = 85.71\%$ the adversary nodes could infer correctly a percentage of 11.3% feature values of victim v. As the number of adversaries increases, the aggregated information from v's model, $\sum_{i=1}^{M} \Theta_{v\mathcal{M}_i}$, becomes more informative.

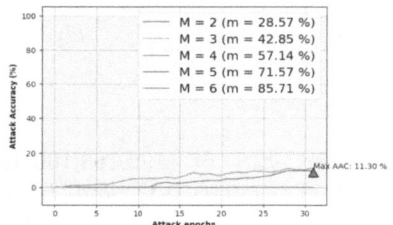
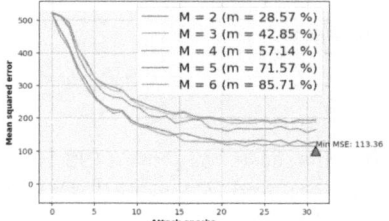

Fig. 10. Measure of AAC per attack epochs (M $= 2 \cdots 6$, $v = $ node1, $|D_{vt}| = 10$, $dim(z_{v,i}) = 2$ for $i = 1 \cdots 10$)

Fig. 11. Measure of MSE per attack epochs (M $= 2 \cdots 6$, $v = $ node1, $|D_{vt}| = 10$, $dim(z_{v,i}) = 2$ for $i = 1 \cdots 10$)

4.5   Discussion

The experiments show that the proposed FLAIR approach allows participating nodes to learn from their federated data without explicitly having access to it. In the case of using GCN to train local models FLAIR reaches an average test accuracy between 63.13%, and 81.36% depending on sample size. Therefore when using LSTM FLAIR attend an average test accuracy between 60.42%, and 73.29%.

In a real-world usage scenario, nodes represent organizations. Each organization can collect their security log and event data, clean it, and collaboratively build the federated learning network. When attending convergence, each organization would have access to a global predictive model that they can deploy on their security infrastructure.

On the other hand FLAIR reaches a resilience against inference between (100–11.3)%, and 100% depending on the number of the malicious nodes. This gives an acceptable trade-off between performance (since we do not bias the aggregated model) and security (MAX AAC=11.3%). Note that the attack is performed on a white-box settings (model parameters, predictions vector, and some feature values are known). However a significant vulnerability is introduced when $m = 100\%$ (all nodes collaborate to infer v's data), each malicious node $\mathcal{M}_i$ has access to its local model Θ_i, and to the global model Θ. Therefore, they can collaboratively compute $\sum_{i=1}^{7} \Theta_i$, then $\Theta - \sum_{i=1}^{7} \Theta_i = \Theta_v$. Accordingly, they can perform the attack with a full knowledge of v's update. This issue will be addressed as a future research work by introducing a masking-based strategy.

5   Related Works

Various studies have shown that FL is vulnerable to different types of inference attacks. Equality solving inference consist of solving one or a set of equations to infer $x = f^{-1}(y, \Theta)$. This attack can be effective when using models with linear transformations. But in this case with the usage of neural network architectures with multiple non linear transformations the attack could be practically impossible. Membership inference [10,12,24,25] aims to infer the presence of a given data record in the data used to train the models. One of the techniques to perform membership inference consists of generating random samples (x, y) with a given distribution D, and learning a threshold λ such that if the loss $L(x, y; \Theta) \leq \lambda$ then (x,y) have been seen by the model Θ. Property inference [28,29,31]: The adversary aims to predict a property related to the distribution of the training data. The method consist of training a meta-classifier A such that given a property $\tilde{Z}_i$ what is the probability $P(\tilde{Z}_i; \Theta)$ that it belongs to i. The adversary aims to predict a property related to the distribution of the training data. For example In [31] the authors train a meta-classifier that analyzes neural networks and infers properties like attractiveness, gender, age by from US-Census Income dataset. And also more sensitive properties like vulnerabilities in a bitcoin mining detector system (property: patch applied or not) with an accuracy $\sim 87\ \%$.

Actual defense strategies against inference attacks use differential privacy based mitigation approaches [27,30] to hide node's inputs. The method consist of adding artificial noise (with a probability density $n(x) \sim \mathcal{N}(0, \sigma^2)$) in client side before exchanging and aggregation. The inconvenient of this method is that it significantly bias the aggregated function ($\tilde{f} = \frac{1}{|U_t|} \sum_{i=1}^{|U_t|} (\Theta_{it} + n_i)$), and decreases model performance. Other methods use homomorphic encryption [32,33] that allows to encrypt model updates before sending it, and performing calculation on encrypted data. This approach requires complex key management according the federated network, increases the size of objects to be send so will require multiple TCP fragments to send it.

6   Conclusion and Future Work

In this work, we studied generative-based inference attacks against federated learning systems, where a malicious subset of participant nodes aim to infer the training data of the victim. The attacker may generate and optimize vectors of features values to infer these data. We proposed FLAIR an approach against inference attacks where the participant nodes are organized as a P2P federated learning architecture. The approach consists in suggesting a novel method to share threat intelligence knowledge that preserves data privacy. We designed a secure multi-party computation to aggregate incoming updates. The choice of a Peer to Peer architecture allows to build a scalable solution. Through an extensive experimental study, we have shown that the defense strategy provides a low accuracy of the data reconstruction due to inference attacks. We have considered the presence of multiple adversaries and studied their impact on attack efficiency. We have also shown that this approach provides a high performance metrics with an accuracy around eighties. We have used separately graph convolutional network model (GCN), and long short-term memory (LSTM) as local models of the participant nodes. In the experiments, we used popular netflow datasets: NF-BoT-IoT, NF-ToN-IoT, NF-UNSW-NB15, and NF-UQ-NIDS.

While progress has been made in the development of FLAIR, as future work we will address the minimization of the attack accuracy even with a high percentage of adversaries. We aim also to extend FLAIR by considering the presence of byzantine nodes that could undermine the learning process. Then, we plan to apply FLAIR to other data types such as images in malware image classification tasks to test the accuracy of the attack in image reconstruction. Finally, as an extension we aim to study the application of FLAIR with heterogeneous models.

References

1. Li, J., Tong, X., Liu, J.,Cheng, L.: An efficient federated learning system for network intrusion detection. IEEE Syst. J. **17**(2), 2455–2464 (2023)
2. Chen, Z., Lv, N., Liu, P., Fang, Y., Chen, K., Pan, W.: Intrusion detection for wireless edge networks based on federated learning. IEEE Access **8** (2020)
3. Verma, P., De Leon, M.P., Breslin, J.G., O'Shea, D.: FedTIU: securing virtualized PLCs against DDoS attacks using a federated learning enabled threat intelligence unit. In: IEEE International Conference on Smart Computing (SMARTCOMP), pp. 233–236 (2023)
4. Rashid, M.M., Khan, S.U., Eusufzai, F., Redwan, M.A., Sabuj, S.R., Elsharief, M.: A Federated learning-based approach for improving intrusion detection in industrial internet of things networks. Network **3**, 158–179 (2023)

5. Wang, X., Wang, N., Wu, L., Guan, Z., Du, X., Guizani, M.: GBMIA: gradient-based membership inference attack in federated learning. In: IEEE International Conference on Communications (ICC), pp. 5066–5071 (2023)
6. Hu, H., Salcic, Z., Sun, L., Dobbie, G., Zhang, X.: Source inference attacks in federated learning. In: IEEE International Conference on Data Mining (ICDM), pp. 1102–1107 (2021)
7. Boenisch, F., Dziedzic, A., Schuster, R., Shamsabadi, A.S., Shumailov, I., Papernot, N.: Reconstructing individual data points in federated learning hardened with differential privacy and secure aggregation. In: IEEE European Symposium on Security and Privacy (EuroS&P), pp. 241–257 (2023)
8. Luo, X., Wu, Y., Xiao, X., Ooi, B.C.: Feature inference attack on model predictions in vertical federated learning. In: IEEE International Conference on Data Engineering (ICDE), pp. 181–192 (2021)
9. Ha, T., Dang, T.K.: Inference attacks based on GAN in federated learning. Int. J. Web Inf. Syst. **18**(2/3), 117–136 (2022)
10. Gu, Y., Bai, Y., Xu, S.: CS-MIA: membership inference attack based on prediction confidence series in federated learning. J. Inf. Secur. Appl. **67**, 103201 (2022)
11. Hatamizadeh, A., et al.: Do gradient inversion attacks make federated learning unsafe?. IEEE Trans. Med. Imaging (2023)
12. Hu, H., Zhang, X., Salcic, Z., Sun, L., Choo, K.K.R., Dobbie, G.: Source inference attacks: beyond membership inference attacks in federated learning. IEEE Trans. Depend. Secure Comput. (2023)
13. Chen, Y., Gui, Y., Lin, H., Gan, W., Wu, Y.: Federated learning attacks and defenses: a survey. In: 2022 IEEE International Conference on Big Data (Big Data), pp. 4256–4265 (2022)
14. Hohman, F., Kery, M.B., Ren, D., Moritz, D.: Model compression in practice: lessons learned from practitioners creating on-device machine learning experiences. arXiv preprint arXiv:2310.04621 (2023)
15. de Vos, M., Dhasade, A., Kermarrec, A.-M., Lavoie, E., Pouwelse, J.A.: MoDeST: bridging the gap between federated and decentralized learning with decentralized sampling. arXiv preprint arXiv:2302.13837 (2023)
16. Wang, P., Sun, W., Zhang, H., Ma, W., Zhang, Y.: Distributed and secure federated learning for wireless computing power networks. IEEE Trans. Veh. Technol. **72**(7), 9381–9393 (2023)
17. McMahan, B., Moore, E., Ramage, D., Hampson, S., Arcas, B.A.: Communication-efficient learning of deep networks from decentralized data. Artif. Intell. Stat. 1273–1282 (2017)
18. Mothukuri, V., Parizi, R.M., Pouriyeh, S., Huang, Y., Dehghantanha, A., Srivastava, G.: A survey on security and privacy of federated learning. Futur. Gener. Comput. Syst. **115**, 619–640 (2021)
19. Blanco-Justicia, A., Domingo-Ferrer, J., Martínez, S., Sánchez, D., Flanagan, A., Tan, K.E.: Achieving security and privacy in federated learning systems: survey, research challenges and future directions. Eng. Appl. Artif. Intell. **106**, 104468 (2021)
20. Tolpegin, V., Truex, S., Gursoy, M.E., Liu, L.: Data poisoning attacks against federated learning systems. In: European Symposium on Research in Computer Security, pp. 480–501 (2020)
21. Hamilton, W.L., Ying, R., Leskovec, J.: Representation learning on graphs: methods and applications. arXiv preprint arXiv:1709.05584 (2017)

22. Herzog, R., Köhne, F., Kreis, L., Schiela, A.: Frobenius-type norms and inner products of matrices and linear maps with applications to neural network training. arXiv preprint arXiv:2311.15419 (2023)

23. Huang, Y., Gupta, S., Song, Z., Li, K., Arora, S.: Evaluating gradient inversion attacks and defenses in federated learning. Adv. Neural. Inf. Process. Syst. **34**, 7232–7241 (2021)

24. Suri, A., Kanani, P., Marathe, V.J., Peterson, D.W.: Subject membership inference attacks in federated learning. arXiv preprint arXiv:2206.03317 (2022)

25. Zari, O., Xu, C., Neglia, G.: Efficient passive membership inference attack in federated learning. arXiv preprint arXiv:2111.00430 (2021)

26. Sarhan, M., Layeghy, S., Moustafa, N., Portmann, M.: NetFlow datasets for machine learning-based network intrusion detection systems. In: Big Data Technologies and Applications (2020)

27. El Ouadrhiri, A., Abdelhadi, A.: Differential privacy for deep and federated learning: a survey. IEEE Access **10**, 22359–22380 (2022)

28. Xu, M., Li, X.: Subject property inference attack in collaborative learning. In: International Conference on Intelligent Human-Machine Systems and Cybernetics (IHMSC), vol. 1 (2020)

29. Suri, A., Evans, D.: Formalizing and estimating distribution inference risks. arXiv preprint arXiv:2109.06024 (2021)

30. Wei, K., et al.: Federated learning with differential privacy : algorithms and performance analysis. IEEE Trans. Inf. Forensics Secur. **15**, 3454–3469 (2020)

31. Ganju, K., Wang, Q., Yang, W., Gunter, C.A., Borisov, N.: Property inference attacks on fully connected neural networks using permutation invariant representations. In: Conference on Computer and Communications Security (CCS) (2018)

32. Jin, W., et al.: FedML-HE: an efficient homomorphic-encryption-based privacy-preserving federated learning system. arXiv preprint arXiv:2303.10837 (2023)

33. Ma, J., Naas, S.A., Sigg, S., Lyu, X.: Privacy-preserving federated learning based on multi-key homomorphic encryption. Int. J. Intell. Syst. **37**(9), 5880–5901 (2022)

34. Yu, Y., Si, X., Hu, C., Zhang, J.: A review of recurrent neural networks: LSTM cells and network architectures. Neural Comput. **31**(7), 1235–1270 (2019)

35. Kipf, T.N., Welling, M.: Semi-supervised classification with graph convolutional networks. arXiv preprint arXiv:1609.02907 (2016)

36. Steinmetz, R., Wehrle, K.: Peer-to-Peer Systems and Applications, vol. 3485 (2005)

37. Ganesh, A.J., Kermarrec, A.M., Massoulié, L.: Peer-to-peer membership management for gossip-based protocols. IEEE Trans. Comput. **52**(2), 139–149 (2003)

38. Eugster, P.T., Guerraoui, R., Kermarrec, A.M., Massoulié, L.: Epidemic information dissemination in distributed systems. Computer **37**(5), 60–67 (2004)

Secure Aggregation of Smartwatch Health Data with LDP

Andres Hernandez-Matamoros[1]([⊠])(iD) and Hiroaki Kikuchi[2](iD)

[1] Organization for the Strategic Coordination of Research and Intellectual Property, Meiji University, Tokyo 164-8525, Japan
`matamoros@meiji.ac.jp`
[2] School of Interdisciplinary Mathematical Sciences, Meiji University, Tokyo 164-8525, Japan
`kikn@meiji.ac.jp`
`https://www.kikn.fms.meiji.ac.jp`

Abstract. This paper evaluates a local differential privacy (LDP) approach designed to address the challenges inherent in smartwatch datasets, particularly those dominated by numerical data. Traditional methods such as Lopub and Locop have demonstrated limitations in accurately estimating joint probability distributions (JPD) within these contexts. The Castell2D approach leverages a refined mechanism for perturbation and aggregation that enhances the precision of numerical data handling while maintaining robust privacy guarantees. In smartwatch datasets, the predominance of numerical data poses significant hurdles for existing LDP techniques, which often work with categorical data but fail with continuous values. By incorporating statistical techniques and noise mechanisms, Castell2D achieves a more accurate estimation of JPD. Comparative analyses with established approaches such as Lopub, Locop, and others show that Castell2D consistently outperforms them in terms of estimation accuracy and privacy preservation. The effectiveness of Castell2D is demonstrated through extensive experiments on real-world open smartwatch datasets from three of the largest companies-Fitbit, Apple Watch, and Garmin-and demonstrates its ability to maintain high utility of the data while ensuring privacy standards. This work represents a significant advancement in the field of LDP, providing a practical and effective solution for privacy-preserving data analysis in environments dominated by numerical data.

Keywords: Local Differential Privacy · SmartWatches · Personal health lifelog data

1 Introduction

The rapid expansion of wearable devices and health-focused applications has led to an unprecedented increase in the collection of personal health lifelog data. Dhingra et al. [10] identify emerging trends in wearable device usage among U.S. adults. According to the Health Information National Trends Survey, nearly one in three Americans uses wearable devices, such as smartwatches or fitness bands,

M. Al-kfairy et al. (Eds.): SocialSec 2024, LNCS 15565, pp. 157–174, 2025.
https://doi.org/10.1007/978-981-96-3774-4_10

to monitor their health and fitness. Notably, over 80% of these users are willing to share their device data with their doctors to aid in health monitoring. This data, which includes a wide range of physiological and behavioral metrics, holds immense potential for transforming healthcare, enabling personalized medicine, and informing public health initiatives [8]. However, the sensitive nature of this data raises significant privacy concerns. It is crucial to develop methods that allow for the aggregation and analysis of health lifelog data while ensuring that individual privacy is not compromised [7].

Local Differential Privacy (LDP) has gained recognition as an effective method for addressing privacy concerns. It is a framework that focuses on privacy at the individual level by obscuring sensitive data before it is transmitted from the user's device [4]. This approach offers strong privacy guarantees while still allowing for the collection of valuable insights from aggregated data [6].

Wearable devices produce various types of data, including categorical data, such as age, and time series data, like Electrocardiogram (ECG) signals. Recent research has concentrated on continual time series analysis under LDP. An initial method introduced in the local setting was based on memoization [30]. Erlingsson et al. [31] investigated a shuffle model for collecting correlated time series data, while Bao et al. [32] introduced a correlated Gaussian mechanism to reduce noise in time series data.

However, applying LDP to datasets with high-cardinality categorical attributes presents significant challenges. These datasets often require fine granularity to maintain utility, but traditional LDP mechanisms introduce noise that can substantially distort the data, resulting in a loss of both accuracy and utility [4,11]. High-cardinality attributes exacerbate this issue because the space of possible values is large, making it difficult to apply standard LDP techniques without either introducing excessive noise or losing the nuanced details of the data [12–14,16].

The primary function in LDP involves the data collector estimating joint probability distributions (JPD). These distributions capture correlations and dependencies between different variables and are essential for various analytical tasks. For instance, an activity recognition model, which is a classification type, aims to predict the type of activity (e.g., walking, running, cycling) based on these metrics or an health risk prediction model, can be either classification or regression, designed to predict health risks such as the likelihood of cardiovascular issues using user metrics.

Techniques like Bloom filters (BF) and randomized response (RR) are commonly employed in current LDP methods [12,14,16] for estimating JPD. BF are efficient probabilistic structures that facilitate privacy-preserving tests of membership, while RR strategically adds noise to an individual's data to conceal their actual values. Although BF are effective for handling moderately sized datasets, they can become memory-intensive under LDP. The need for larger BF escalates with the increase in elements or a lower tolerance for false positives, leading to greater memory demands. The dimensionality issue in BF can cause a rise in spatial complexity and computational efforts, especially as the dataset expands, necessitating larger bit arrays to keep the false positive rate minimal. This can result in increased memory usage and slower operations, as explored by Hernandez-Matamoros et al. [23].

Consequently, it is crucial to devise new LDP mechanisms that effectively manage high-cardinality numerical data, ensuring an optimal balance between preserving privacy and maintaining data utility [15]. This is particularly critical in domains like health informatics, where precise data is necessary for meaningful analysis and decision-making. To address the challenges associated with dimensionality, Kikuchi et al. [1] (preprint) have explored innovative approaches, specifically through the development of Castell2D, it processes a dataset of randomized data from smartwatch users, transforming it to more accurately reflect the original data structure despite the randomization. This is achieved by defining a probability matrix for each attribute in the dataset. These matrices are constructed such that diagonal elements represent the probability of an attribute value remaining unchanged, while off-diagonal elements reflect the probability of changing to any other possible value, governed by a privacy parameter.

In the transformation phase, the algorithm employs these probability matrices to methodically adjust each attribute's data. Initially, empirical values are calculated and organized into a matrix format. Then, starting with the first attribute, the algorithm applies the inverse of its probability matrix to transform the data. This step is repeated iteratively for each attribute, adjusting and reorganizing the data to align with subsequent attributes. This iterative process ensures that the transformation respects the original data's structure, effectively reverting the data to a form that closely approximates its pre-randomization state, thereby enabling more accurate data analysis while maintaining privacy.

This papers examines the effectiveness of various methods including Lopub [12], Br [16], Locop [14], and Castell2D [1](preprint) when applied to open smartwatch datasets under LDP. The distinctions among these methods are detailed in Table 1. The key findings of this research are:

Improved Accuracy. Castell2D yields more precise estimates of JPD under LDP conditions compared to conventional BF-RR.

Tested in Open Datasets. The datasets used in this analysis differ in terms of the number of users, the number of attributes, the cardinality of those attributes, and their possible applications.

Performance Analysis of LDP Approaches for Future Research Applications - We analyze the performance of LDP approaches without considering which variables are independent or dependent, allowing for a focus on specific applications in future research.

The structure of the paper is as follows: Sect. 2 presents the preliminaries. Section 3 outlines the various methods used to anonymize user data and estimate JPD, employed by different approaches including Lopub, Locop, Br, and Castell2D. In Sect. 4, we detail the experiments conducted, including the datasets utilized and the metrics used to assess the performance of each approach. Section 5 provides an in-depth discussion. The paper concludes with a summary of findings in the Conclusion section.

Table 1. Difference between Lopub, Locop, Br, and Castell2D.

Approach	Perturbation	Estimation
Lopub [12]	Bloom Filter Randomized Response	Lasso with EM
Locop [14]		Lasso with Gaussian Copula
Br [16]		Bayesian Ridge Regression
Castell2D [1] (preprint)	Randomized Response	Reshaping the data into 2D

2   Preliminaries

2.1   Health Lifelog Data

Health lifelog data refers to the continuous stream of information generated by individuals through wearable devices, mobile applications, and other health-related tools [9]. This data encompasses a wide range of personal health metrics, including physiological data (heart rate, blood pressure, body temperature, sleep patterns, and respiratory rate), activity data (steps taken, distance traveled, calories burned, active minutes, and exercise intensity), dietary data (food intake, macronutrient breakdown, micronutrient intake, and hydration levels), environmental data (location, air quality, exposure to pollutants, and ambient temperature), and self-reported data (mood, stress levels, pain levels, medication adherence, and symptom logs).

2.2   Potential Healthcare Applications

Smartwatch data sets offer several potential applications in healthcare, providing valuable insights and improving patient outcomes. These applications include:

- Fitness and activity monitoring involves tracking daily steps, distance, calories burned, and activity type to provide personalized fitness plans and monitoring cadence and speed to improve athletic performance.
- Chronic disease management can benefit from monitoring heart rate data (average, min, max) to manage conditions such as hypertension or heart disease, tracking resting heart rate to detect early signs of potential health issues, and using heart rate variability and its entropy to assess stress levels and autonomic nervous system function.
- Weight management can be personalized by combining demographic data (height, weight) with activity data (steps, calories burned).
- Sleep quality assessment can use heart rate data and its variability during night hours to infer sleep quality and patterns.
- General health and wellness can be enhanced by providing insights on overall health by correlating heart rate and step data and monitoring daily activity levels to encourage a more active lifestyle.
- Rehabilitation can be tracked by monitoring progress in patients undergoing physical rehabilitation through daily activity, steps, and heart rate.

2.3   Why Do We Need LDP on Smartwatches?

LDP ensures privacy preservation by keeping individual health records confidential and mitigating the risk of re-identification or misuse [4]; it builds trust between individuals and data collectors, fostering broader participation in health data initiatives [2]; it maintains data utility by allowing the collection of accurate and statistically relevant insights without compromising individual privacy, thus enabling valuable research and healthcare advancements [3]; and it ensures regulatory compliance by aligning with stringent data protection regulations, such as GDPR, which emphasize the importance of privacy-preserving technologies [5].

Additionally, LDP approaches [1,12,14,16] compute JPD, which can be used to create synthetic data [26]. This synthetic data can then feed machine learning and deep learning systems, enabling the development of healthcare applications.

2.4   Local Differential Privacy (LDP)

LDP [19] provides a robust privacy assurance, enabling users to place trust in their own systems instead of depending on a central authority.

Definition 1 (Local Differential Privacy). *An algorithm $\mathcal{F}$ satisfies ϵ-LPD if, for any two track records q and w and any output $\tilde{q}$ within the range of outputs of the algorithm $\mathcal{F}(\tilde{q} \subset Range(\mathcal{F}))$, the Eq. (1) holds:*

$$Pr[\mathcal{F}(q) \in \tilde{q}] \leq e^{\epsilon} Pr[\mathcal{F}(w) \in \tilde{q}]. \tag{1}$$

3   LDP Approaches

The following subsections offer a concise overview of the anonymization algorithms used for smartwatch users, including Lopub [12], Locop [14], Br [16], and Castell2D [1] (preprint), along with the methods employed for computing the JPD.

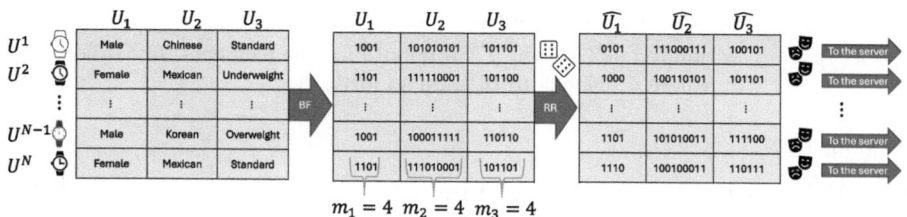

$$m_1 = 4 \quad m_2 = 4 \quad m_3 = 4$$

Fig. 1. The user's flowchart utilized by Lopub [12], Locop [14] and Br [16].

Table 2. Notations

Notation	Description
U	dataset
$\hat{U}$	randomized dataset
N	number of users
d	number of attributes in U
U_j	j^{th} attribute in U
u_j^i	record of ith user with attribute j^{th} in U
$\hat{u}_j^i$	randomized record of ith user with attribute j^{th} in $\hat{U}$
Ω_j	domain of U_j
$\mathcal{H}_j$	Hash Functions for U_j
f	represents the probability of randomly flipping
p	false positive probability using to calculate m_j
m_j	length of s_j^i
s_j^i	bloom filter of u_j^i, $s_j^i = \mathcal{H}_j(u_j^i)$
$s_j^i[b]$	b^{th} bit of s_j^i
$\hat{s}_j^i$	randomized bloom filter of u_j^i
$\hat{s}_j^i[b]$	b^{th} bit of $\hat{s}_j^i[b]$
$\hat{y}$	counts the number of frequencies of $\hat{s}_j^i$
$\hat{y}[b]$	b^{th} bit of $\hat{y}[b]$
y	original count
$y[b]$	b^{th} bit of y
M	candidate bit matrix
$\hat{R}$	Pearson correlation coefficient matrix
F_j	marginal distribution function of U_j
F_j^{-1}	inverse cumulative distribution function of U_j
P_j	probability matrix of jth attribute
$X_{a,b,c}$	empirical values of elements a, b, and c, where a belongs to U_1, b to U_2, and so forth
$\tau_{a,b,c}^j$	estimated JPD of the jth attribute for the elements a, b, and c, where a belongs to U_1, and so forth

3.1   Privacy Preserving Algorithms

In this subsection details the algorithms utilized by the methods analyzed in this study. We explore two main approaches: the first involves Bloom filters and randomized response (BF-RR), employed by Lopub, Locop, and Br; the second approach directly applies RR into the raw data, as used by Castell2D. Figures 1,2 present the flowchart of BF-RR and RR for anonymizing patient data across

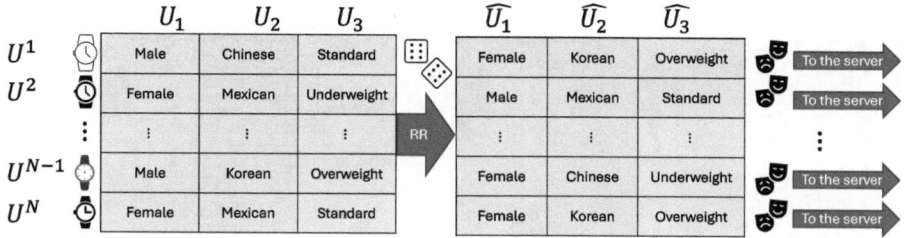

Fig. 2. The user's flowchart utilized by Castell2D [1] (preprint).

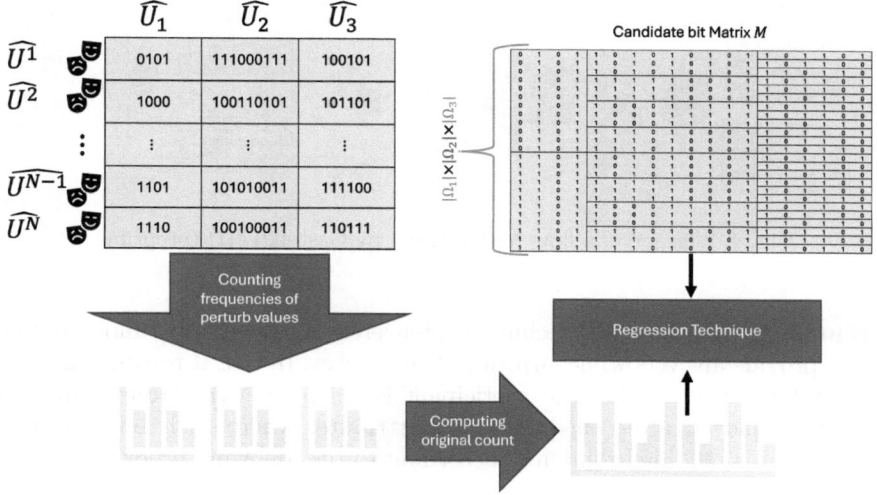

Fig. 3. The server's flowchart utilized by Lopub [12], Locop [14] and Br [16].

three attributes, and Table 2 enumerates the key notations used throughout this paper.

BF-RR. We detail the algorithm developed by Ren et al. [12], which is similarly utilized by Locop [14] and Br [16]. This section outlines how users encode and then perturb their data.

Encoding User Information. In a dataset U containing N users, each user record u^i for the ith user consists of d attributes, represented as $u_j^i (j = 1, \ldots, d)$, which are encoded and stored using BF [17]. Each user applies h hash functions $\mathcal{H}_h (h = 1, \ldots, 4)$ to map u_j^i to a bit string s_j^i of length m_j. Here, $s_j^i[b]$ indicates the bth bit of the bit string s_j^i. The BF's length (m_j) for U_j is calculated using the formula $m_j = \frac{\ln \frac{1}{p}}{(\ln 2)^2} |\Omega_j|$, where $|\Omega_j|$ represents the cardinality of the attribute U_j and p denotes the false positive probability. In our experiments, we set p to 0.022.

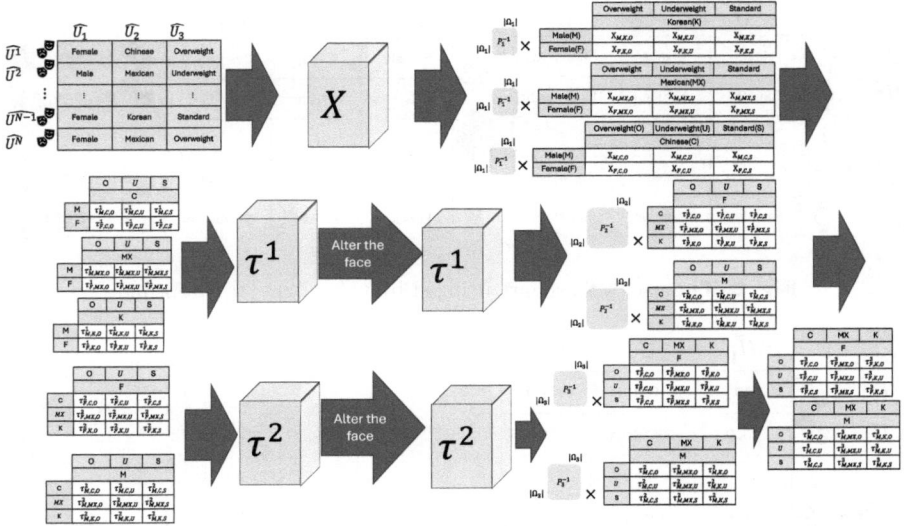

Fig. 4. The server's flowchart utilized by Castell2D [1] (preprint).

Perturbing the Data. RR technique, pioneered by Warner [18], allows individuals to provide answers while ensuring their privacy. In RR, it remains unknown to the interviewer whether the participant is responding truthfully. This technique is employed after encoding each attribute, where each bit $s_j^i[b], (b = 1, 2, \ldots, m_j)$ is modified randomly according to the following probabilities:

$$\hat{s}_j^i[b] = \begin{cases} s_j^i[b] & \text{with probability } 1 - f, \\ 1 & \text{with probability } f/2, \\ 0 & \text{with probability } f/2. \end{cases} \tag{2}$$

The $f \in [0, 1]$ signifies the probability of randomly flipping a bit of $s_j^i[b], (b = 1, 2, \ldots, m_j)$. Once the randomized BF $\hat{s}_j^i$ is obtained for each attribute j (ranging from 1 to d), the ith user combines $\hat{s}_1^i$ through $\hat{s}_d^i$ to create the bit vector $(\hat{s}_1^i || \ldots || \hat{s}_d^i)$ consisting of $(\sum_{j=1}^d m_j)$ bits. This combined vector is then sent to the data collector. Privacy for users is preserved by guaranteeing confidentiality through personalized local randomization techniques, which are independently implemented by users on their data entries. Local alteration of d attributes can secure ϵ-LDP, where h denotes the count of hash functions in the BF, and f signifies the probability of flipping a bit, expressed as $\epsilon = 2dh \ln \frac{2-f}{f}$.

RR. Let u_j^i denote the real data for the jth attribute of the ith patient. Each patient employs a biased coin flip, using a probability $p = \frac{e^\epsilon}{e^\epsilon + |\Omega_j| - 1}$, where ϵ represents the privacy budget. If the coin lands on heads, the patient reports their true value $\hat{u}_j^i$. If it lands on tails, the patient chooses a random value $\hat{u}_j^i$

from the set of Ω_j possible responses. The final step involves the smartwatch users sending this data to the server.

3.2   Estimating Joint Probability Distributions (JPD)

This subsection clarifies the algorithms used by the methods examined in this paper to estimate JPD. Three different approaches are discussed: Regression analysis (utilized by Lopub and Br), Lasso regression combined with Gaussian copula (used by Locop), and Castell2D. Figures 3,4 present the flowchart of these approaches for estimating the JPD of three attributes.

Regression Algorithms. [12,16] The data collector will receive $\hat{s}_j^i[b]$ from the users after they have encrypted and perturbed their data. For each bit b in attribute j, the frequency of the perturbed value $\hat{s}_j^i$ is determined by $\hat{y}_j[b] = \sum_{i=1}^N \hat{s}_j^i[b]$. The original count $y_j[b]$ is then estimated as $y_j[b] = \frac{\hat{y}_j[b] - \frac{fN}{2}}{1-f}$. Once the original counts are computed, the candidate bit matrix M is constructed as $M = [\mathcal{H}_1(\Omega_1) \times \mathcal{H}_2(\Omega_2) \times \cdots \times \mathcal{H}_d(\Omega_d)]$, where $\mathcal{H}_j(\Omega_j)$ represents a matrix for each attribute j (where $j = 1, \ldots, d$). Here, d denotes the number of attributes. Then, the coefficients β for the regression algorithm-Lasso regression [20] for Lopub and Bayesian ridge regression [21] for Br-are derived by solving the equation $y = M\beta$. The JPD is then calculated as $JPD = \frac{\beta}{\text{sum}(\beta)}$. Figure 3 presents an example where the distributions of attributes U_1, U_2, and U_3 are assessed to compute the JPD from data that has been modified by noise. This depiction illustrates the approach used to extract the JPD from the distorted data.

Lasso Regression and Gaussian Copula. [14] This subsection outlines the algorithm employed by Locop to estimate the JPD. Once the central server receives the perturbed data from smartwatch users, it begins by estimating the one-dimensional and two-dimensional distributions using the methodology detailed in [12], as described previously. Subsequently, the server calculates the Pearson correlation coefficient matrix $\hat{R}$ for the d attributes. This matrix must be positive definite (PDM), meaning all its eigenvalues are positive. PDMs are crucial in copula theory [22] because they model the dependency structure between random variables. It is therefore necessary to ensure that $\hat{R}$ is a PDM. If $\hat{R}$ fails to meet the criteria, a post-processing step is carried out to convert it into a positive definite matrix. This modification guarantees that the copula function precisely represents the JPD.

After calculating the correlation coefficient matrix R, the multivariate Gaussian copula is constructed based on the Gaussian joint distribution $\Phi(0, R)$. The sampling and synthesis procedure uses the matrix $\tilde{U}$, which represents anonymized users with rows as users and columns as attributes. This matrix is crucial for calculating the Joint Probability Distribution (JPD) of the original dataset while maintaining the privacy of the smartwatch users. To compute the

JPD of two or more attributes in $\tilde{U}$, the total number of users (sample size) is tallied, and the occurrence of each attribute value combination among smartwatch users is documented to derive the JPD.

Castell2D [1]. The term "Castell2D" refers to the fact that the algorithm uses a 2D matrix format, even though the original data is multi-dimensional. The algorithm processes and transforms this multi-dimensional data, ultimately organizing it into a 2D matrix for easier analysis and computation. This naming emphasizes the goal of simplifying high-dimensional data into a more manageable 2D structure.

In the example in Fig. 4, the geometric figure represented is a cube because we have three attributes. However, for k attributes, we can conceptualize a hypercube, where each additional dimension represents a new attribute. A hypercube is a generalization of a cube in higher dimensions and is useful for visualizing data in multidimensional spaces. For simplicity, we assume $X_{|\Omega_1|,|\Omega_2|,|\Omega_3|} = X$ throughout the remainder of this paper, where $|\Omega_1|$, $|\Omega_2|$, and $|\Omega_3|$ are the cardinality of three somattributes and represent the dimensions of X. The same assumption applies to the variable τ^j.

After the central server recevied the dataset $\hat{U}$, which contains the randomized data of the smartwatch's users. For each jth attribute in $\hat{U}$ a probability matrix P_j is defined as:

$$P_{j_{v,l}} = \begin{cases} \frac{1-p}{|\Omega_j|-1} & \text{if } v \neq l, \\ p & \text{if } v = l, \end{cases} \tag{3}$$

Here, $p = \frac{e^\epsilon}{e^\epsilon + |\Omega_j| - 1}$ defines the setup where P_j is a square matrix of size $|\Omega_j| \times |\Omega_j|$. In this matrix, $P_{j_{v,l}}$ indicates the probability of moving from state v to l. The diagonal entries of matrix P_j denote the probability of remaining in the same state, equal to p, whereas the off-diagonal elements signify the probability of transitioning to a different state, calculated as $\frac{1-p}{|\Omega_j|-1}$.

Initially, we compute the empirical values for $\hat{U}$ across its entirety. These values are systematically arranged into a two-dimensional matrix, X, such that the rows of X are indexed by the elements of the first attribute, while the columns correspond to the combined indices of the remaining two attributes.

To facilitate a transformation that reflects the interdependencies and structure within $\hat{U}$, we apply a matrix inversion operation. Specifically, X is multiplied by the inverse of matrix P_1, denoted as P_1^{-1}. This operation yields a transformed matrix τ, encapsulating new values that better represent the underlying statistical relationships:

$$\tau^1 = P_1^{-1} \cdot X$$

Following the initial transformation, τ^1 undergoes a systematic reorganization. The matrix is rearranged so that the rows now represent the elements of the second attribute. This restructured matrix is then subject to further transformation by multiplication with P_2^{-1}, enhancing the attribute specific representations:

$$\tau^2 = P_2^{-1} \cdot \tau^1_{\text{reordering}}$$

Next, τ^2 undergoes a systematic reorganization. The matrix is rearranged so that the rows now represent the elements of the third attribute. This restructured matrix is then subject to further transformation by multiplication with P_3^{-1}, enhancing the specific representations:

$$\tau^3 = P_3^{-1} \cdot \tau^2_{\text{reordering}}$$

This iterative process is continued until j attributes have sequentially occupied the row indices in the transformation matrices. The final matrix τ^j is achieved after successive applications of the respective inverse probability matrices for each attribute, culminating in a comprehensive analytical representation of $\hat{U}$. The general Castell2D algorithm is described in Algorithm 1.

Algorithm 1 Castell2D

Input: Dataset $\hat{U}$ containing randomized data from smartwatch users
Output: Transformed dataset τ^j
Initialization: Receive the dataset $\hat{U}$
$U_i(i = 1, ..., d)$
for each jth attribute in $\hat{U}$ **do**
    Define a probability matrix P_j as:

$$P_{j_{v,l}} = \begin{cases} \frac{1-p}{|\Omega_j|-1} & \text{if } v \neq l, \\ p & \text{if } v = l, \end{cases}$$

    where $p = \frac{e^\epsilon}{e^\epsilon + |\Omega_j| - 1}$
end for
Compute the empirical values for $\hat{U}$ and arrange them into X such that one dimension of the cube represents the elements of the $(1)^{\text{st}}$ attribute, while the other dimensions represent the combinations of the remaining attributes.
Transformation:
for each jth attribute in $\hat{U}$ **do**
    if $j = 1$ **then**
        $\tau^1 = P_1^{-1} \cdot X$
    else
        $\tau^j = \cdot P_j^{-1} \cdot \tau^{j-1}$
    end if

    if $(j + 1) \in \hat{U}$ **then**
        Reorder the dimensions of τ^j so that one dimension now represents the elements of the $(j + 1)^{\text{th}}$ attribute, while the other dimensions represent the combinations of the remaining attributes
    end if

end for
Final Output: τ^j

---

4   Experiments

All experiments were conducted using an AMD EPYC 7543P 32-core processor with 512GB of RAM, operating on Ubuntu 22.04.3 and Python 3.11.

4.1   Datasets Overview

The datasets used in our study include the Fitbit, Apple Watch, Fitbit+Apple Watch, and Garmin datasets. Through a discretization process, the datasets have been transformed, converting their continuous attributes into five distinct categories. For example, the attribute "Age" is divided into equal intervals. If the variable ranges from 0 to 100, it can be categorized into five classes: 0–20, 21–40, 41–60, 61–80, and 81–100.

4.2   Fitbit Dataset

The Fitbit dataset [24] consists of data from 2609 users. The dataset includes a wide range of attributes such as age, gender, height, weight, steps, heart rate, calories, distance, and various entropy and correlation metrics. These attributes provide detailed insights into users' daily activities and physiological parameters.

4.3   Apple Watch Dataset

The Apple Watch dataset [24] comprises data from 3657 users. Similar to the Fitbit dataset, it includes attributes such as age, gender, height, weight, steps, heart rate, calories, distance, and various entropy and correlation metrics. The data is useful for analyzing users' health and fitness levels, providing personalized fitness recommendations, detecting heart rate anomalies, and predicting daily activity levels.

4.4   Fitbit+Apple Watch Datasets

Combining Fitbit and Apple Watch datasets to leverage the strengths of both data sources, enabling a more comprehensive analysis. The combined dataset includes overlapping attributes such as age, gender, height, weight, steps, heart rate, calories, and distance, as well as unique features from each device. This combined dataset facilitates a richer understanding of user behavior and health metrics, allowing for more robust predictive modeling and personalized health insights.

4.5   Garmin Dataset

The Garmin dataset [25] contains 298 activities, focusing on detailed activity metrics. The attributes include activity type, start time, end time, average altitude, minimum altitude, maximum altitude, ascent, descent, distance, duration, heart rate (average, minimum, maximum), calories, speed (average), and cadence (average, maximum). This dataset is valuable for classifying activity types and predicting performance metrics.

Table 3 provides a summary of each dataset and includes a comparison table that outlines their features.

Table 3. Comparison of Dataset Characteristics

Datasets	#Smart Watch Users (N)	#Attributes (d)	#Continuous Att
Fitbit	2609	18	17
Apple Watch	3657	17	16
Fitbit+Apple Watch	6266	17	16
Garmin	298	12	11

4.6 JPD Estimation

In this paper, we analyze the performance of LDP approaches without considering which variables are independent and which are dependent. This allows us to focus on specific applications in future research. As mentioned in Sect. 2.2, these applications may involve a particular target variable and several dependent variables as features.

A subset of k attributes is randomly chosen from each dataset, and their JPD is estimated in a k-way manner, repeating this process one hundred times. To assess the accuracy of the JPD estimation, the average variant distance (AVD) metric is employed to quantify the difference between the true and estimated JPD. The AVD, as utilized by [1,12,14,16,26], is defined as $AVD = \frac{1}{2}\sum_{\omega \in \Omega} |O(\omega) - S(\omega)|$. A value close to zero indicates a more accurate JPD. We evaluate the performance of four approaches: the simple Lopub, which relies solely on LASSO regression; the standard Locop; Br; and Castell2D. The results are displayed in Figs. 5 and 6.

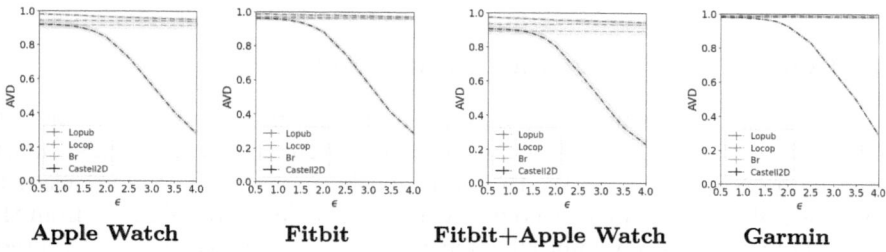

Apple Watch   **Fitbit**   **Fitbit+Apple Watch**   **Garmin**

Fig. 5. AVD vs Privacy Budget (ϵ) per attribute with 6-way.

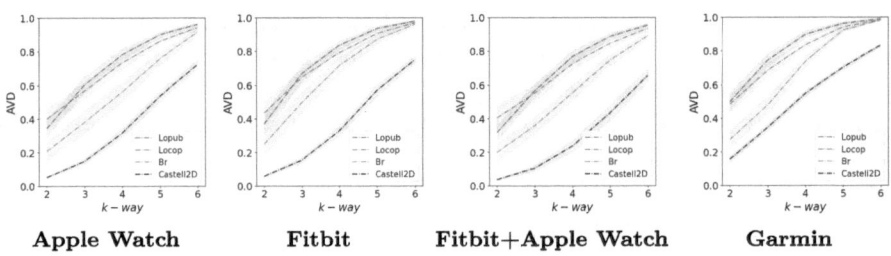

Fig. 6. AVD vs k-way, with $\epsilon = 2.5$.

Figure 5 shows the relationship between the AVD and the privacy budget (ϵ) for each dataset (Apple Watch, Fitbit, Fitbit+Apple Watch, and Garmin) with a 6-way attribute combination. The y-axis represents the AVD, where values closer to zero indicate more accurate estimations of the JPD. The x-axis represents the privacy budget (ϵ), where lower values imply greater privacy. As the privacy budget increases, the AVD generally decreases, indicating that higher privacy budgets allow for more accurate JPD estimations. Among the methods compared (Lopub, Locop, Br, and Castell2D), Castell2D consistently shows the lowest AVD across all datasets, suggesting it provides the most accurate JPD estimations while maintaining a balance between privacy and utility.

Figure 6 examines the impact of the k-way evaluation on AVD for each dataset with $\epsilon = 2.5$. The y-axis represents the AVD, where lower values denote better performance, and the x-axis represents the k-way evaluation (number of attributes). As the number of attributes increases, the AVD also increases, indicating that estimating JPD with more attributes is more challenging and leads to less accurate estimations. Castell2D again demonstrates superior performance, maintaining the lowest AVD across different k-way evaluations. This suggests that Castell2D is particularly effective at handling the complexity of higher-dimensional JPD estimations compared to the other methods.

In summary, both Figs. 5, 6 highlight the effectiveness of the Castell2D method in providing accurate JPD estimations while balancing privacy and utility. The results suggest that Castell2D performs better across various privacy budgets and attribute combinations, making it a robust choice for privacy-preserving data analysis.

4.7 Comparison with Original Healthcare Data

To comprehensively validate the usefulness of LDP in the context of medical analysis, we conducted a series of comparative experiments using original smartwatch datasets as benchmarks. By meticulously applying LDP approaches to these original datasets, we observed that the JPD calculations derived from the Castell2D method closely approximated the real data, surpassing the accuracy of other methodologies when the privacy budget ϵ was set to values greater than 2. Our empirical results substantiated that the loss in data utility was minimal, thereby demonstrating the effectiveness of LDP in preserving both the integrity and the practical utility of smartwatch data. Furthermore, the comparative analysis revealed that the error introduced through LDP perturbation remained within acceptable bounds, which is crucial for ensuring that the medical insights from smartwatches and decisions drawn from the anonymized data are reliable. This finding underscores the potential of LDP as a robust privacy-preserving mechanism for smartwatches that can maintain high data quality standards, even under stringent privacy requirements, thereby supporting its application in sensitive domains such as healthcare.

4.8   Comparison with Other Approaches

To protect user privacy in wearable device data collection, Li et al. [27] proposed a LDP approach for numerical stream data. Their experiments on a time-series heart rate dataset demonstrated that with a privacy budget of 0.5, the error rate was significantly reduced, thereby improving data usability while ensuring robust privacy protection.

Wook et al. [28] also introduced a method for collecting data from wearables using LDP, specifically targeting time-series daily step counts. Their approach involves sampling a small number of salient data points that best represent the original health data, mitigating the error introduced by the LDP perturbation mechanism.

Marchioro et al. [29] evaluated a crowdsourcing platform designed to collect wearable IoT data with LDP. Their experiments compared the true sample mean for steps with the estimated mean across varying privacy budgets.

Unfortunately, we are unable to compare our approach directly with those of Li et al. [27], Wook et al. [28], and Marchioro et al. [29] because our focus is on tabular data, whereas their focus is on time-series data.

5   Discussion

Castell2D applies RR technique directly to the raw data, which offers a simplified and effective way to anonymize smart watch data while preserving privacy. Castell2D's approach involves using a probability matrix to transform the data iteratively, ensuring that the original data distribution is accurately represented in the anonymized dataset. This method maintains high data utility and privacy by systematically transforming the dataset while preserving the statistical relationships among the attributes.

5.1   Why Does Castell2D Outperform LoPub, Locop, and Br?

Castell2D outperforms LoPub, Locop, and Br for several reasons:

- Unlike the BF-RR method used by LoPub, Locop, and Br, Castell2D directly applies the Randomized Response (RR) technique to the raw data. This eliminates the complexity and potential errors associated with encoding and perturbing data through Bloom filters, resulting in a more streamlined and accurate anonymization process.
- Castell2D's approach is more straightforward, involving fewer steps than the combined Bloom Filter (BF) and RR techniques used by other methods. This simplicity reduces computational overhead, minimizes potential sources of error, and improves algorithmic efficiency.

6 Conclusions

The evaluation of various LDP algorithms has demonstrated the effectiveness of the Castell2D method in estimating JPD accurately while maintaining a balance between privacy and utility. Among the methods analyzed, including Lopub, Locop, and Br, Castell2D consistently outperforms in terms of accuracy across different datasets and privacy settings.

A key factor in Castell2D's success is its direct application of the RR technique to raw data, bypassing the complexities introduced by additional layers like Bloom filters.

Moreover, Castell2D employs a sophisticated method involving probability matrices and re-order operations that accurately model and subsequently reverse the noise introduced during data randomization. This methodological precision allows Castell2D to reconstruct the underlying data distribution effectively.

The algorithm's capability extends further through iterative reorganizations and transformations of data matrices across all attributes. This ensures that the intrinsic characteristics of each attribute and their interdependencies are preserved and accurately represented. Additionally, Castell2D's adaptability to handle multiple attributes efficiently makes it particularly effective in complex datasets where the statistical dependencies among attributes vary.

In future work, we plan to compare Castell2D with popular LDP approaches such as GRR, OLH, and OUE, examining how small changes in the privacy budget affect performance. This will help guide users in selecting optimal privacy parameters for specific applications. Additionally, we aim to use the accurate JPD generated by Castell2D to create synthetic data for training machine learning and deep learning models. For instance, to create a model beneficial for patients, we can focus on tracking the rehabilitation progress of those undergoing physical therapy by monitoring daily activities, steps, and heart rate. By analyzing these features, the model can offer valuable insights into the rehabilitation process, enabling timely interventions and enhancing overall health outcomes. This approach is expected to enhance model performance by providing more robust and realistic data representations, thereby bridging the gap between privacy-preserving techniques and advanced predictive analytics.

Overall, Castell2D provides a robust solution for privacy-preserving data analysis, proving to be highly effective in managing the trade-offs between data privacy and the accuracy of statistical estimations.

Acknowledgements. This work was supported by JST, CREST Grant Number JPMJCR21M1, Japan.

References

1. Kikuchi, H.: Castell: scalable joint probability estimation of multi-dimensional data randomized with local differential privacy. arXiv preprint (2022). https://arxiv.org/abs/2212.01627
2. Apple Differential Privacy Team. (2017). Learning with Privacy at Scale
3. Ding, B., Kulkarni, J., Yekhanin, S.: Collecting telemetry data privately (2017)
4. Erlingsson, Ú., Pihur, V., Korolova, A.: RAPPOR: randomized aggregatable privacy-preserving ordinal response (2014)
5. European Union. General Data Protection Regulation (2016)
6. Dwork, C., Roth, A.: The algorithmic foundations of differential privacy (2014)
7. Fredrikson, M., Jha, S., Ristenpart, T.: Model inversion attacks that exploit confidence information and basic countermeasures (2014)
8. Li, X., et al.: Digital health: tracking physiomes and activity using wearable biosensors reveals useful health-related information (2019)
9. Choi, E., Lee, S., Lee, Y.: Personal health records: a systematic review. J. Med. Internet Res. **18**(5), e105 (2016)
10. Dhingra, L.S., Aminorroaya, A., Oikonomou, E.K., et al.: Use of wearable devices in individuals with or at risk for cardiovascular disease in the US, 2019 to 2020. JAMA Netw. Open **6**(6), e2316634 (2023). https://doi.org/10.1001/jamanetworkopen.2023.16634
11. Wang, T., Blocki, J., Li, N., Jha, S.: Locally differentially private protocols for frequency estimation. In: 26th Annual Network and Distributed System Security Symposium (NDSS 2019) (2019)
12. Ren, X., et al.: LoPub: high-dimensional crowdsourced data publication with local differential privacy. IEEE Trans. Inf. Forensics Secur. **13**, 2151–2166 (2018). https://doi.org/10.1109/TIFS.2018.2812146
13. Qin, Z., Yang, Y., Feng, W., Lei, X., Hu, S.: Heavy hitter estimation over set-valued data with local differential privacy. In: Proceedings of the 2016 ACM SIGSAC Conference on Computer and Communications Security, pp. 192–203 (2016)
14. Wang, T., Yang, X., Ren, X., Yu, W., Yang, S.: Locally private high-dimensional crowdsourced data release based on copula functions. IEEE Trans. Serv. Comput. **15**, 778–792 (2022). https://doi.org/10.1109/TSC.2019.2961092
15. Kulkarni, M., Li, C., Yang, Y.: Achieving information-theoretic local differential privacy with high utility. IEEE Trans. Inf. Forensics Secur. **16**, 1716–1731 (2021)
16. Hernandez-Matamoros, A., Kikuchi, H.: Comparative analysis of local differential privacy schemes in healthcare datasets. Appl. Sci. **14**(7), 2864 (2024). https://doi.org/10.3390/app14072864
17. Bloom, B.H.: Space/time trade-offs in hash coding with allowable errors. Assoc. Comput. Mach. **13**, 422–426 (1970)
18. Warner, S.L.: Randomized response: a survey technique for eliminating evasive answer bias. J. Am. Stat. Assoc. **60**, 63–69 (1965)
19. Kasiviswanathan S.P., Lee, H.K., Nissim, K., Raskhodnikova, S., Smith, A.: What can we learn privately? In: Proceedings of the 49th Annual IEEE Symposium on Foundations of Computer Science, Philadelphia, PA, USA (2008)

20. Zou, H., Hastie, T., Tibshirani, R.: On the "degrees of freedom" of the LASSO. In: The Annals of Statistics, vol. 35. Institute of Mathematical Statistics, Hayward (2007)
21. Michimae, H., Emura, T.: Bayesian ridge estimators based on copula-based joint prior distributions for regression coefficients. Comput. Stat. **37**, 2741–2769 (2022)
22. Sutikno, S., Kuswanto, H., Ratih, I.: Gaussian Copula Marginal Regression for modeling extreme data with application. J. Math. Stat. **10**, 192–200 (2014). https://doi.org/10.3844/jmssp.2014.192.200
23. Hernandez-Matamoros, A., Kikuchi, H.: Meaningful performance analysis on healthcare data under local differential privacy. In: New Trends in Intelligent Software Methodologies, Tools and Techniques 2024. IOS Press (2024)
24. Fuller, D.: Replication Data for: Using machine learning methods to predict physical activity types with Apple Watch and Fitbit data using indirect calorimetry as the criterion (2020). https://doi.org/10.7910/DVN/ZS2Z2J, https://dataverse.harvard.edu/dataset.xhtml?persistentId=doi%3A10.7910/DVN/ZS2Z2J
25. Jarnoma, Data World. Activity Data from Garmin Devices (2021). https://data.world/jarnoma/activity-history/workspace/project-summary?agentid=jarnoma&atasetid=activity-history
26. Xue, J., Zhou, X., Grossklags, J.: Privacy-preserving highdimensional data collection with federated generative autoencoder. Proc. Priv. Enhanc. Technol. 481–500 (2022). https://doi.org/10.2478/popets-2022-0024
27. Li, Z., Wang, B., Li, J., Hua, Y., Zhang, S.: Local differential privacy protection for wearable device data. PLOS ONE **17**(8), e0272766 (2022). https://doi.org/10.1371/journal.pone.0272766
28. Kim, J.W., Moon, S.-M., Kang, S., Jang, B.: Effective privacy-preserving collection of health data from a user's wearable device. Appl. Sci. **10**(18), 6396 (2020). https://doi.org/10.3390/app10186396
29. Marchioro, T., Kazlouski, A., Markatos, E.P.: Practical crowdsourcing of wearable IoT data with local differential privacy. In: Proceedings of the 8th ACM/IEEE Conference on Internet of Things Design and Implementation (IoTDI 2023), pp. 275–287. Association for Computing Machinery, New York (2023). https://doi.org/10.1145/3576842.3582367
30. Ding, B., Kulkarni, J., Yekhanin, S.: Collecting telemetry data privately. In: NIPS, pp. 3574–3583 (2017)
31. Erlingsson, U., Feldman,V., Mironov, I., Raghunathan, A., Talwar, K., Thakurta, A.: Amplification by shuffling: from local to central differential privacy via anonymity. In: Annual ACM-SIAM Symposium on Discrete Algorithms, pp. 2468–2479. SIAM (2019)
32. Bao, E., Yang, Y., Xiao, X., Ding, B.: CGM: an enhanced mechanism for streaming data collection with local differential privacy. PVLDB **14**(11), 2258–2270 (2021)

Author Index